NORTH AMERICAN WILDLIFE
WILDFLOWERS

READER'S DIGEST

NORTH AMERICAN

WILDLIFE

WILDFLOWERS

Reader's
Digest

The Reader's Digest Association, Inc.
Pleasantville, New York/Montreal

A READER'S DIGEST BOOK

Edited and designed by Media Projects Incorporated

Editors:
Edward S. Barnard
Sharon Fass Yates

Managing Editor:
Lelia Mander

Assistant Editor:
Aaron Murray

Production Manager:
Laura Smyth

Design:
Design Oasis

Copy Editor:
Charlotte Maurer

Consultant for revised edition:
Robert E. Budliger
Dir. of Environmental
Education(retired)
NY State Department of
Environmental Conservation

The credits and acknowledgments that appear on page 479 are hereby made a part of this copyright page.

Library of Congress Cataloging in Publication Data
Wildflowers.
    p. cm. (North American Wildlife)
   Includes Index.
   ISBN 0-7621-0034-6
   1. Wildflowers—North America—Identification. I. Reader's Digest Association.
QK110.N868   1998
582.13'097—dc21   97-32727

This book contains revised material originally published in 1982 in the Reader's Digest book, NORTH AMERICAN WILDLIFE.

Printed in the United States of America
Second Printing, April 2000

CONTENTS

WILDFLOWERS is a book for browsing and for identifying flowers. Use it to discover remarkable species like the Bloodroot, which the Algonquian Indians applied to their faces and bodies as a ceremonial paint, or the Puttyroot, from which early American settlers made glue. Use it to name the many different species of lilies, from the Tiger Lily to the Leopard Lily, and learn the legend of where the Tiger Lily got its name. Unique in its coverage, this book includes nearly 700 wildflowers—from common backyard species like the Daylily to the exotic Sandfood, which looks like a fuzzy, gray tennis ball covered with tiny purple flowers half-buried in the sand of the Colorado Desert.

Since no single book could cover all the species of North American wildflowers, the focus in this volume is on the species that are common, conspicuous, or important in some other way.

The introduction to WILDFLOWERS explains how the book is organized and provides general identification tips. The species entries are carefully written so that all the salient facts are easy to find. Information important for identification (size, markings, and the like) is placed in compact **identification capsules**. These are intended to be used together with the color portraits, for certain features mentioned in the capsules have been highlighted with check marks on the art. The **idento-checks** point out particular traits to be observed when identifying a species.

In this book there are certain species, such as the long-stemmed Goatsbeard, with its Dandelion-like flower, that can be easily recognized. Where you find these plants doesn't much matter (for identification purposes, at least). For others, where you find them is often an important clue to what they are. The range maps help out here. Much easier to use than lengthy written descriptions of ranges, these maps show the areas where particular species are likely to be. Flowers travel as seeds, so the ranges shown on the maps should be considered approximations only.

HELPFUL IDENTIFICATION FEATURES

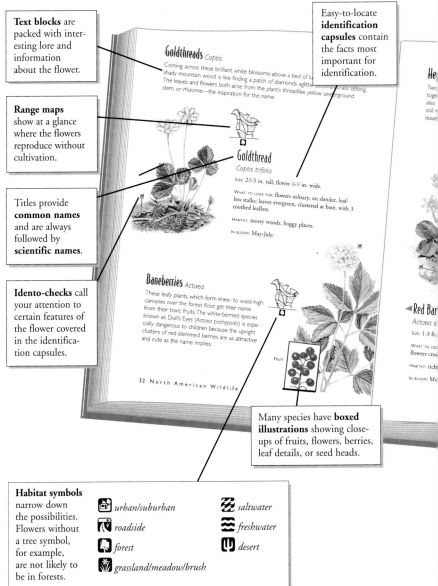

Text blocks are packed with interesting lore and information about the flower.

Easy-to-locate **identification capsules** contain the facts most important for identification.

Range maps show at a glance where the flowers reproduce without cultivation.

Titles provide **common names** and are always followed by **scientific names**.

Idento-checks call your attention to certain features of the flower covered in the identification capsules.

Goldthreads Coptis

Coming across these brilliant white blossoms above a bed of lush shady mountain wood is like finding a patch of diamonds aglitter in the second setting. The leaves and flowers both arise from the plant's threadlike yellow underground stem, or rhizome—the inspiration for the name.

Goldthread
Coptis trifolia

Size: 2½-5 in. tall; flower ¼-½ in. wide.

WHAT TO LOOK FOR: flowers solitary, on slender, leafless stalks; leaves evergreen, clustered at base, with 3 toothed leaflets.

HABITAT: mossy woods, boggy places.

IN BLOOM: May-July.

Baneberries Actaea

These leafy plants, which form knee- to waist-high canopies over the forest floor, get their name from their toxic fruits. The white-berried species known as Doll's Eyes (*Actaea pachypoda*) is especially dangerous to children because the upright clusters of red-stemmed berries are as attractive and cute as the name implies.

FRUIT

32 North American Wildlife

He
Two
toge
also
soil
leave

◄ Red Ba[r]
Actaea s

Size: 1-3 ft.

WHAT TO LO[OK]
flowers crea

HABITAT: rich

IN BLOOM: Ma

Many species have **boxed illustrations** showing close-ups of fruits, flowers, berries, leaf details, or seed heads.

Habitat symbols narrow down the possibilities. Flowers without a tree symbol, for example, are not likely to be in forests.

🏠 *urban/suburban*   🐾 *saltwater*

🌿 *roadside*   🌊 *freshwater*

🌲 *forest*   🌵 *desert*

🌼 *grassland/meadow/brush*

For the purposes of this book, a wildflower is any flowering plant that grows outside cultivation and is neither a tree nor a tall shrub. More than 15,000 such species grow north of the Mexican border.

Plants in this book are arranged by botanical family, a scheme that involves consideration of both flower and fruit. This arrangement may take some getting used to. The chart that begins on the following page will help you make the most of this book.

Range maps show the zones where species are most likely to occur. A plant is not necessarily found throughout a zone. Similarly, plants growing in an area may bloom for a shorter time than the blossoming period indicated for the species as a whole.

For centuries, wildflowers have been used as food and medicine. Many such uses are mentioned in this book as items of interest only. Because there are dangers involved, we advise *against* trying any of them.

The Anatomy of Flowers

Most flowers need an insect or bird to transfer pollen from the stamen of a blossom to the pistil of another. Blossom parts are arranged to encourage pollination, and the flower offers a nectar reward.

The Wild Geranium (below left) illustrates the parts of a typical flower. The Daisy (below right) bears a composite flowerhead, made up of many small 5-petalled flowers.

Flower colors, shapes, textures, and scents serve one function: to produce seed for a new generation. Flowers contain ovule- ("egg-") producing female organs (pistils), pollen-producing male organs (stamens), or both. To set seed, the ovule, or ovules, at the base of the pistil must be fertilized by a grain of pollen from an anther. Exceptions to this rule, such as Dandelions, set seed without pollination.

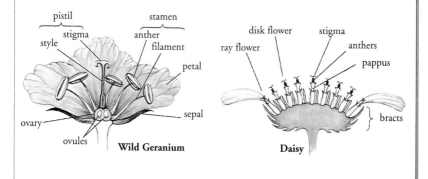

WILDFLOWER IDENTIFICATION CHART

To help you use this book, most of the species shown in it are listed below, arranged by color (yellow to orange, white, red, pink to lavender, blue to purple, and green to brown) and then by overall structure (either small flowers in clusters or a certain number of petals or petallike parts). The symbols used to define flower shapes are explained below.

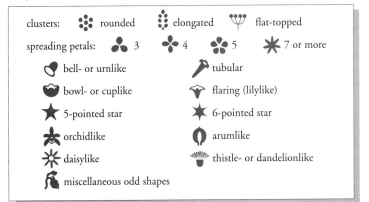

clusters: ⚬ rounded   ⚬ elongated   ⚘ flat-topped

spreading petals: ❀ 3   ❀ 4   ❀ 5   ✳ 7 or more

♥ bell- or urnlike   ↗ tubular

♥ bowl- or cuplike   ⚘ flaring (lilylike)

★ 5-pointed star   ✶ 6-pointed star

⚜ orchidlike   ⚘ arumlike

✳ daisylike   ⚘ thistle- or dandelionlike

⚜ miscellaneous odd shapes

CLUSTERS

⚬ Cushion Buckwheat p.81
⚬ Black Mustard p.107
⚬ Western Wallflower p.110
⚬ Tufted Loosestrife p.126
⚬ Wall Pepper p.131
⚬ Gordon's Ivesia p.135
⚬ Round-headed Bush Clover p.161
⚬ Orange Milkwort p.191
⚬ Butterfly Pea p.152
⚬ Desert Milkweed p.217
⚬ Navarretia p.233
⚬ Spotted Horsemint p. 257
⚬ Birdbeak p.270

⚬ Alpine Goldenrod p.309
⚬ Desert Plume p.108
⚬ Swamp Candles p.127
⚬ Canyon Dudleya p.132
⚬ Wild Senna p.142
⚬ Milk Vetch p.147
⚬ Yellow Lupine p.155
⚬ Wild Indigo p.153
⚬ Hoary Puccoon p.238
⚬ Horse Balm p.255
⚬ Downy Paintbrush p.262
⚬ Common Mullein p.276
⚬ Goldenrods pp.308-311
⚬ Golden Club p.385
⚬ California Bog Asphodel p.417

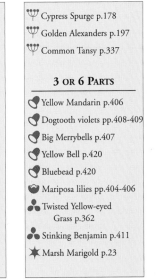

⚘ Cypress Spurge p.178
⚘ Golden Alexanders p.197
⚘ Common Tansy p.337

3 OR 6 PARTS

♥ Yellow Mandarin p.406
♥ Dogtooth violets pp.408-409
♥ Big Merrybells p.407
♥ Yellow Bell p.420
♥ Bluebead p.420
♥ Mariposa lilies pp.404-406
❀ Twisted Yellow-eyed Grass p.362
❀ Stinking Benjamin p.411
✶ Marsh Marigold p.23

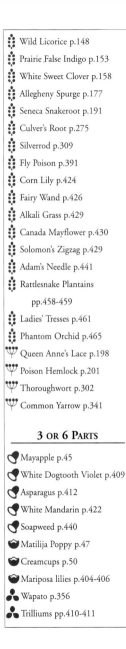
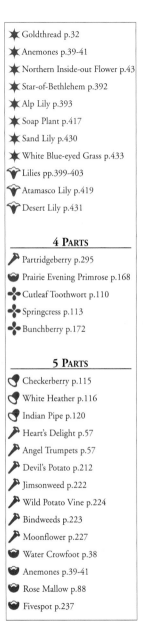

- ✴ Rock Sandwort p.63
- ✴ Common Chickweed p.63
- ✴ Starry Campion p.64
- ✴ Star Cucumber p.105
- ✴ One-flowered Wintergreen p.119
- ✴ Grass of Parnassus, p.135
- ✴ Buckbean p.208
- ✴ Black Nightshade p.219
- ✴ Horse Nettle p.219
- ❉ Bladder Campion p.66
- ❉ Bouncing Bet p.67
- ❉ White Campion p.69
- ❉ Leadwort p.82
- ❉ Roundleaf Sundew p.94
- ❉ Venus Flytrap p.95
- ❉ Violets pp.96-100
- ❉ Pipsissewa p.117
- ❉ Wild Strawberry p.136
- ❉ Tall Cinquefoil p.139
- ❉ Quail Plant p.240

7 OR MORE PARTS

- ✳ Yerba Mansa p.16
- ✳ White Water-lily p.20
- ✳ Elkslip p.23
- ✳ Rue Anemone p.28
- ✳ Goldthread p.32
- ✳ Carolina Anemone p.41
- ✳ Twinleaf p.46
- ✳ Bloodroot p.50
- ✳ Ice Plant p.76
- ✳ Starflower p.132
- ✳ Desert Chicory p.353

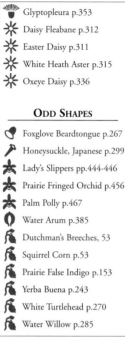

- ✴ Glyptopleura p.353
- ✴ Daisy Fleabane p.312
- ✴ Easter Daisy p.311
- ✴ White Heath Aster p.315
- ✴ Oxeye Daisy p.336

ODD SHAPES

- Foxglove Beardtongue p.267
- Honeysuckle, Japanese p.299
- Lady's Slippers pp.444-446
- Prairie Fringed Orchid p.456
- Palm Polly p.467
- Water Arum p.385
- Dutchman's Breeches, 53
- Squirrel Corn p.53
- Prairie False Indigo p.153
- Yerba Buena p.243
- White Turtlehead p.270
- Water Willow p.285

CLUSTERS

- Four O'Clock p.56
- Crimson Clover p.156
- Trumpet Honeysuckle p.298
- Firecracker Flower p.398
- Snow Plant p.122
- Canyon Dudleya p.132
- Cardinal Spear p.151
- Indian Pink p.195
- Indian paintbrush p.261-263
- Leafless Beaked Orchid p.460

3 OR 6 PARTS

- Red Prickly Poppy p.47

- Mariposa lilies p.404-406
- Wood Lily p.403

4 PARTS

- Scarlet Clematis p.25
- Hummingbird Trumpet p.165
- Trompetilla p.295

5 PARTS

- Wild Columbine p.30
- Prairie Smoke p.141
- Indian Pink p.195
- Cypress Vine p.227
- Standing Cypress p.232
- Cross Vine p.283
- Trumpet Creeper p.283
- Poppy Mallow p.90
- Scarlet Globe Mallow p.90
- Scarlet Pimpernel p.128
- Fire Pink p.65
- Round-leaved Catchfly p.65
- Prairie Bur p.194
- Rose Moss p.72
- Nama p. 236

7 OR MORE PARTS

- Strawberry Hedgehog p.61
- Claret Cup Cactus p.60
- Firewheel p.335

ODD SHAPES

- Tropical sage p.259
- Scarlet Bugler, 266

7 OR MORE PARTS

* Sacred Lotus p.22
* Hepatica p.33
* Carolina Anemone p.41
* Peyote p.59
* Pincushion Cactus p.62
* Fishhook Cactus p.62
* Bitterroot p.73
* Ice Plant p.76
* Maypop p.101
* Large Marsh Pink p.211
* Skeleton Plant p.348
* Dusty Maiden p.335
* Spotted Knapweed p.341
* Nodding Thistle p.342
* Thistles pp. 342, 344-345
* Daisy Fleabane p.312
* Easter Daisy p.311
* Asters pp.314-316
* Pale Purple Coneflower p.324

ODD SHAPES

* Rosebud Orchid p.449
* Lady's slippers pp.444-446
* Three Birds, 448
* Calypso p.443
* Dragon's Mouth p.448
* Rose Pogonia p.447
* Large Twayblade p.451
* Showy Orchis p.456
* Grass Pink p.462
* Stream Orchid p.468
* Western Bleeding Heart p.52

* Pale Corydalis p.54
* Locoweed p.146
* Crown Vetch p.149
* Butterfly Pea p.152
* Gaywings p.190
* Obedience p.251
* Beardtongues pp.266-268
* Towering Lousewort p.278
* Elephant Heads p.279
* Unicorn Plant p.286

CLUSTERS

* Roseroot p.130
* Ground Plum p.147
* Groundnut p.152
* Purple Prairie Clover p.159
* Bottle Gentian p.204
* Bluestar p.209
* Miami Mist p.235
* Blueweed p.238
* Rose Vervain p.242
* Heal-all p.246
* Gill-over-the-ground p.251
* Chia p.258
* Blue-eyed Mary p.261
* Escobita p.271
* Tall Ironweed p.303
* Lupines pp.154-155
* American Wisteria p.161
* Spiked Loosestrife p.171
* Purple Fringe p.234
* Hoary Vervain p.242
* Woundwort p.247

* Carpet Bugleweed p.249
* Mountain Kittentails p.272
* Louisiana Broomrape p.280
* Venus' Looking Glass p.290
* Great Blue Lobelia p.293
* Blazing Stars p.306
* Pickerelweed p.389
* Camases p.426-427
* Mistflower p.301

3 OR 6 PARTS

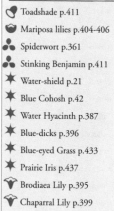

* Toadshade p.411
* Mariposa lilies p.404-406
* Spiderwort p.361
* Stinking Benjamin p.411
* Water-shield p.21
* Blue Cohosh p.42
* Water Hyacinth p.387
* Blue-dicks p.396
* Blue-eyed Grass p.433
* Prairie Iris p.437
* Brodiaea Lily p.395
* Chaparral Lily p.399

4 PARTS

* Leatherflower p.24
* Fringed Gentian p.205
* Desert Candle p.109
* Winecup Clarkia p.167
* Birdseye Speedwell p.274
* Quaker Ladies p.294

5 Parts

- Northern Pitcher Plant p.92
- Prairie Smoke p.141
- Explorer's Gentian p.206
- Greek Valerian p.231
- Virginia Bluebells p.239
- Southern Harebell p.289
- Desert Four O'Clock p.56
- Morning glories pp.224-225
- Pale Trumpets p.232
- Ruellia p.284
- Blue Columbine p.31
- Baby Blue-eyes p.237
- Marsh Cinquefoil p.138
- Downy Gentian p.206
- Bluestar p.209
- Bittersweet Nightshade p.221
- Tall Bellflower p.288
- Larkspurs p.35
- Rose Moss p.72
- Violets pp.96-100
- Violet Wood Sorrel p.189
- Common Flax p.187
- Running Myrtle p. 211
- Phlox pp.228-230
- Nama p. 236
- Forget-me-not p.239

7 or More Parts

- Strawberry Hedgehog p.61
- Maypop p.101
- Thistles pp. 342, 344-345
- Common Chicory p.352
- Asters pp.314-316

Odd Shapes

- Spotted Coralroot p.453
- Showy Orchis p.456
- Purple Fringed Orchid p.455
- Cranefly Orchid p.458
- Stream Orchid p.468
- Jack-in-the-pulpit p.386
- Monkshoods p.29
- Downy Skullcap p.251
- Blue Curls p.253
- Bladder Sage p.255
- Blue Sage p.259
- Allegheny Monkey Flower p.264
- Towering Lousewort p.278
- Butterwort p.286
- Downingias p.291
- Asiatic Dayflower p.363
- Irises pp.434-437

Clusters

- Snow-on-the-mountain p.179
- American Spikenard p.193
- Green Milkweed p.217
- Lamb's Quarters p.69
- One-sided Pyrola p.119
- Deertongue p.203
- Common Plantain p.243
- Common Ragweed p.320
- Cattails p.381
- Indian Poke p.425
- Bunchflower p.428

3 or 6 Parts

- Wild Gingers p.17
- Indian Cucumberroot p.407
- Toadshade p.411
- Solomon's Seal p.421

5 Parts

- Cobra Plant p.93

7 or More Parts

- Teddy Bear Cholla p.58
- Hen and Chickens Cactus p.61

Odd Shapes

- Heartleaf Twayblade p.450
- Puttyroot p.457
- Butterfly Orchid p.464
- Vanilla Orchid p.466
- Skunk Cabbage p.387
- Green Dragon p.386
- Green Arrow p.389
- Dutchman's Pipe p.18
- Indian Root p.19

Lizard's Tails *Saururus*

The Lizard's Tail takes its name from the graceful plumes of delicately scented flowers that have made it a popular plant for pools and water gardens. (It is sometimes sold under the less picturesque name of Swamp Lily.) Spreading by means of branches that form just above the roots, it occasionally escapes from cultivation and is therefore found growing in wetlands well outside its native range.

Lizard's Tail *Saururus cernuus*

SIZE: 1-3 ft. tall; flower plume 3-6 in. long.

WHAT TO LOOK FOR: flowers tiny, cream-colored, in drooping plumes; leaves heart-shaped, leathery.

HABITAT: pond edges, swampy forests.

IN BLOOM: June-Sept.

Yerba Mansa *Anemopsis*

The alkaline soil of the New Mexico section of the Rio Grande Valley is bound tightly together by the spreading root systems of clusters of Yerba Mansa. Bricks cut from this soil are more waterproof than plain mud adobe, and so they were preferred as building material—first by the Indians and later by the Spanish, who christened the plant *yerba del manso*, or plant of the farmhouse.

Yerba Mansa *Anemopsis californica*

SIZE: 2-6 in. tall; flower head 1-2 in. wide.

WHAT TO LOOK FOR: flower heads white or pinkish, composed of many tiny flowers clustered above petallike bracts; leaves long-stalked, oval.

HABITAT: wet meadows, streambanks.

IN BLOOM: Mar.-Aug.

Wild Gingers *Asarum*

The sharply acrid taste of these plants, reminiscent of the unrelated tropical spice for which they are named, protects them against most plant eaters. Humans, however, dig the spreading underground stems (called rhizomes), boil the pieces in sugar water, and use the decoction in place of true ginger. The ground-hugging flowers have a fetid odor, like rotting meat, and attract pollinating flies. After the seeds have formed, ants carry them away but eat only the seed coats, thus spreading the plant.

Wild Ginger

Asarum canadense

Size: 4-7 in. tall;
flower ½-1½ in. wide.

What to look for: leaves large, hairy, kidney-shaped; flowers red-brown to purple, urn-shaped, each borne on short stem between 2 leaves.

Habitat:
rich woods.

In bloom:
Mar.-June.

Western Wild Ginger

Asarum caudatum

Size: 4-8 in. tall; flower 2-5 in. wide.

What to look for:
leaves slightly hairy, heart-shaped; flowers brownish purple, urn-shaped, with 3 thin "tails."

Habitat:
rich woods.

In bloom:
Apr.-July.

Birthworts *Aristolochia*

According to the Doctrine of Signatures, a concept prevalent in the 17th century, plants proclaimed their medicinal values by some aspect of their appearance. Because the flowers of birthwort seemed to resemble pregnant wombs, women in labor were advised to chew the roots to ease the pain of childbirth. But the birthwort flower is in fact a flytrap that ensures cross-pollination. In the depths of each blossom is the pistil, or female organ, which matures before the stamens (male organs). The pistil is located at the end of a narrow passageway lined with downward-pointing hairs. Attracted by the fetid-smelling nectar, a fly enters the flower but cannot escape. While imprisoned it feeds on nectar and deposits any pollen it may have carried from another blossom. Later, when the pollen-producing stamens have matured, the flower opens fully. On the way out, the fly picks up fresh pollen to carry to another flower.

Dutchman's Pipe

Aristolochia durior

SIZE:
vine to 60 ft. high;
flower 1-1½ in. long.

WHAT TO LOOK FOR:
flowers pipe-shaped, purple to greenish yellow; leaves heart-shaped, to 1 ft. wide.

HABITAT:
rich woods, swampy forests.

IN BLOOM:
May-July.

Virginia Snakeroot

Aristolochia serpentaria

SIZE:
6-30 in. tall;
flower ½-¾ in. long.

WHAT TO LOOK FOR:
flowers brownish purple, S-shaped, borne on
stalks near ground; leaves arrow- to heart-shaped.

HABITAT:
dry to wet forests; often in leaf litter.

IN BLOOM:
May-July.

Indian Root

Aristolochia watsoni

SIZE: vine 1-3 ft. long;
flower ¾-1½ in. long.

WHAT TO LOOK FOR: stems trailing; flowers tubular with
narrow opening, brown to greenish purple; leaves
hairy, triangular, lobed at base.

HABITAT: warm deserts, mountain scrublands.

IN BLOOM: Apr.-Aug.

Water-lilies *Nymphaea*

Among the many plants that grow rooted to the bottoms of ponds, lakes, and sluggish rivers, these are best beloved, with their bright, floating blossoms and deeply notched pads. When the flower fades, its stalk shrinks, submerging the hard-cased fruit while the edible seeds mature. Then the case opens, and the seeds float free until they finally become waterlogged, sink, and take root.

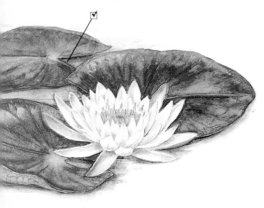

White Water-lily
Nymphaea odorata

SIZE:
flower 2-6 in. wide;
leaf 3-20 in. across.

WHAT TO LOOK FOR:
flowers white, floating; leaves shiny green, oval, notched, floating.

HABITAT:
still freshwater to 8 ft. deep.

IN BLOOM:
Mar.-Oct.

Yellow Water-lily
Nymphaea mexicana

SIZE: flower 3-4 in. wide;
leaf 4-8 in. across.

WHAT TO LOOK FOR: flowers yellow, floating or slightly above water surface; leaves green blotched with brown, notched, floating.

HABITAT: still freshwater to 4 ft. deep.

IN BLOOM: Mar.-Sept.

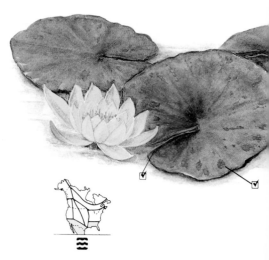

Water-shields *Brasenia*

The single species of Water-shield grows wild on every continent except Antarctica, known by such names as Deerfood, Frogleaf, Little Water-lily, Purple Dock, and Water Target. The hard round seeds are eaten by ducks the world over, and people of many lands eat the roots and leaves. The undersides of the leaves, stems, and other submerged parts are protected from snails, insect larvae, and many other water animals by a gelatinous coating.

Pond-lilies *Nuphar*

These plants, also known as spatterdocks, grow so rampantly that they are often eradicated as weeds. Where wildlife is abundant, however, this vigor is of value. Ducks eat the seeds. Moose and deer graze on the greens. Muskrats and beavers relish the sweet rootstocks, storing caches of them for winter. (Indians and frontiersmen, who cooked and ate the rootstocks like potatoes or pounded them into flour, sometimes raided the animal stockpiles.)

Water-shield

Brasenia schreberi

SIZE: flower ½ in. wide; leaf 2-4 in. across.

WHAT TO LOOK FOR: flowers dull reddish purple, held slightly above water on stout stems; leaves medium green, elliptical, floating on surface.

HABITAT: still freshwater to 10 ft. deep.

IN BLOOM: June-Sept.

Yellow Pond-lily

Nuphar luteum

SIZE: flower ½-2½ in. wide; leaf 2-18 in. across.

WHAT TO LOOK FOR: flowers cup-shaped, held above water; heart-shaped leaves submerged, floating, or above water.

HABITAT: still freshwater to 15 ft. deep.

IN BLOOM: May-Oct.

Lotuses *Nelumbo*

Larger than this entire page, lotus leaves and flowers rise above the water on stout stalks. In the center of each blossom is a structure that looks like a salt shaker. After pollination, the petals fall away, leaving this structure standing naked above the water, filled with seeds that can remain viable for centuries.

Sacred Lotus

Nelumbo nucifera

SIZE:
flower 6-9 in. wide; leaf 12-24 in. across.

WHAT TO LOOK FOR:
flowers pink, held above water; leaves leathery, umbrellalike.

HABITAT:
still freshwater to 8 ft. deep.

IN BLOOM:
June-Aug.

Yellow Lotus

Nelumbo lutea

SIZE:
flower 6-8 in. wide; leaf 12-24 in. across.

WHAT TO LOOK FOR:
flowers yellow, held up to 10 ft. above surface; leaves umbrellalike.

HABITAT:
still freshwater to 8 ft. deep.

IN BLOOM:
June-Sept.

Marsh Marigolds *Caltha*

Although these plants are called marigolds, they actually belong to the buttercup family. Crowds of their cheery flowers and glistening leaves brighten wetlands throughout the Northern Hemisphere. The leaves are often eaten cooked, but are poisonous to humans and most animals if eaten raw. Elk and moose, however, feed with impunity on the Elkslip.

Marsh Marigold

Caltha palustris

SIZE:
6-30 in. tall; flower 1-2 in. wide.

WHAT TO LOOK FOR:
flowers bright yellow; leaves round or heart-shaped, toothed, clustered at plant base and scattered along stem.

HABITAT:
marshes, swamps, ditches.

IN BLOOM:
Apr.-Aug.

Elkslip

Caltha leptosepala

SIZE: 6-12 in. tall; flower ¾-2 in. wide.

WHAT TO LOOK FOR: flowers white, with yellow center; leaves oblong to heart-shaped, clustered at plant base.

HABITAT: mountain streams, marshes.

IN BLOOM: May-Aug.

Clematises *Clematis*

These plants are unique among the buttercup family in that they are twining vines. They climb trees, arbors, and other supports by what seem to be leafy, coiling branches. When Charles Darwin studied the Virgin's Bower, he found that each new leafstalk revolves as it grows, making a full circle every five or six hours until it finds a solid object to climb. The technical term for this searching pattern of growth is thigmotropism.

FRUIT

Virgin's Bower
Clematis virginiana

SIZE: vine 3-15 ft. high; flower ½-¾ in. wide.

WHAT TO LOOK FOR: flowers white, on dense, tangled vine; leaves divided into 3 leaflets; fruit white, feathery.

HABITAT: thickets, fencerows, roadsides.

IN BLOOM: July-Sept.

Leatherflower
Clematis viorna

SIZE: vine 3-6 ft. high; flower ¾ in. wide.

WHAT TO LOOK FOR: flowers pinkish purple with creamy tips, urn-shaped, nodding; leaves divided into several large egg-shaped leaflets.

HABITAT: rich woods; rich thickets.

IN BLOOM: May-Aug.

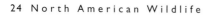

Scarlet Clematis

Clematis texensis

Size: vine 1-6 ft. high; flower ½-¾ in. wide.

What to look for: flowers red, urn-shaped, single or clustered; leaves divided into 3-5 pairs of rounded leaflets; stems sprawling or climbing.

Habitat: cliffs, wooded slopes near streams in Texas.

In bloom: May-June.

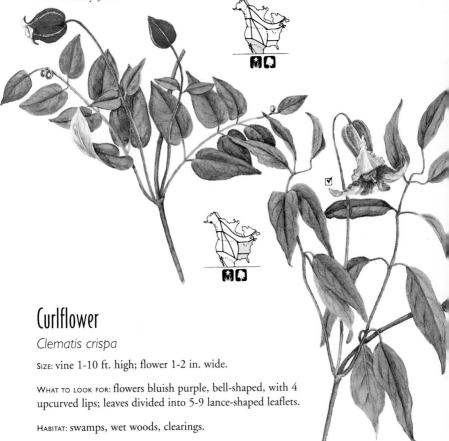

Curlflower

Clematis crispa

Size: vine 1-10 ft. high; flower 1-2 in. wide.

What to look for: flowers bluish purple, bell-shaped, with 4 upcurved lips; leaves divided into 5-9 lance-shaped leaflets.

Habitat: swamps, wet woods, clearings.

In bloom: Apr.-Aug.

Goldenseals *Hydrastis*

Once abundant, the only American goldenseal is rare now because its thick yellow roots have had great commercial value. They were used to treat dyspepsia, skin eruptions, and hemorrhage, and were also a source of yellow dye and an insect repellent. Lewis and Clark described Goldenseal to Thomas Jefferson as a "sovereign remidy [*sic*] for sore eyes."

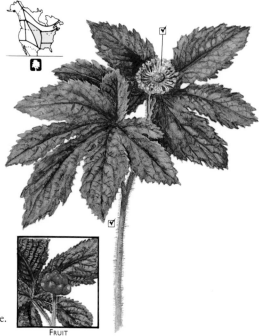

FRUIT

Goldenseal

Hydrastis canadensis

SIZE:
6-18 in. tall; flower ½-¾ in. wide.

WHAT TO LOOK FOR:
flower creamy yellow, solitary, atop hairy stem with 2 hand-shaped hairy leaves; fruit cluster of red berries (summer).

HABITAT:
rich woods.

IN BLOOM:
Apr.-May.

Meadow Rues *Thalictrum*

Several of these stately perennials bear the male (pollen-producing) flowers on one plant and the seed-producing female flowers on the other, and thus depend on wind and—to a lesser extent—on insects to carry pollen from plant to plant. Most other species bear both kinds of flowers on one plant, and a few high mountain species bear "perfect" flowers (each bloom has both male and female parts).

Purple Meadow Rue

Thalictrum dasycarpum

SIZE:
2-7 ft. tall; flower ¼-½ in. wide.

WHAT TO LOOK FOR:
male flowers showy, with threadlike drooping stamens; female flowers (dull green buttons) sometimes on same plant; leaves dark green, much divided; stems purplish.

HABITAT:
moist meadows, thickets, marshes.

IN BLOOM:
May-July.

Rue Anemones *Anemonella*

Neither a rue nor an anemone, the one species in this group gets its compound name from its ruelike leaves and anemonelike flowers. The False Rue Anemone (*Isopyrum biternatum*) resembles this plant (its flowers are smaller), and it has a similar range.

Rue Anemone

Anemonella thalictroides

SIZE:
2-8 in. tall; flower ½-¾ in. wide.

WHAT TO LOOK FOR:
flowers white, in 2's or 3's, surrounded by whorl of leaflets atop wiry black stem; leaves from base much divided.

HABITAT: rich woods. IN BLOOM: Apr.-May.

Globeflowers *Trollius*

Occasionally seen in cultivation, globeflowers are rather rare in the wild. There is only one species in North America; a white-flowered variety of this species is found high in the Rocky Mountains. Its flowers appear in profusion after the snow melts.

American Globeflower

Trollius laxus

SIZE: 4-20 in. tall; flower ¾-1½ in. wide.

WHAT TO LOOK FOR: flowers greenish yellow, cup-shaped, scattered on plants; leaves sharply segmented, toothed.

HABITAT: marshes, swampy woods, streams.

IN BLOOM: Apr.-June.

Monkshoods *Aconitum*

The "hood" of the monkshood is technically a sepal that covers the true petals. In some species it more nearly resembles a crested helmet, inspiring such names as Thor's Hat and Helmetflower. Monkshoods are pollinated mainly by bumblebees, which are among the few insects strong enough to enter the hood. The plants are hazardous to both humans and livestock; they contain a deadly substance called aconite, which has been used as arrow poison.

Blue Monkshood

Aconitum columbianum

SIZE:
1-7 ft. tall; flower ¾-1 in. wide.

WHAT TO LOOK FOR:
flowers blue or purple (occasionally white), hooded, on tall stalk; leaves lobed, toothed.

HABITAT:
streambanks, moist woods, meadows.

IN BLOOM:
June-Aug.

Wild Monkshood

Aconitum uncinatum

SIZE:
2-4 ft. tall; flower ¾-1 in. wide.

WHAT TO LOOK FOR:
flowers blue-purple, with helmetlike hoods on weak (often reclining) stem; leaves lobed.

HABITAT:
rich woods, unwooded streambanks.

IN BLOOM:
July-Oct.

Columbines *Aquilegia*

Each of the five petals of a columbine flower stretches back into a distinctive spur, and deep within these spurs is the nectar that attracts pollinating animals. The nectar of some species can be reached by bees. Other species attract long-tongued moths. Still others—all in the New World—are pollinated by hummingbirds. The five spurs give the flowers a birdlike form that inspired both the common and scientific names: "columbine" means dove, and *Aquilegia* is from the Latin for eagle. The petals are surrounded by five broad sepals of the same or a different color. Blue Columbine is Colorado's state flower.

Yellow Columbine

Aquilegia flavescens

SIZE:
1-2½ ft. tall;
flower ¾-1½ in. wide.

WHAT TO LOOK FOR:
flowers yellow, nodding, with spurs
½-¾ in. long; leaves much divided.

HABITAT: open woods, meadows.

IN BLOOM: June-Aug.

Wild Columbine

Aquilegia canadensis

SIZE:
1-4 ft. tall; flower ½-1 in. wide.

WHAT TO LOOK FOR:
flowers red and yellow, nodding; leaves divided,
subdivided into 3's, almost fernlike.

HABITAT: rocky woods, clearings; shaded cliffs, ledges.

IN BLOOM: Apr.-June.

Blue Columbine

Aquilegia coerulea

SIZE:
1-2 ft. tall; flower 1-2 in. wide.

WHAT TO LOOK FOR:
flowers blue, white, or blue and white, with
1- to 2-in. spurs; leaves divided into many leaflets.

HABITAT: mountain woods and clearings.

IN BLOOM: June-Aug.

Longspur Columbine

Aquilegia longissima

SIZE:
2-4 ft. tall; flower 1½-3 in. wide.

WHAT TO LOOK FOR:
flowers yellow, erect, with 4- to 8-in. spurs.

HABITAT:
streambanks, rocky canyons.

IN BLOOM:
June-Nov.

Goldthreads *Coptis*

Coming across these brilliant white blossoms above a bed of lustrous green leaves in a shady mountain wood is like finding a patch of diamonds aglitter in an emerald setting. The leaves and flowers both arise from the plant's threadlike yellow underground stem, or rhizome—the inspiration for the name.

Goldthread

Coptis trifolia

SIZE: 2½-5 in. tall; flower ¼-½ in. wide.

WHAT TO LOOK FOR: flowers solitary, on slender, leafless stalks; leaves evergreen, clustered at base, with 3 toothed leaflets.

HABITAT: mossy woods, boggy places.

IN BLOOM: May-July.

Baneberries *Actaea*

These leafy plants, which form knee- to waist-high canopies over the forest floor, get their name from their toxic fruits. The white-berried species known as Doll's Eyes (*Actaea pachypoda*) is especially dangerous to children because the upright clusters of red-stemmed berries are as attractive and cute as the name implies.

FRUIT

Hepaticas *Hepatica*

Two forms of hepatica grow in the same general range (though seldom together) and look very much alike except for their leaf shapes. The Hepatica, also called Liverleaf, grows in acid soil; the Sharp-lobed Hepatica flourishes in soil with a limestone base. The flowers of both open in spring before new leaves appear, above a flat blanket of last year's foliage.

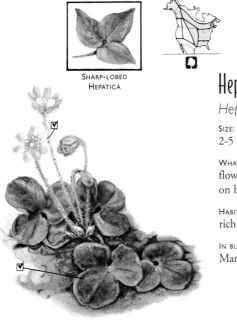

SHARP-LOBED
HEPATICA

Hepatica
Hepatica nobilis

SIZE:
2-5 in. high; flower ½-¾ in. wide.

WHAT TO LOOK FOR:
flowers blue, purple, pinkish, or white, on hairy stalks; leaves leathery, 3-lobed.

HABITAT:
rich woods.

IN BLOOM:
Mar.-Apr.

◄ Red Baneberry
Actaea spicata

SIZE: 1-3 ft. tall; flower ¼ in. wide.

WHAT TO LOOK FOR: leaves divided into toothed leaflets; flowers creamy white in rounded clusters; berries red.

HABITAT: rich woods, streambanks.

IN BLOOM: May-June.

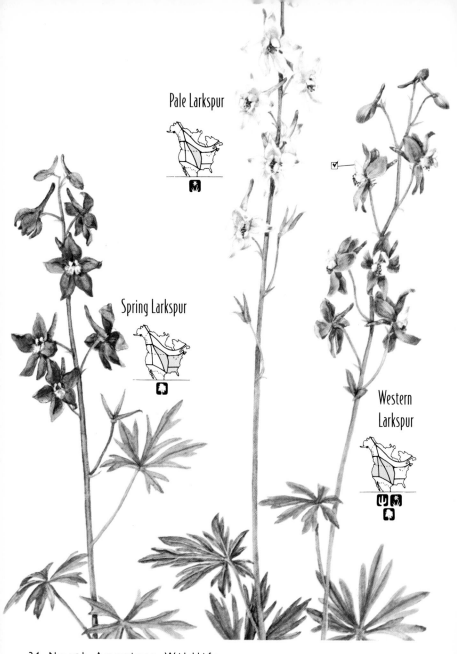

Pale Larkspur

Spring Larkspur

Western
Larkspur

Larkspurs *Delphinium*

Shakespeare knew them as lark's heels. Their modern name describes the same characteristic spur, which is formed by the upper sepal of the flower. (There are five sepals, all of the same color.) In the center of each flower are four small petals. The upper two petals extend back to line the inside of the spur, where nectar awaits those insects that can reach it—long-tongued butterflies and moths, and strong, aggressive bumblebees. Because all parts of the plants are poisonous to livestock, as well as to humans, they are among the many plants known in western cattle country as locoweeds, staggerweeds, or cow poisons. The Hopi Indians extracted a blue dye from the flowers of larkspur, and settlers later mixed this extract with a fixative to make blue ink.

Spring Larkspur

Delphinium tricorne

SIZE:
6-36 in. tall; flower 1-1½ in. long.

WHAT TO LOOK FOR:
flowers purple or blue (rarely white), loosely clustered along upper part of wandlike stem; leaves divided, scattered on stem.

HABITAT:
rich woods, clearings.

IN BLOOM: Apr.-May.

Pale Larkspur

Delphinium virescens

SIZE:
18-48 in. tall; flower ¾-1 in. long.

WHAT TO LOOK FOR:
flowers white to light lavender (greenish tinge), clustered along wandlike stem; leaves at base of stem, finely divided.

HABITAT:
dry prairies.

IN BLOOM: June-July.

Western Larkspur

Delphinium nuttallianum

SIZE:
6-30 in. tall; flower 1-1½ in. long.

WHAT TO LOOK FOR:
flowers bright blue to purplish with white upper petals, loosely clustered along wandlike stem; leaves at base of stem, divided into sharp-tipped leaflets.

HABITAT:
sagebrush, grassy prairies, open mountain woods.

IN BLOOM: May-Aug.

Buttercups *Ranunculus*

There are more than 300 species of buttercups. Some grow on land, some in water, and the majority in the moist and marshy places that lie between. Most are notable for their splayed leaves—for which some species are called crowfoot—and cupped flowers. Many contain an acrid juice that can poison cattle and blister human skin. Beggars once used the Tall Buttercup and the aptly named Cursed Crowfoot (*Ranunculus sceleratus*) to induce ulcerous sores on their bodies and faces. Among botanists, buttercups are believed to represent a primitive, nonspecialized stage of evolution. Many species have petals and similar-looking sepals that open to reveal a central mound of multiple stamens and pistils crowded together; a disturbance will shake pollen from one to the other. In more highly evolved plants, the parts are adapted to perform special functions in the process of cross-pollination.

Swamp Buttercup

Ranunculus hispidus

SIZE:
1-3 ft. long; flower ¾-1 in. wide.

WHAT TO LOOK FOR:
flowers bright yellow, with 5 petals much longer than sepals; stems usually sprawling; leaves divided into 3 stalked leaflets.

HABITAT:
marshes, ditches, wet woods, meadows.

IN BLOOM:
Apr.-June.

Prairie Buttercup

Ranunculus rhomboideus

SIZE:
2-7 in. tall; flower ½-¾ in. wide.

WHAT TO LOOK FOR:
flowers light yellow, with 5 narrow petals and
5 short, lavender-tinged sepals around spherical
center clusters; stems hairy; leaves lobed near
flower, spoon-shaped near base of plant.

HABITAT:
grasslands, dry prairies.

IN BLOOM:
Apr.-May.

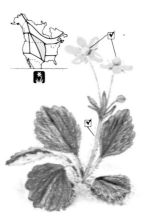

Tall Buttercup

Ranunculus acris

SIZE:
1-3 ft. tall; flower ¾-1 in. wide.

WHAT TO LOOK FOR:
flowers waxy, bright yellow or white,
on slender, branched stems; leaves
divided into 5-7 toothed leaflets.

HABITAT:
meadows, fields, roadsides.

IN BLOOM:
May-Sept.

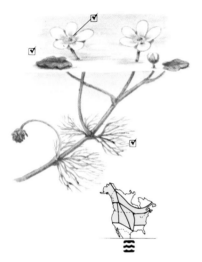

Water Crowfoot

Ranunculus trichophyllus

SIZE:
1-3 ft. long; flower ½ in. wide.

WHAT TO LOOK FOR:
flowers white with yellow centers, held just
above water; leaves round-lobed on surface,
hairlike underwater.

HABITAT:
ponds, marshes.

IN BLOOM:
May-July.

Bristly Crowfoot

Ranunculus pensylvanicus

SIZE:
1-2 ft. tall; flower ¼-½ in. wide.

WHAT TO LOOK FOR:
flowers pale yellow, with petals shorter than sepals;
stems bristly; leaves hairy, cleft into 3 sharp-pointed lobes.

HABITAT:
marshes, ditches, wet meadows.

IN BLOOM:
July-Aug.

Anemones *Anemone*

Anemones are known as windflowers because their fluffy seeds are blown about and carried by the wind. In some species the petalless flowers (the sepals look like petals) are borne on short hairy stalks until they are pollinated by crawling insects; as the seedheads develop, the stalks stretch upward a few inches, allowing the feathery fruits to be caught by a passing breeze. (The appearance of the seedheads has inspired descriptive names for several species: the Pasqueflower is sometimes known as Prairie Smoke, and the Western Anemone is also called Old Man of the Mountains.) Other anemones, pollinated by bees and various other flying insects, stand tall from the beginning; many are known as Thimbleweed because of their compact seedheads. The Pasqueflower is the state flower of South Dakota and the provincial emblem of Manitoba.

Pasqueflower

Anemone patens

SIZE:
2-10 in. tall; flower 1-2 in. wide.

WHAT TO LOOK FOR:
flowers lavender with yellow centers, opening on silky stalks before leaves appear; leaves with strap-shaped lobes; seedheads feathery.

HABITAT:
dry prairies to mountain slopes.

IN BLOOM:
Apr.-May.

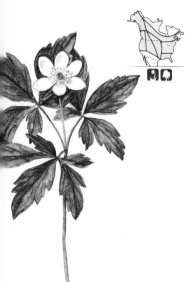

Wood Anemone

Anemone quinquefolia

SIZE:
3-10 in. tall; flower ½-1 in. wide.

WHAT TO LOOK FOR:
flowers white, starlike, solitary on delicate 3-leaved stem; each leaf divided into 3 or 5 leaflets.

HABITAT:
rich woods, wet meadows.

IN BLOOM:
Apr.-June.

Western Anemone

Anemone occidentalis

SIZE:
6-24 in. tall; flower 1½-2 in. wide.

WHAT TO LOOK FOR:
flowers showy, creamy white with golden centers, on densely hairy stems; seedheads with long white hairs; leaves divided, like lace.

HABITAT:
damp mountain slopes, grassy hills.

IN BLOOM:
June-Aug.

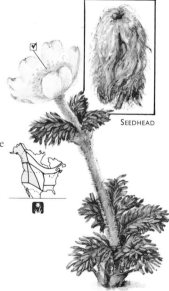

SEEDHEAD

WHITISH FORM

Carolina Anemone

Anemone caroliniana

SIZE:
1-12 in. tall; flower ¾-1½ in. wide.

WHAT TO LOOK FOR:
flowers white, pink, or purplish, with 10-20 sepals; leaves much divided, at base of woolly stems.

HABITAT:
dry prairies, clearings.

IN BLOOM:
Apr.-May.

Thimbleweed

Anemone cylindrica

SIZE:
1-2½ ft. tall; flower ¾-1 in. wide.

WHAT TO LOOK FOR:
flowers white, with greenish, thimble-shaped center; seedheads cylindrical, 1-1½ in. long; plant robust, with divided leaves.

HABITAT:
dry woods, prairies, mountain slopes.

IN BLOOM:
June-Aug.

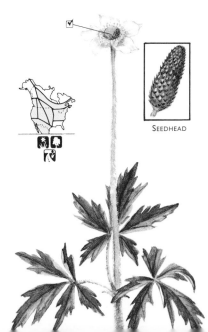

SEEDHEAD

Blue Cohoshes *Caulophyllum*

Indians gave the name cohosh to several unrelated plants with two things in common: they serve medicinal purposes, and they bear poisonous berries. The Blue Cohosh, which is the only species of *Caulophyllum,* is also called Papoose Root because Indians used it to hasten childbirth.

FRUIT

Blue Cohosh

Caulophyllum thalictroides

SIZE:
1-4 ft. tall; flower ½ in. wide.

WHAT TO LOOK FOR:
plant erect, branching; leaves divided into many lobed leaflets; flowers greenish purple; fruit berrylike blue seeds in loose clusters.

HABITAT: rich woods.

IN BLOOM: April-May.

Inside-out Flowers *Vancouveria*

The three species in this group grow in shaded forests of the Pacific Northwest. All bear similarly odd flowers, in which six backswept sepals hide six small petals. The Northern Inside-out Flower dies back in autumn; the Redwood Inside-out Flower (*Vancouveria planipetala*) and the Golden Inside-out Flower (*Vancouveria chrysantha*) are evergreen.

Northern Inside-out Flower

Vancouveria hexandra

SIZE:
4-20 in. tall; flower ½-¾ in. wide.

WHAT TO LOOK FOR:
flowers white, clustered along straight, branching stalk; leaves leathery, much divided.

HABITAT: rich, shady woods.

IN BLOOM: May-July.

Vanilla Leaves *Achlys*

There are two kinds of vanilla leaf in North America. The California Vanilla Leaf (*Achlys californica*), found only along the Pacific Coast, looks very much like this one, but its leaves are divided into more segments. Both are named for the pleasant fragrance of the leaves when dried, and both grow in dense groups on the moist floors of shady forests.

Vanilla Leaf

Achlys triphylla

SIZE:
1-2 ft. tall; flower ¼ in. wide.

WHAT TO LOOK FOR:
leaves large, with 3 fan-shaped leaflets on slim stalk; flowers white, petalless, clustered in dense spike atop leafless stalk.

HABITAT:
dense to open woods.

IN BLOOM:
Apr.-June.

Mayapples *Podophyllum*

The 19th-century botanist Asa Gray described the flavor of the Mayapple's ripe fruit as "somewhat mawkish, beloved of pigs, raccoons, and small boys." Immature fruits, seeds, and all other plant parts are poisonous. In the past, mild infusions have been used medicinally as a powerful purgative.

FRUIT

Mayapple

Podophyllum peltatum

SIZE:
6-20 in. tall; flower 1-2 in. wide.

WHAT TO LOOK FOR:
flowers cup-shaped, showy, borne singly between 2 large leaves; fruits lemon-yellow when ripe, as plants die back.

HABITAT: rich woods, clearings.

IN BLOOM: Apr.-June.

Twinleaves *Jeffersonia*

These woodland plants look much like miniature Mayapples and were, in fact, first included in the same group. William Bartram, the scientist who decided that they belonged in their own category, was a friend and colleague of Thomas Jefferson—himself a botanist of note—and so he called the new group *Jeffersonia*. The only other *Jeffersonia* species—*J. dubia*—occurs in Japan.

Twinleaf

Jeffersonia diphylla

SIZE:
4-18 in. tall; flower ¾-1 in. wide.

WHAT TO LOOK FOR:
leaves shiny, shaped like butterfly wings; solitary white flowers on leafless stalks, lasting 1 day.

HABITAT:
rich, moist woods, limestone cliffs.

IN BLOOM:
Apr.-May.

Prickly Poppies *Argemone*

Such impressive armaments as the prickly poppies' coats of stiff spines are not unusual among plants of the desert, where growth is slow, conditions are harsh, and the least palatable plants are often the most likely to survive.

Matilija Poppies *Romneya*

Hikers in the gorges, canyons, and dry washes of southern California's arid mountains—and even occasionally in Arizona's Grand Canyon—may chance upon a fragrant cluster of this spectacular member of the poppy family.

Red Prickly Poppy

Argemone sanguinea

SIZE:
1-4 ft. tall; flower 2-3 in. wide.

WHAT TO LOOK FOR:
flowers red-purple to pinkish white; leaves lobed, with prickly tips; stems spiny.

HABITAT: chaparral, deserts, roadsides, disturbed areas.

IN BLOOM: Feb.-Apr.

Matilija Poppy

Romneya coulteri

SIZE: 2-8 ft. tall; flower 4-8 in. wide.

WHAT TO LOOK FOR: flowers profuse, with 6 peculiarly crimped white petals around yellow center; leaves divided.

HABITAT: chaparral, scrubland, desert canyons.

IN BLOOM: May-July.

California Poppies *Eschscholzia*

At night and on cloudy days, California's state flower remains
closed, its blossom nightcap-shaped. At the first touch of sunlight,
vast fields and hillsides blaze with open poppies. California Poppies
are low-growing annuals on the southern coast and in sand
dunes. Farther north they are tall perennials.

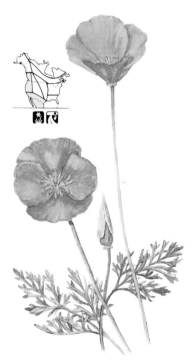

California Poppy

Eschscholzia californica

SIZE:
5-24 in. tall; flower 1-2 in. wide.

WHAT TO LOOK FOR:
flowers brilliant yellow to deep
orange, shaped like shallow teacups;
leaves minutely divided.

HABITAT:
grasslands, meadows, dunes.

IN BLOOM:
Feb.-Sept.

Celandines *Chelidonium*

European colonists brought this tough poppy with its fragile-looking flowers to these shores because of its medicinal properties. They used its caustic yellow juice in eyedrops and in the treatment of such skin disorders as warts—hence the alternative name of Wartwort. It is often grown in gardens.

Greater Celandine

Chelidonium majus

SIZE:
8-30 in. tall; flower ½-¾ in. wide.

WHAT TO LOOK FOR:
flowers yellow, 4-petaled; leaves deeply lobed; stem much branched.

HABITAT:
moist fields, urban lots, waste places.

IN BLOOM:
Apr.-Sept.

Creamcups *Platystemon*

Botanists debate whether there are as many as 60 creamcups species or only one. Those who say that the tiny plants along clay cliffs, the taller, hairy ones of sand dunes, and the gangly ones in shady woods are examples of separate species are known as "splitters." "Lumpers" say that all are mere variations.

Creamcups

Platystemon californicus

SIZE: 3-12 in. tall; flower ½-1 in. wide.

WHAT TO LOOK FOR: flowers usually cream-colored (ranging from yellow to white), 6-petaled; leaves hairy, lance-shaped; stems often branching, hairy.

HABITAT: dunes, chaparral, grasslands, oak woods.

IN BLOOM: Mar.-May.

Bloodroots *Sanguinaria*

Algonquian Indians called this member of the poppy family *puccoon*, as they did almost any plant that was a source of dye. They used its copious red latex to color clothing and baskets, and applied it to their bodies and faces as ceremonial paint. In the latter capacity, it also served as an insect repellent.

Bloodroot

Sanguinaria canadensis

SIZE: 2-8 in. tall; flower 1-2 in. wide.

WHAT TO LOOK FOR: flowers white with golden centers, each on a single stem enfolded in a blue-green leaf; roots and stems filled with red latex.

ROOT

HABITAT: rich woods. IN BLOOM: Mar.-May.

Allegheny Vines *Adlumia*

Although the only species in this group was first found in the Allegheny Mountains, it is not restricted to that area. The plant has become even more widespread since gardeners have adopted it as an ornamental climbing vine, often sold under the name of Mountain Fringe or Climbing Fumitory.

Allegheny Vine
Adlumia fungosa

SIZE:
to 12 ft. high; flower ½-¾ in. long.

WHAT TO LOOK FOR:
flowers pale pink, bottle-shaped, hanging in loose clusters; stems viny, climbing by means of divided leaves.

HABITAT:
mountain woodlands, open hillsides.

IN BLOOM:
June- Oct.

Bleeding Hearts *Dicentra*

The shapes of their flowers have inspired names for these plants that range from poetic (Bleeding Heart) to humorous (Dutchman's Breeches). An exception is Squirrel Corn, named not for the flowers but for the kernel-sized yellow corms, or swellings in the stem, that develop beneath the soil. Practical-minded ranchers call them all staggerweeds because cattle are poisoned by their toxic juices. The eastern Wild Bleeding Heart (*Dicentra eximia*) is similar to the western species, but its flowers are a softer pink.

WILD
BLEEDING
HEART

Western Bleeding Heart

Dicentra formosa

SIZE:
8-15 in. tall; flower ½-¾ in. long.

WHAT TO LOOK FOR:
flowers pinkish purple, heart-shaped, with spreading lower lobes; leaves springing from stem base, divided.

HABITAT:
dense woods, redwood forests.

IN BLOOM:
Mar.-July.

Squirrel Corn
Dicentra canadensis

SIZE:
4-12 in. tall; flower ½-¾ in. long.

WHAT TO LOOK FOR:
flowers white, heart-shaped, nodding; leaves springing from stem base, much divided.

HABITAT:
rich woods.

IN BLOOM:
Apr.-May.

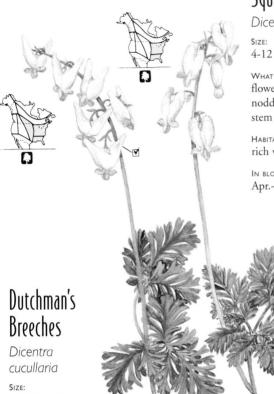

Dutchman's Breeches
Dicentra cucullaria

SIZE:
4-12 in. tall; flower ½-¾ in. long.

WHAT TO LOOK FOR:
flowers white, waxy, with 2 spurred petals like baggy trouser legs; leaves springing from stem base, much divided.

HABITAT:
rich woods, shaded moist ledges.

IN BLOOM:
Apr.-May.

Corydalises *Corydalis*

There are several species of corydalis native to North America. Only the Pale Corydalis has pink flowers; the others bear bright yellow blossoms. These plants are closely related to the bleeding hearts but differ in that only one petal has a spur.

Pale Corydalis

Corydalis sempervirens

SIZE: 4-24 in. tall; flower ⅜-½ in. long.

WHAT TO LOOK FOR: flowers pink, with rounded spur extending behind stalk; leaves blue-green, divided and lobed.

HABITAT: open woods; clearings.

IN BLOOM: May-Sept.

Nettles *Urtica*

The downy hairs that cover the plant inject a severe irritant when bruised. The young shoots and tender top leaves, however, make a good soup or cooked green. Boiling takes out the sting.

Stinging Nettle

Urtica dioica

SIZE: 2-8 ft. tall; flower ⅛ in. wide.

WHAT TO LOOK FOR: leaves paired, toothed, covered with stinging hairs; flowers green, in long clusters.

HABITAT: wetlands, meadows, edges of woods.

IN BLOOM: June-Sept.

STINGING HAIR

Pokeweeds *Phytolacca*

"Useful but dangerous" best characterizes these weedy plants. In pioneer days the purple berries of North America's only species were used for ink, and so the plant came to be known as Inkweed. Young shoots and leafy tips are edible if boiled in at least two changes of water, but children have died from eating the berries. The seeds and roots are also quite poisonous, and so are the mature stems and leaves.

FRUIT CLUSTER

Pokeweed

Phytolacca americana

SIZE: 1-10 ft. tall; flower ⅛-¼ in. wide.

WHAT TO LOOK FOR: flowers greenish white, in upright spikes; berries purple, hanging downward; stems reddish; leaves oval, pointed.

HABITAT: waste places, edges of woods, fields.

IN BLOOM: June-Sept.

Four O'Clocks *Mirabilis*

Like the popular garden species imported from the tropics, the native wild four o'clocks blossom in late afternoon, though seldom at exactly 4 P.M. The time varies daily, depending on the moment of sunset the day before. The flowers remain open through the evening and night, and are pollinated by hummingbirds, bees, and night-flying moths.

Four O'Clock

Mirabilis nyctaginea

SIZE:
1-4 ft. tall; flower ½ in. wide.

WHAT TO LOOK FOR:
flowers lavender to red, 2-5 small blossoms in each star-shaped green cup, the cups forming loose clusters; leaves arrow-shaped, in pairs.

HABITAT:
prairies, cultivated areas, waste places.

IN BLOOM: May-Oct.

Desert Four O'Clock

Mirabilis froebelii

SIZE:
6-24 in. tall; flower 1-1½ in. wide.

WHAT TO LOOK FOR:
flowers rose-purple, showy, profuse on sticky stem; leaves oval.

HABITAT:
dry grasslands, desert scrub, pinyon woods.

IN BLOOM: Apr.-Aug.

Sand Verbenas *Abronia*

The fragrant sand verbenas, like the rest of the four o'clock family, have no petals. The sepals look remarkably like petals and also attract pollinating insects as petals would, but they retain more moisture. The juicy stems and leaves of sand verbenas are adapted to minimize water loss, helping these creepers to blanket the dry sandy areas where they flourish.

Heart's Delight

Abronia fragrans

SIZE:
4-10 in. tall; flower ½-1 in. long.

WHAT TO LOOK FOR:
flowers tubular with lacy white or pale lavender sepals, in caplike clusters; leaves oval; stem covered with sticky hairs.

HABITAT: dry grasslands. IN BLOOM: Apr.-Aug.

Angel Trumpets *Acleisanthes*

Each elegant "trumpet" lasts but a single night. During the day, the bud is a dull green tube arising from the base of a leaf. The petallike sepals spread at dusk to attract night-flying moths, which sip the nectar with their long tongues and often pollinate the flower in the process. By the first light of dawn, the flower has collapsed into a limp heap.

Angel Trumpets

Acleisanthes longiflora

SIZE: to 3 ft. long; flower 4-6 in. long.

WHAT TO LOOK FOR: flowers trumpetlike, white-belled on dull green tubes; leaves triangular to long and thin; stems sprawling on ground.

HABITAT: dry rocky soil, sand, deserts.

IN BLOOM: Apr.-Aug.

Opuntia Cacti _Opuntia_

The upright, cylindrical plants in this group are called chollas; those with flat stems are known as prickly pears because of their edible fruit. Although chollas are densely covered with formidable barbed spines, Cactus Wrens nest among their branches, and a pack rat may protect its burrow with broken-off joints. The stiff spines of prickly pears are grouped in bunches. Peccaries, deer, and cattle feed on the plants, and the pulp of the pads is used to make candy and syrup.

Teddy Bear Cholla
Opuntia bigelovii

SIZE:
2-5 ft. tall; flower 1-2 in. wide.

WHAT TO LOOK FOR:
stem treelike, with many detachable joints clustered at top; spines white to yellow; flowers yellow to greenish purple.

HABITAT: warm deserts, scrublands.

IN BLOOM: Feb.-May.

Plains Prickly Pear
Opuntia polyacantha

SIZE:
4-12 in. tall; flower 2-3 in. wide.

WHAT TO LOOK FOR: stems flattened into 3- to 6-in.-long oval pads, sprawling in dense mats; flowers pale yellow; spines in clusters of 5-11.

HABITAT: deserts, dry grasslands, dry mountain slopes.

IN BLOOM: May-July.

Peyotes *Lophophora*

The ancient Indians of Mexico and Texas called these soft cacti *mezcal*, or mushrooms. The "buttons" were cut from the turniplike taproots, dried, and eaten for their intense hallucinatory effect. The cacti are still valued by mystics and thrill-seekers, although their use is now illegal except as part of the religious rites of the Native American Church.

Peyote

Lophophora williamsii

SIZE:
1-4 in. tall; flower ½-1 in. wide.

WHAT TO LOOK FOR:
stems gray-green to chalky blue, fleshy, spineless, with tufts of woolly white hairs; flowers purple to creamy white, with yellow centers.

HABITAT: deserts, dry scrublands.

IN BLOOM: Mar.-Oct.

Barrel Cacti *Ferocactus*

These slow-growing giants (an 8-foot plant may be more than 500 years old) are legendary emergency water sources. But it is hard work to cut off the top and to pound juice from the inner pulp—and the result is less than pleasant tasting. Because barrel cacti lean southward toward the sun, they are also known as compass cacti.

Candy Barrel Cactus

Ferocactus wislizenii

SIZE:
1-9 ft. tall; flower 1-2 in. wide.

WHAT TO LOOK FOR:
stems columnar, ribbed; spines to 2 in. long, some hooked; flowers orange.

HABITAT: warm deserts, dry mountain slopes.

IN BLOOM: July-Sept.

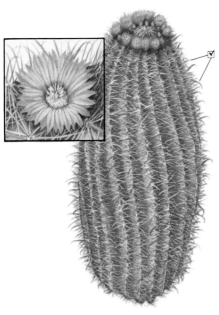

Wildflowers 59

Hedgehog Cacti *Echinocereus*

Cacti have developed a unique set of water-hoarding traits, typified by the hedgehog cacti. The thick pulpy stems are ribbed or segmented, expanding quickly when water is available and shrinking slowly in dry times. Photosynthesis takes place in the tough skin of the stems, close to the water source. The spines are actually modified leaves, shaped and arranged differently in each species. Not only do they protect the plants from browsing animals, they also prevent water loss by shading the stem. Each spine, in fact, collects a little water from the morning dew.

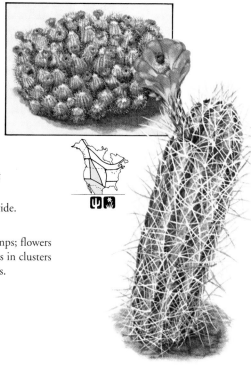

Claret Cup Cactus

Echinocereus triglochidiatus

SIZE:
6-12 in. tall; flower 1½-1¾ in. wide.

WHAT TO LOOK FOR:
stems upright, in mounded clumps; flowers bright red, funnel-shaped; spines in clusters of 3-6, pale, varying in thickness.

HABITAT:
deserts, dry grasslands.

IN BLOOM:
May-June.

Strawberry Hedgehog
Echinocereus engelmannii

SIZE:
1-12 in. tall; flower 1-2½ in. wide.

WHAT TO LOOK FOR:
stems upright, in large clumps; flowers showy, red to maroon; spines in clusters of 10-12 (about half long, slightly curved), spines of different colors (white, yellow, tan, gray) on the same plant.

HABITAT:
rocky slopes, cliffs, deserts, scrublands.

IN BLOOM:
Feb.-June.

Hen and Chickens Cactus
Echinocereus viridiflorus

SIZE:
1-10 in. tall; flower 1-1½ in. wide.

WHAT TO LOOK FOR:
stems sharply ribbed, sometimes spiraling; flowers green, long, many-petaled; spines white or brown, short, flattened against stem, in clusters of 10-20.

HABITAT:
deserts, dry grasslands, rocky hillsides.

IN BLOOM:
Apr.-July.

Pincushion Cacti *Coryphantha*

These miniature cacti, their stems all but hidden by overlapping spines that radiate from clusters like spokes from a wheel hub, are favorites of those who collect and cultivate desert plants. Like most cacti, they do best in neutral to somewhat alkaline soil.

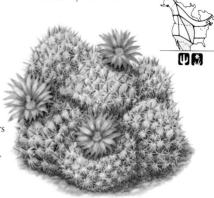

Pincushion Cactus

Coryphantha vivipara

SIZE: 1-3 in. tall; flower 1-1½ in. wide.

WHAT TO LOOK FOR: stems spherical or barrel-shaped, densely covered with spines; flowers rose to purplish, many-petaled; spines to 1 in. long, in clusters of 3-10, surrounded by 12-40 short, white hairlike spines.

HABITAT: dry prairies, rocky slopes.

IN BLOOM: May-July.

Nipple Cacti *Mammillaria*

Botanists classify cacti according to the way the spines are clustered, the exact points on the stem where the flowers grow, and the placement of the stamens in the flowers. The most notable feature of the nipple cacti is that the spines are clustered at the tips of small bumps arranged in rows along the stems.

Fishhook Cactus

Mammillaria microcarpa

SIZE: 1-6 in. tall; flower 1-1½ in. wide.

WHAT TO LOOK FOR: stem knobby, barrel-shaped, alone or in dense clumps; flowers pink with yellow centers, forming crown at top of stems; spines in clusters, with 1-2 hooked spines at center and many short ones radiating outward.

HABITAT: deserts, scrublands.   IN BLOOM: Apr.-May.

Sandworts *Arenaria*

There are more than 150 species of these small, sandloving members of the pink family. Most of them are, like the Rock Sandwort, low-growing, with creeping stems that form dense mats. Several, including the delicate Creeping Sandwort (*Arenaria humifusa*) and the wiry Mountain Sandwort (*Arenaria capillaris*), are common high in the northern Rockies.

Rock Sandwort
Arenaria stricta

SIZE: stem 4-16 in. long; flower ½ in. wide.

WHAT TO LOOK FOR: flowers white, 5-petaled, on threadlike stalks; leaves small, needle-like, in clusters along creeping stem; plant forms bushy mats.

HABITAT: sandy prairies, meadows, shores.

IN BLOOM: June-July.

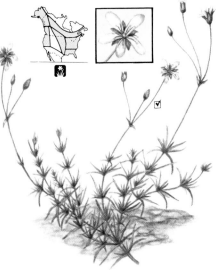

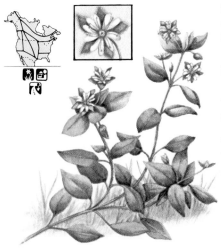

Chickweeds *Stellaria*

These delicate-looking edible weeds are bespangled from early spring to late fall with white, five-petaled flowers. Each petal is so deeply cleft, however, that there seem to be 10 of them. The weak, reclining stems and tender leaves may be added raw to salads but taste best when boiled briefly in salted water.

Common Chickweed
Stellaria media

SIZE: stem to 2½ ft. long; flower ¼ in. wide.

WHAT TO LOOK FOR: flowers profuse, small, white, with 5 deeply cleft petals; stems sprawling, forming large tangles; leaves oval to elongate.

HABITAT: lawns, meadows, pastures.

IN BLOOM: Feb.-Dec.

Catchflies *Silene*

The plants of this diverse group are known by a variety of names, nearly all of which are misleading. Many are called campions because they look like members of the genus *Lychnis*. Bright-flowered species are often called pinks, although that name properly belongs to the genus *Dianthus*. The many species known as catchflies are so called because small flying insects do indeed find themselves stuck in the spittle-like secretion that coats the hairy stems, flower tubes, and leaves. However, these plants are not insect eaters like sundews. Their stickiness keeps crawling insects from the flowers, and thus facilitates cross-pollination by airborne insects.

Starry Campion
Silene stellata

SIZE:
1-3 ft. tall; flower ¾-1 in. wide.

WHAT TO LOOK FOR:
flowers white, with 5 fringed petals; leaves lance-shaped, usually in 4's.

HABITAT:
open woods, clearings.

IN BLOOM:
July-Sept.

Fire Pink

Silene virginica

SIZE: 6-30 in. tall;
flowers 1-1½ in. wide.

WHAT TO LOOK FOR: flowers
bright red, with 5 notched
petals; stems and leaves hairy,
sticky.

HABITAT: open woods, clearings,
rocky slopes.

IN BLOOM: Apr.-June.

Round-leaved Catchfly

Silene rotundifolia

SIZE: stem 6-24 in. long;
flower ¾-1¼ in. wide.

WHAT TO LOOK FOR: flowers scarlet,
with 5 deeply notched petals; leaves
spoon-shaped; stems weak, reclining.

HABITAT: rocky
cliffs, open
slopes.

IN BLOOM: May-July.

Common Pink

Silene caroliniana

SIZE:
2-10 in. tall; flower ¾-1 in. wide.

WHAT TO LOOK FOR:
flowers pink, with 5 wedge-shaped petals; leaves
spatula-shaped to oblong, clustered at base.

HABITAT:
clearings, open woods, rocky slopes.

IN BLOOM:
Apr.-June.

Bladder Campion

Silene vulgaris

SIZE:
8-20 in. tall; flower ½-1 in. wide.

WHAT TO LOOK FOR:
flowers white, with 5 deeply notched petals emerging
from melonlike swelling; leaves oblong, pointed.

HABITAT:
roadsides, open fields.

IN BLOOM:
Apr.-Aug.

Soapworts *Saponaria*

When mixed with water, the bruised leaves of these European weeds produce a soapy lather that has been used since ancient times for laundry and bathing. Bouncing Bet came to North America with the colonists and went west with the pioneers, spreading quickly from their gardens along the way. Its cleansing action makes it a useful home remedy for Poison Ivy.

Pinks *Dianthus*

The flowers in this group were not named for their color, but for the frilled, or pinked, appearance of their petals. The color was later named for the flowers. The name of the Deptford Pink celebrates bygone days when its blossoms blanketed the open fields near Deptford, England—now part of urban London.

Bouncing Bet

Saponaria officinalis

SIZE:
1-2 ft. tall; flower ¾-1 in. wide.

WHAT TO LOOK FOR:
flowers white or pinkish, 5-petaled, in dense clusters; leaves elliptical to lance-shaped.

HABITAT:
streets, roadsides, railways, pastures.

IN BLOOM:
July-Sept.

Deptford Pink

Dianthus armeria

SIZE:
6-24 in. tall; flower ½ in. wide.

WHAT TO LOOK FOR:
flowers bright pink, starlike, loosely clustered; leaves strap-shaped.

HABITAT:
fields, waste places.

IN BLOOM:
June-Aug.

Corn Cockles *Agrostemma*

Despite its pretty pink flower, the one Corn Cockle species is more often cursed than admired because it is a dangerous weed around winter wheat. Its poisonous seeds mature along with the grain, and because they are the same size and weight they cannot easily be winnowed out.

Corn Cockle

Agrostemma githago

SIZE:
1-3 ft. tall; flower 1-1½ in. wide.

WHAT TO LOOK FOR:
flowers pink, with pale centers; stems and slender paired leaves covered with silky hairs.

HABITAT:
grainfields, waste places, roadsides.

IN BLOOM:
July-Sept.

Campions *Lychnis*

The campions include such popular garden flowers as Scarlet Maltese Cross (*Lychnis chalcedonica*) and Rose of Heaven (*Lychnis coeli-rosa*). The night-blooming White Campion differs from its close relatives the catchflies in that its male and female flowers are borne on separate plants.

Goosefoots _Chenopodium_

These widespread, leafy weeds, relatives of beets, spinach, and Swiss chard, are prized by outdoorsmen for their young leaves and shoots. When boiled until tender and served like spinach, they are a tasty substitute for garden-grown greens and are rich in vitamins A and C. Indians ground the seeds into flour.

Lamb's Quarters

Chenopodium album

SIZE:
6-72 in. tall; flower minute.

WHAT TO LOOK FOR:
leaves diamond-shaped, toothed, with white to pink mealy coating when young; flowers in dense clusters.

HABITAT: fields, yards, waste places.

IN BLOOM: June-Oct.

◄White Campion

Lychnis alba

SIZE: 1-4 ft. tall; flower ¾-1¼ in. wide.

WHAT TO LOOK FOR: flowers white, with 5 notched petals emerging from swollen pouch; leaves in pairs, downy.

HABITAT: waste places, fields.

IN BLOOM: May-Sept.

Spring Beauties *Claytonia*

These dainty heralds of spring form large colonies, spreading underground by means of bulblike swellings just above the roots. The swellings, called corms, look like small new potatoes and taste like sweet chestnuts when boiled, earning at least two species the nickname Fairy Spuds. Gathering them is tedious, however, and it takes a great many to make a satisfying meal.

Spring Beauty

Claytonia virginica

SIZE:
2-10 in. tall; flower ½ in. wide.

WHAT TO LOOK FOR:
flowers pink to white with dark pink veins, in loose clusters; 2 narrow, slightly succulent leaves on each slender stem.

HABITAT:
meadows, streambanks, woods.

IN BLOOM:
Mar.-June.

Montias *Montia*

Of the several edible montias, none is more easily recognized than
Miner's Lettuce—so called because it was a dietary staple of the
forty-niners in California's gold rush days. What appears to be a single
leaf pierced by the stem is actually two leaves fused together. This is
the choice part for salads, but the entire plant—flowers included—is
edible and flavorsome, whether eaten raw or lightly steamed.

Miner's Lettuce

Montia perfoliata

SIZE:
3-12 in. tall; flower ¼-½ wide.

WHAT TO LOOK FOR:
flowers cream-colored, loosely clustered on stalk
arising from center of umbrellalike, leafy collar;
lower leaves narrow.

HABITAT:
forests, streambanks, meadows, grasslands.

IN BLOOM:
Feb.-May.

Purslanes *Portulaca*

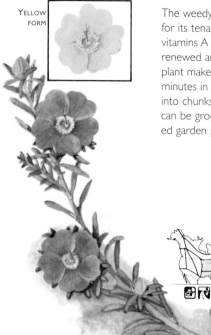

YELLOW FORM

The weedy Common Purslane, despised by gardeners for its tenacity, can be a rich source of iron and of vitamins A and C. The tender, leafy tips are a quickly renewed and very tasty salad green, and the entire plant makes a good potherb when simmered for a few minutes in salted water. The thick stems can be cut into chunks and pickled like cucumbers, and the seeds can be ground into flour. The Rose Moss is an imported garden plant that has spread to the wild.

Rose Moss
Portulaca grandiflora

SIZE: 3-6 in. tall; flower 1-2 in. wide.

WHAT TO LOOK FOR: flowers red, pink, white, yellow, or purple; leaves narrow, succulent, on creeping or ascending reddish stems.

HABITAT: fields, waste places.

IN BLOOM: Apr.-Sept.

Common Purslane
Portulaca oleracea

SIZE: 1-2 in. tall; flower ¼-½ in. wide.

WHAT TO LOOK FOR: stems reddish, creeping, covered with fleshy, wedge-shaped leaves; flowers small, yellow.

HABITAT: lawns, fields, waste places.

IN BLOOM: Apr.-Oct.

Rock Purslanes *Calandrinia*

Most rock purslanes are relatively large-flowered natives of Australia and South America. (The spectacular rock-garden plant *Calandrinia grandiflora* is in this category.) Red Maids, however, are among California's most abundant spring wildflowers. Their short-lived blossoms, which last but a single sunny day, produce masses of shiny black seeds that are eaten by many kinds of songbirds and rodents.

Lewisias *Lewisia*

Montana's official flower, the Bitterroot, was first collected in 1806 by Capt. Meriwether Lewis from what is now called the Bitterroot Valley. (A mountain range is also named for the plant.) Its rosette of narrow, succulent leaves, which die back as the flowers appear, crowns the starchy edible root for which the plant is named. The bitterness is mostly in the husk, which can be stripped off after boiling.

LEAFY ROSETTE

Red Maids

Calandrinia ciliata

SIZE: 4-16 in. long; flower ¾-1 in. wide.

WHAT TO LOOK FOR: flowers red to rose-purple with pale starlike centers, on spreading, leafy stalks; leaves narrow, spreading from base.

HABITAT: gravelly ground, moist grasslands.

IN BLOOM: Feb.-May.

Bitterroot

Lewisia rediviva

SIZE: 1-3 in. tall; flower 1-2 in. wide.

WHAT TO LOOK FOR: flowers rose to creamy white, in showy bunches at or near ground level; leaves narrow, dying back early.

HABITAT: dry rocky slopes, open areas.

IN BLOOM: Mar.-July.

Pussy Paws *Calyptridium*

These ground-huggers are ideally suited to the well-drained and windswept places where they grow, including the steep ridges between glaciers high on the peaks of the Pacific Northwest. The succulent leaves radiate in a flat rosette from the top of a taproot that may delve 12 feet deep for water. The flowering stalks may also lie flat; and the petals, instead of falling, form a protective cap over the seedpods.

Pussy Paws

Calyptridium umbellatum

SIZE:
2-10 in. tall; flower cluster 1½-2½ in. wide; leaf 1-3 in. long.

WHAT TO LOOK FOR:
flowers white to pink, in dense fuzzy clusters at ends of reddish stalks; leaves fleshy, spoon-shaped, in flat rosettes.

HABITAT:
mountain tundra, meadows, pine forests.

IN BLOOM:
May-Aug.

Fameflowers *Talinum*

Though not strictly desert plants, fameflowers grow in rocky or sandy places where a few rainless days constitute a drought. They store water in their thick, succulent leaves, which are almost round in cross section. The small five-petaled flowers are short-lived—they open about noon and fade before sunset—but their bright colors attract enough pollinating insects to perpetuate the species.

Fameflower

Talinum calycinum

SIZE:
4-12 in. tall; flower ¾-1 in. wide.

WHAT TO LOOK FOR:
flowers rose-pink with yellow centers, loosely clustered on slender stalks; leaves tiny, succulent, fingerlike, at base of stem.

HABITAT:
dry prairies, rocky exposed places.

IN BLOOM:
May-July.

Carpetweeds *Mollugo*

If you have ever wielded a hoe, you have probably met up with these low-growing weeds, which quickly carpet newly cultivated ground from coast to coast. At each fork in the stem is a whorl of leaves. The small flowers rise from the center of the whorl.

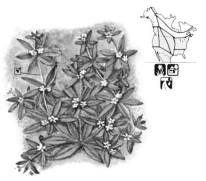

Carpetweed

Mollugo verticillata

SIZE: stem to 1 ft. long; flower ⅛ in. wide.

WHAT TO LOOK FOR: stems prostrate, spreading; leaves in whorls; flowers white, on short stalks.

HABITAT: roadsides, cultivated ground, sandy places.

IN BLOOM: June-Nov.

Midday Flowers *Mesembryanthemum*

A few species of these African succulents now grow wild in California and Mexico. The flowers open around midday, not by a time clock but in response to the sun's warmth. The Ice Plant's glistening beads are swollen droplets of stored water.

Ice Plant

Mesembryanthemum crystallinum

SIZE: 2½-3 in. high; stem to 3 ft. long; flower 1 in. wide.

WHAT TO LOOK FOR: plant creeping, covered with shiny beads; flowers white to pink.

HABITAT: beaches, dunes, roadsides.

IN BLOOM: Mar.-Oct.

Knotweeds *Polygonum*

Although knotweeds are named for their knotlike stem joints, some are also called smartweeds—an allusion to the sharp taste of the foliage. Knotweeds range from open waters to deep forests, supplying food for songbirds, waterfowl, and mammals.

Water Smartweed
Polygonum amphibium

SIZE:
stem to 8 ft. long; flower ⅛ in. wide.

WHAT TO LOOK FOR:
flowers pink, in dense spikes; stems spreading underwater or on banks.

HABITAT: lakes, ponds, swamps.

IN BLOOM: June-Sept.

Pinkweed
Polygonum pensylvanicum

SIZE:
1-6 ft. tall; flower ⅛ in. wide.

WHAT TO LOOK FOR:
flowers pink, in dense spikes; stems branched, with knotlike joints.

HABITAT:
fields, roadsides, clearings.

IN BLOOM:
June-Aug.

Copperleaves *Alternanthera*

Several of these spreading tropical plants are used by gardeners as summer ground covers that die back in autumn. One species, the aquatic Alligator Weed, has found a home in the Deep South, where it is rapidly choking bayous, streams, and other waterways. It spreads by means of horizontal stems as well as seeds.

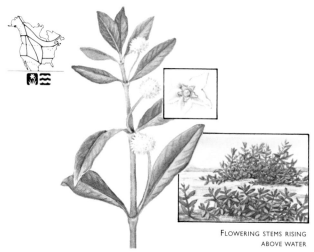

FLOWERING STEMS RISING
ABOVE WATER

Alligator Weed

Alternanthera philoxeroides

SIZE: 6-24 in. tall; flower ¼-½ in. wide.

WHAT TO LOOK FOR:
flowers silvery to pinkish green, in rounded clusters from spreading, matted stems.

HABITAT: wet meadows, ditches, swamps, waterways, lakeshores.

IN BLOOM: all year.

Docks *Rumex*

There are few places where docks do not grow. Their rhubarblike leaves have been prized as cooked greens since antiquity, and their wandlike clusters of brown seeds were gathered, hand-winnowed, and stone-ground into flour by Indians and settlers. The bitter taste of the young leaves is not unpleasant, but older leaves must be boiled in at least two changes of water to make them palatable.

FLOWER

FRUIT

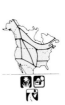

Curly Dock
Rumex crispus

SIZE:
1-5 ft. tall; flower minute.

WHAT TO LOOK FOR:
leaves large, dark green, crisped and curled; flowers green and red, in upright clusters; fruits brown, heart-shaped, winged.

HABITAT:
ditches, roadsides, fields, waste places.

IN BLOOM:
May-Sept.

Wild Buckwheats *Eriogonum*

With hairy, densely matted leaves well adapted for retaining moisture, these plants inhabit dry, open areas from deserts to mountain tundra. Wild buckwheats have little in common with the cultivated grain (*Fagopyrum*). Although their seeds are of value only to birds and rodents, bees make wild buckwheat nectar into an excellent honey. There are about 200 wild buckwheat species in North America, many of which are hard to tell apart without a magnifying glass.

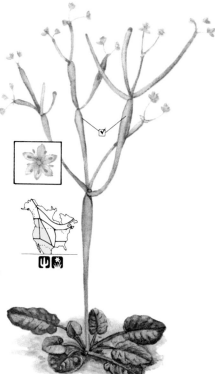

Desert Trumpet

Eriogonum inflatum

SIZE:
4-40 in. tall; flower ⅛ in. wide.

WHAT TO LOOK FOR:
flowers cream-yellow, in flaring clusters at ends of branches; stem swollen just below branches; leaves at base.

HABITAT:
deserts, scrublands.

IN BLOOM:
Mar.-Oct.

Skeletonweed

Eriogonum deflexum

SIZE:
3-25 in. tall; flower ⅛ in. wide.

WHAT TO LOOK FOR:
flowers white or pink, hanging in clusters
from leafless, branching stem; leaves oval,
at base of stem.

HABITAT:
deserts, mountain slopes.

IN BLOOM:
all year.

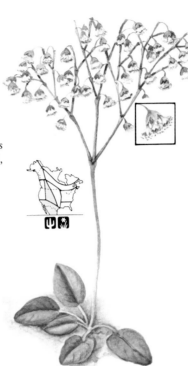

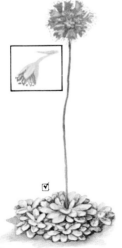

Cushion Buckwheat

Eriogonum caespitosum

SIZE:
2-7 in. tall; flower ⅛ in. wide.

WHAT TO LOOK FOR:
flowers yellow (turning orange), in dense,
round clusters on leafless stalks; leaves small,
woolly, white, in cushiony mats.

HABITAT:
deserts; dry, rocky slopes.

IN BLOOM:
Apr.-July.

Leadworts *Plumbago*

Most members of this largely tropical group are woody vines and shrubs, but one low-growing species qualifies as a North American wildflower. The calyx, or outer coat, of each of its flowers is covered with rows of stalked glands. When the seeds mature, the glands secrete a sticky substance that adheres to the fur or feathers of passing creatures, who thus serve to spread the seeds.

Leadwort

Plumbago scandens

SIZE: to 3 ft. long; flower ½ in. wide.

WHAT TO LOOK FOR: stems spreading, viny; flowers white, with petals spreading from tube; leaves oval, with pointed tips.

HABITAT: groves, thickets, woods.

IN BLOOM: all year in Florida; Mar.-Sept. elsewhere.

Thrifts *Armeria*

Wild Thrift thrives in North America on rocky western cliffs and salt-sprayed bluffs overlooking the Pacific. The English have, over the centuries, known it by such names as Cliff Rose, Sea Pink, Ladies' Cushion, and Midsummer Fairmaid. The plant also grows along the coast of northern Europe and in Iceland, where it is eaten boiled in milk. Like the sea lavenders, thrifts are often sold under the name statice.

Sea Lavenders

Limonium

Like a low, blue-gray mist moving in from the Atlantic, dense colonies of these shrubby perennials cover coastal salt marshes and alkaline meadows with their lavender-pink bloom in late summer. The thick rootstocks yield an astringent that was once a popular mouthwash. Some cultivated species, known as statice ("stopping"), were used in ancient times to treat dysentery, hemorrhage, and other ailments.

Sea Lavender

Limonium carolinianum

SIZE: 8-20 in. tall; flower ⅛ in. wide.

WHAT TO LOOK FOR: flowers lavender-pink, borne along side of branches; leaves spoon-shaped, at base of plant.

HABITAT: salt marshes, dunes, salt meadows along coast.

IN BLOOM: July-Oct.

◄ Wild Thrift

Armeria maritima

SIZE: 4-18 in. tall; flower ⅛ in. wide.

WHAT TO LOOK FOR: flowers lilac-pink, in dense spherical clusters on leafless stalks; leaves grasslike, at base of plant.

HABITAT: coastal bluffs, dunes.

IN BLOOM: Apr.-Aug.

St. Johnsworts *Hypericum*

"Trefoil, johnswort, vervaine, dill/Hinder witches of their will." The festival day of St. John the Baptist occurs on June 24, when the sun is high and days are long. The bright flowers of St. Johnswort open about this time in England, and so— as the ancient couplet indicates—they came to embody the power of light over darkness. The plants actually contain a most unusual toxin. Eaten in the flowering stage, they sensitize nerve endings in the skin and cause inflammation and open sores in light-skinned animals and humans exposed to sunlight. Dark skins are seldom affected, and light skins are immune if they are kept shaded.

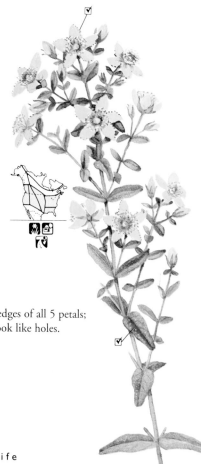

St. Johnswort

Hypericum perforatum

SIZE:
12-32 in. tall; flower ¾-1 in. wide.

WHAT TO LOOK FOR:
flowers yellow, with black dots at edges of all 5 petals; leaves with translucent dots that look like holes.

HABITAT: fields, meadows, roadsides.

IN BLOOM: June-Sept.

Pineweed

Hypericum gentianoides

SIZE:
4-16 in. tall; flowers ⅛-¼ in. wide.

WHAT TO LOOK FOR:
flowers yellow, scattered along delicately branched stems; leaves small, scalelike.

HABITAT: sandy meadows, clearings.

IN BLOOM: June-Sept.

St. Peterswort

Hypericum crux-andreae

SIZE:
12-30 in. tall; flower ¾-1 in. wide.

WHAT TO LOOK FOR:
flowers yellow, 4-petaled, borne at ends of stout, wiry stems; leaves oval, in pairs.

HABITAT: dry clearings, coastal areas.

IN BLOOM: July-Aug.

Peonies *Paeonia*

Among the first plants known to have been cultivated for their flowers, peonies were grown by the rulers of China more than 4,000 years ago. Although most horticultural varieties originated in Asia, there are two native North American species. The California Peony (*Paeonia californica*), limited to that state, is taller and leafier than the Western Peony. Its flowers are deep red outside, with black centers.

Western Peony

Paeonia brownii

SIZE:
8-24 in. tall; flower 1-1½ in. wide.

WHAT TO LOOK FOR:
flowers maroon with yellow-green centers, globelike, solitary, nodding on ends of leafy stalks; leaves blue-green, much divided.

HABITAT:
sagebrush, chaparral, open pine forests.

IN BLOOM:
Apr.-June.

Velvetleaves *Abutilon*

These aggressive weeds are the bane of corn and soybean farmers across the continent. Although they do not appear until the crop plants have started to grow, they then flourish, flower, and bear fruit with amazing speed, consuming much of the soil's nutrients. The seeds are released from the crimped capsules gradually over the winter, and can remain viable in the soil for as long as 60 years.

Velvetleaf

Abutilon theophrasti

SIZE:
1-5 ft. tall; flower ½-1 in. wide.

WHAT TO LOOK FOR:
leaves heart-shaped, velvety; flowers yellow; fruits crownlike.

HABITAT:
fields, waste places.

IN BLOOM:
July-Aug.

Rose Mallows *Hibiscus*

These leafy, stout-stemmed plants are marked as members of the mallow family by the odd cylinder, called a stamen column, that projects from the center of the flower. In the rose mallows, this column, fuzzy with pollen from base to tip, completely surrounds the seed-producing pistil. The five rounded tips of the pistil, called the stigmas, emerge from the end of the column. A bee or butterfly, making its rounds in search of nectar, touches the stigmas with pollen from another flower, then burrows deeper into the blossom and picks up a new load of pollen.

Halberdleaf Rose Mallow

Hibiscus militaris

SIZE:
2-5 ft. tall; flower 4-6 in. wide.

WHAT TO LOOK FOR:
flowers pink, with wine-red centers; leaves 3-lobed, like blades of a halberd.

HABITAT:
marshes, shallow freshwater.

IN BLOOM:
Aug.-Sept.

Swamp Rose Mallow

Hibiscus moscheutos

SIZE:
2-8 ft. tall; flower 4-8 in. wide.

WHAT TO LOOK FOR:
flowers white, with burgundy centers (entirely pink in north); leaves toothed, heart-shaped; stems canelike.

HABITAT:
salt and freshwater marshes; lakeshores.

IN BLOOM: July-Sept.

Flower-of-an-hour

Hibiscus trionum

SIZE:
6-20 in. tall; flower 1-2½ in. wide.

WHAT TO LOOK FOR:
flowers yellow with brown centers, open briefly in morning; leaves with fingerlike lobes; stems erect or sprawling.

HABITAT:
yards, waste places.

IN BLOOM:
July-Sept.

Musk Mallows *Malva*

These European natives were imported for gardens, but long ago escaped to the wild in the New World. Their flowers differ from those of American mallows in that the petals are scalloped and the stamen column is rounder. The stamens completely enclose the pistil until they have finished producing pollen. Then they roll back to allow the stigmas at the tip of the pistil to receive pollen from another blossom.

Musk Mallow

Malva moschata

SIZE:
1-3 ft. tall; flower 1½-2 in. wide.

WHAT TO LOOK FOR:
flowers pink, lavender, or white, with notched petals; leaves with fingerlike lobes.

HABITAT:
grasslands, waste places.

IN BLOOM:
June-Sept.

Globe Mallows *Sphaeralcea*

Among Spanish-speaking Americans, globe mallows are sometimes known as *plantas muy malas* ("very bad plants"), for they are densely covered with detachable hairs that irritate the eyes. These hairs also tend to discourage many animals from eating the plants. The several kinds of globe mallow are often difficult to tell apart because the plants hybridize.

Scarlet Globe Mallow

Sphaeralcea coccinea

SIZE: 1-2 ft. tall; flower 1 in. wide.

WHAT TO LOOK FOR: flowers brick-red with pale centers, clustered atop slender stalks; leaves hairy, divided into narrow lobes.

HABITAT: dry grasslands, scrub.

IN BLOOM: May-Aug.

Poppy Mallows *Callirhoë*

The showy poppy mallows are also known as wine-cups for the shape and color of their flowers. Unlike the rose mallows, these flowers have stamen columns that become pollen-covered only about halfway down from the tip. It takes a magnifying glass to see that the long, threadlike stigmas emerge, not from the end of the column but along its length.

Poppy Mallow

Callirhoë involucrata

SIZE: 1-3 ft. long; flower 1-2½ in. wide.

WHAT TO LOOK FOR: flowers wine-red, saucer shaped; stems spreading; leaves with fingerlike lobes.

HABITAT: dry prairies, deserts.

IN BLOOM: June-Aug.

Checker Mallows *Sidalcea*

The 20 species of checker mallow, all native to western North America, are commonly known as wild hollyhocks, for at first glance they do indeed look like miniature versions of the garden Hollyhock (*Alcea rosea*). The stamen column in the center of the flowers, unlike that of most other mallows, has two separate groups of pollen-bearing heads.

Checker Mallow

Sidalcea neomexicana

Size: 8-36 in. tall; flower ¾-1 in. wide.

What to look for: flowers rose-colored, with petals slightly fringed; upper leaves hand-shaped, lower leaves rounded.

Habitat: streambanks, moist meadows. In bloom: June-Sept.

BASAL LEAF

Marsh Mallows *Althaea*

The roots of these Old World plants were the original source of the gummy confection now synthesized from sugar, gelatin, and other ingredients. It was made from the white core of the root; first the rind was peeled away, and then the core was cut into small pieces and boiled in sugar water until it was thick enough to form blobs. Its use was medicinal—as a laxative and as a treatment for sore throat.

Marsh Mallow

Althaea officinalis

Size: 2-4 ft. tall; flower 1-1½ in. wide.

What to look for: flowers lavender to pink, in clusters along stem; leaves toothed, slightly lobed, with soft hairs.

Habitat: brackish or freshwater marshes near coast.

In bloom: July-Sept.

Pitcher Plants *Sarracenia*

In the boggy, acid soil where most insect-eating plants grow, decay takes place quite slowly, and little nitrogen is therefore available to the roots of plants. Pitcher plants make up for this deficiency by holding small pools of water in their modified leafstalks, or pitchers. Insects are attracted to the pitchers, often by the odor of decay within, and are forced into the water by a lining of stiff, downward-pointing hairs. There a narcotic kills them, bacteria begin to decompose them, and enzymes convert their protein into usable nitrogen. Some insects, however, have a different relationship with these plants. Certain moth caterpillars feed on the inside of the pitcher. When the adult moths emerge, they pollinate the flowers.

Northern Pitcher Plant

Sarracenia purpurea

SIZE: 1-2 ft. tall; flower 2-3 in. wide.

WHAT TO LOOK FOR: flowers purple to brick-red, nodding, on leafless stalks; leaves clustered at base, pitcher-shaped with flared tops and red veins.

HABITAT: bogs, marshes.

IN BLOOM: May-Aug.

Trumpets

Sarracenia flava

SIZE: 1-3 ft. tall; flower 3-4 in. wide.

WHAT TO LOOK FOR: flowers greenish yellow, large, nodding, on leafless stalks; leaves trumpet-shaped, erect, green to yellow.

HABITAT: marshes, bogs, shallow water, wet pinelands. IN BLOOM: Apr.-June.

Cobra Plants *Darlingtonia*

The manner in which the Cobra Plant traps flying insects is as diabolical as the plant's appearance is bizarre. An insect, lured by fragrant nectar, lands on the cobra's "tongue" and is guided into the "head" by slanting hairs, which then block its escape. At the top and rear of the head are translucent spots. When the insect tries to fly out through one of these false windows, it falls into the water below and is slowly digested.

Cobra Plant

Darlingtonia californica

SIZE:
1-3 ft. tall; flower 2-2½ in. wide.

WHAT TO LOOK FOR:
leaves tubular, erect, hooded, with 2 tonguelike lobes at mouth, pale green to pinkish; flowers yellow-green with brownish or maroon centers, nodding, on leafless stalks.

HABITAT:
cool bogs, seepage areas.

IN BLOOM:
Apr.-June.

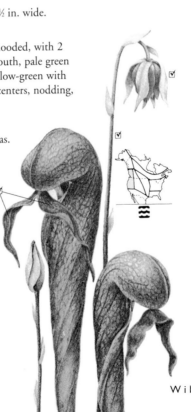

Sundews *Drosera*

The droplets that glisten on the leaves of these delicate-looking plants serve to attract and entrap the small insects upon which they feed. The sweet, sticky fluid is exuded at the tips of the glandular hairs that cover the leaves. When an insect, attracted by the appetizing odor, becomes stuck among the hairs, neighboring hairs are triggered to bend like tentacles, further binding the insect and eventually suffocating it. Protein-digesting enzymes are then secreted, which cause the release of nitrogen and other vital elements that are absorbed by the leaves.

Roundleaf Sundew

Drosera rotundifolia

Size: 1-12 in. tall; flower ¼-½ in. wide.

What to look for: leaves reddish, glistening, in ring at ground level; flowers white to pink, 5-petaled, opening one at a time in a wandlike cluster atop straight stalk.

Habitat: bogs, moist open sand, mossy hummocks.

In bloom: June-Sept.

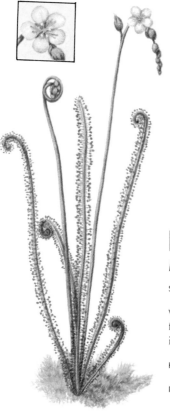

Dewthread

Drosera filiformis

Size: 5-25 in. tall; flower ¼-½ in. wide.

What to look for: leaves stringy, erect, glistening; flowers lavender-pink, opening 1 or 2 at a time in nodding clusters.

Habitat: bogs, damp sandy soil.

In bloom: June-Sept.

Venus Flytraps *Dionaea*

This most dramatic of all carnivorous plants—the only one of its kind on earth—traps and digests its prey in hinged leaves. Near the central vein of each leaf are several sensitive hairs that, in response to slight pressure, trigger the leaf to fold shut in less than a second. Bristles along the edges interlock, trapping the unwary insect. The leaf remains closed for about a week while antibacterial substances prevent putrefaction, and enzymes dissolve all but the external skeleton. Then the leaf reopens and readies itself for another visitor. The Venus Flytrap has become an endangered species in its native bogs and savannas, a victim of overzealous admirers.

Venus Flytrap

Dionaea muscipula

SIZE:
4-12 in. tall; flower ¾-1 in. wide.

WHAT TO LOOK FOR:
leaves traplike, green outside and often red inside; flowers white, 5-petaled, in rounded cluster atop straight stalk.

HABITAT:
sandy bogs, low pinelands, savannas in North and South Carolina.

IN BLOOM:
May-June.

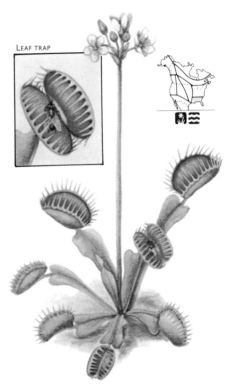

LEAF TRAP

Violets *Viola*

There are more than 500 species of violets worldwide, including more than 60 in North America. Four states—Illinois, New Jersey, Rhode Island, and Wisconsin—have violets as their state flowers. Violets have five petals, with the lowest reminiscent of a landing platform complete with lines that guide a bee into a nectar-filled inner spur. The spur, formed by the two side petals, points upward, and the bee must turn upside down to reach the nectar. In the process any pollen carried by the bee is dusted onto the seed-producing pistil; the bee then receives a fresh coat of pollen from the stamens. Many species also bear flowers that never open (some are even underground) but produce seeds by self-pollination. In such cases, insects are helpful but not necessary in perpetuating the species.

TWO-COLOR FORM

Beckwith's Violet

Viola beckwithii

SIZE:
2-5 in. tall; flower ¾-1 in. wide.

WHAT TO LOOK FOR:
flowers lilac or white, with upper 2 petals purple; leaves from base of plant, in 3 lacy lobes.

HABITAT:
dry pine forests; grassy slopes.

IN BLOOM:
Mar.-May.

Birdfoot Violet

Viola pedata

SIZE:
2-10 in. tall; flower ¾-1½ in. wide.

WHAT TO LOOK FOR:
flowers lavender, upper 2 petals slanting backward and often darker; leaves arising from base of plant, finely cut.

HABITAT:
dry woods, clearings, prairies.

IN BLOOM:
Mar.-June.

CONFEDERATE VIOLET

Common Blue Violet

Viola sororia

SIZE:
3-12 in. tall; flower ¾-1 in. wide.

WHAT TO LOOK FOR:
flowers purple, lavender, or white (the variety called Confederate Violet is grayish white with lavender center), with spreading petals; leaves heart-shaped, toothed, at base of plant.

HABITAT:
woods, meadows, lawns, swamps, waste ground.

IN BLOOM:
Mar.-June.

Arrowleaf Violet

Viola sagittata

SIZE:
2-10 in. tall; flower ½-¾ in. wide.

WHAT TO LOOK FOR:
flowers purple with white centers; leaves arrowhead-shaped, toothed, long-stalked from base of plant.

HABITAT:
moist meadows, open woods, prairies.

IN BLOOM:
Apr.-June.

Prairie Violet
Viola pedatifida

SIZE:
2-10 in. tall; flower ½-1¼ in. wide.

WHAT TO LOOK FOR:
flowers blue-violet, on leafless stalks;
leaves long-stalked from base of plant,
with fingerlike sections.

HABITAT:
prairies.

IN BLOOM:
Apr.-June.

White Violet
Viola macloskeyi

SIZE: 1-6 in. tall; flower ¼-½ in. wide.

WHAT TO LOOK FOR: flowers white, with
maroon veins on lowest petal; leaves
oval to heart-shaped, from base of plant.

HABITAT: swamps, marshes, wet woods.

IN BLOOM: Apr.-July.

Lanceleaf Violet
Viola lanceolata

SIZE: 1-8 in. tall;
flower ¼-¾ in. wide.

WHAT TO LOOK FOR: flowers
white, with maroon veins
on lowest petal; leaves
long, lance-shaped, from
base of plant.

HABITAT: meadows, wet open
sand, peat.

IN BLOOM: Mar.-July.

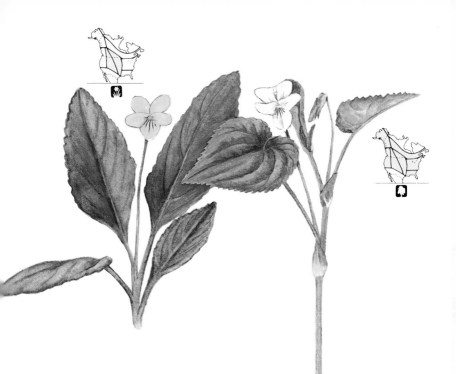

Yellow Prairie Violet

Viola nuttallii

SIZE:
1-10 in. tall; flower ¼-½ in. wide.

WHAT TO LOOK FOR:
flowers yellow, on leafless stalks; leaves
long, lance-shaped, arising from base
of plant.

HABITAT:
prairies, mountain grasslands.

IN BLOOM:
Apr.-May.

Canada Violet

Viola canadensis

SIZE:
2-18 in. tall;
flower ½-1 in. wide.

WHAT TO LOOK FOR:
flowers white with blue-violet tint,
on leafy stems; leaves heart-shaped.

HABITAT:
forests, streambanks.

IN BLOOM:
May-July.

YELLOW FORM

Downy Yellow Violet

Viola pubescens

SIZE:
3-16 in. tall;
flower ½-¾ in. wide.

WHAT TO LOOK FOR:
flowers yellow with purple veins in
center, on leafy stems; leaves and
stems covered with soft hairs; leaves
heart-shaped.

HABITAT: rich woods.

IN BLOOM: Apr.-July.

Wild Pansy

Viola rafinesquii

SIZE: 2-12 in. tall; flower ¼-½ in. wide.

WHAT TO LOOK FOR: flowers blue-violet to cream
(often with yellow centers), profuse, on leafy,
branching stem; leaves small, some lobed, some
deeply divided.

HABITAT: clearings, roadsides, meadows, lawns.

IN BLOOM: Apr.-Aug.

Passionflowers *Passiflora*

The first Europeans to describe and name New World plants were scholar-priests who accompanied the Spanish conquistadores. In the intricate blossoms of these climbing vines, they saw elaborate symbols of the passion of Christ. The three stigmas in the center represented nails, the five stamens beneath them were Christ's wounds, the fringe was the crown of thorns, and the ten petallike parts behind the fringe were the apostles (excluding Judas and Peter).

Maypop

Passiflora incarnata

SIZE:
to 20 ft. high; flower 1½-4 in. wide.

WHAT TO LOOK FOR:
flowers cream-colored and purple, with fringe of tentacles; stems trailing or climbing by means of curly tendrils; leaves 3-lobed.

HABITAT:
open thickets, roadsides.

IN BLOOM:
June-Sept.

False Heathers *Hudsonia*

These sprawling, mat-forming evergreens are easy to tell from true Heather (*Calluna vulgaris*) by their five-petaled yellow flowers. (Those of Heather are pink or white, bell-shaped, and clustered.) The Beach Heather is also known as Poverty Grass because it is able to flourish in sandy, nutrient-poor soil. As a hummock-former, it tends to slow the erosion of dunes.

Beach Heather

Hudsonia tomentosa

SIZE:
2-8 in. tall; flower ¼ in. wide.

WHAT TO LOOK FOR:
flowers sulfur-yellow, profuse, on dense mat of sprawling stems; leaves scalelike.

HABITAT: beaches, shifting sands.

IN BLOOM: May-July.

Rockroses *Helianthemum*

Rockroses bear two types of flowers. The showy five-petaled blossoms appear first (each lasting only a single day) and are pollinated by flying insects. Then come small budlike flowers, which never open but produce seeds by self-pollination. Some species are known as frostweeds because ribbons of ice extrude from their stems in winter. Water is carried upward in wicklike fashion, and as it freezes is forced out through cracks in the husk.

Frostweed

Helianthemum canadense

SIZE:
8-16 in. tall; flower 1-1¼ in. wide.

WHAT TO LOOK FOR:
yellow flowers at stem tips, with closed ones clustered at leaf bases; leaves narrow, fuzzy.

HABITAT:
dry open woods, sandy meadows, clearings.

IN BLOOM: May-July.

CLOSED FLOWERS

Stickleaves *Mentzelia*

Stickleaves are largely desert plants, although many are also found in dry areas of surrounding mountains and plains. Their leaves are covered with small barbed hairs, causing them to stick to clothing and animal fur. Several species are also known as blazing stars for their bright, distinctive blossoms.

Giant Blazing Star

Mentzelia laevicaulis

SIZE:
1-4 ft. tall; flower 3-6 in. wide.

WHAT TO LOOK FOR:
flowers star-shaped, yellow; leaves toothed; stems whitish.

HABITAT:
deserts, streambeds, rocky hills.

IN BLOOM:
July-Sept.

Wild Cucumbers *Echinocystis*

Each flower cluster on the Wild Cucumber comprises many male blossoms and few females, from only one of which the prickly fruit develops. Although the vine is a cousin of the garden Cucumber (*Cucumis sativus*), its fruit is inedible—and, in fact, explosive. As the fruit ripens, tension develops between its interwoven fibers until it bursts, hurling its four seeds as far as 20 feet or more.

FRUIT

Wild Cucumber

Echinocystis lobata

SIZE: to 20 ft. high; flower ½-¾ in. wide.

WHAT TO LOOK FOR: climbing vine; flowers greenish white, in clusters; leaves star-shaped; fruit prickly.

HABITAT: streambanks, moist woods, marshes.

IN BLOOM: June-Oct.

Squashes *Cucurbita*

This valuable group of plants includes garden squashes as well as the familiar jack-o'-lantern pumpkin. Although the fruit of the Stinking Gourd is inedible, it is not useless; it contains a lathery substance that can be used as a sub-stitute for soap.

FRUIT

Bur Cucumbers *Sicyos*

Several of these vines are also known as Nimble Kate for the agility with which they climb, clamber, and creep over almost anything. This quality has made them popular among some gardeners as fast-growing ornamental coverings for walls and latticework—and unpopular among others as incursive weeds. The inedible fruit has barbed bristles, which cling to the fur of animals and help spread the seeds.

Star Cucumber

Sicyos angulatus

SIZE:
to 25 ft. high; flower ¼-½ in. wide.

WHAT TO LOOK FOR:
climbing vine; flowers white, with green centers; leaves maplelike; fruit spiny, clustered.

HABITAT: riverbanks, fencerows, clearings, waste places.

IN BLOOM: July-Sept.

FRUIT CLUSTER

◄ Stinking Gourd

Cucurbita foetidissima

SIZE: to 20 ft. long; flower 3-4 in. wide.

WHAT TO LOOK FOR: trailing vine; flowers yellow; fruit striped; leaves triangular.

HABITAT: dry prairies, grasslands.

IN BLOOM: May-Aug.

Spiderflowers *Cleome*

These tall plants of the plains have two sets of names describing very different qualities. The flower clusters, with their leggy-looking stamens and protruding pistils and seedpods, evoke the name spiderflowers; the rich nectar within earns the name bee plants. (The odor of the crushed leaves, however, inspires additional epithets like stinkweed, skunkweed, and stinking clover.)

Rocky Mountain Bee Plant

Cleome serrulata

SIZE: 1-5 ft. tall; flower ½ in. wide.

WHAT TO LOOK FOR: flowers pink to white, clustered, with long stamens; seedpods long, thrust from center of flowers; leaflets in 3's.

HABITAT: riverbanks, prairies, roadsides.

IN BLOOM: May-Aug.

Radishes *Raphanus*

Although the garden Radish (*Raphanus sativus*) has been grown for food since ancient times, the Wild Radish, with its slender, inedible taproot, is considered a noxious weed. Its small seeds remain viable in the ground for decades, sprouting only when they work their way to the surface. In some areas the young leaves are cooked as a potherb, and immature seedpods are diced into salads for sharp flavor.

Wild Radish

Raphanus raphanistrum

SIZE: 8-30 in. tall; flower ½-¾ in. wide.

WHAT TO LOOK FOR: flowers yellow, in clusters atop branched stem; leaves lobed.

HABITAT: waste places, fields.

IN BLOOM: Apr.-Nov.

Winter Cress *Barbarea*

The glossy, edible leaves of these plants stay green in flat rosettes beneath ice and snow, and new ones appear during brief thaws. All winter long they can be used raw in salads or cooked. But from flowering time until killing frost, they are too bitter to be palatable.

Winter Cress

Barbarea vulgaris

SIZE: 1-4 ft. tall; flower ½ in. wide.

WHAT TO LOOK FOR: flowers yellow, clustered atop erect stems; leaves glossy, deeply lobed, rounded.

HABITAT: waste places, fields.

IN BLOOM: Apr.-Aug.

Mustards *Brassica*

This group includes such familiar garden vegetables as broccoli, brussels sprouts, cabbage, cauliflower, kale, kohlrabi, rutabagas, and turnips. Black Mustard's young leaves are cooked and eaten as greens.

Black Mustard

Brassica nigra

SIZE: 1-6 ft. tall; flower ½-¾ in. wide.

WHAT TO LOOK FOR: flowers bright yellow, clustered atop branched stems; leaves rough, lobed, divided at base.

HABITAT: fields, meadows.

IN BLOOM: Mar.-Oct.

WINTER CRESS

BLACK MUSTARD

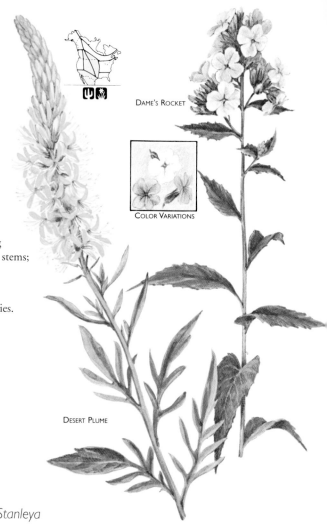

Desert Plume

Stanleya pinnata

SIZE:
1-5 ft. tall;
flower ½ in. wide.

WHAT TO LOOK FOR:
flowers yellow, in long
spires atop blue-green stems;
leaves much divided.

HABITAT:
desert scrub, dry prairies.

IN BLOOM:
Apr.-Sept.

DAME'S ROCKET

COLOR VARIATIONS

DESERT PLUME

Prince's Plumes *Stanleya*

The leaves of most plants in the mustard family make good
potherbs if boiled in two changes of water. The prince's plumes, sometimes
called Paiute cabbages, are no exception. But because these plants accumulate the poisonous element selenium, often found in the desert soils and dry
plains where they grow, they may be toxic if eaten raw or undercooked.

Rockets *Hesperis*

One species in this Old World group, brought to the Americas as a garden flower, spread quickly into the wild. It had been cultivated in ancient Rome.

◄ Dame's Rocket
Hesperis matronalis

SIZE:
2-4 ft. tall;
flower ½-1 in. wide.

WHAT TO LOOK FOR:
flowers red-purple to white, clustered atop tall, leafy stems; leaves lance-shaped, toothed.

HABITAT:
roadsides, wet ditches, fields, woods.

IN BLOOM:
May-Aug.

Squaw Cabbages *Caulanthus*

Like most members of the mustard family, these bizarre desert plants start out as dense leafy clusters produced from seeds. Then a stout stem arises, and four-petaled flowers appear at its tip. They become long seedpods as the stem grows beyond them and more blossoms are produced.

Desert Candle
Caulanthus inflatus

SIZE: 1-3 ft. tall;
flower ¼-½ in. wide.

WHAT TO LOOK FOR: stems greenish yellow, like erect cucumbers; flowers purple and white; leaves clasp stem near base.

HABITAT: deserts. IN BLOOM: Feb.-May.

Toothworts *Dentaria*

Pepperroot and wild horseradish are among the many names given to these small, early-blooming members of the mustard family. The names refer to the ivory-colored underground stems, or rhizomes. These root-like parts bear sharp knobs like little teeth, and their peppery taste has made them popular snack foods for children, campers, and long-distance hikers.

Cutleaf Toothwort

Dentaria laciniata

SIZE:
4-15 in. tall; flower ½-¾ in. wide.

WHAT TO LOOK FOR:
flowers white to pinkish, clustered atop slender stalk; 3 leaves near top of stalk, each with 5 toothed lobes.

HABITAT:
rich woods, river floodplains.

IN BLOOM:
Mar.-June.

Wallflowers *Erysimum*

These tough, colorful plants share the name wallflower with their close cousins *Cheiranthus,* and plants of both groups are listed interchangeably in many garden catalogs. Both are sun-lovers, known for pushing their way between the rocks of old drywalls and for brightening the bases of rocky cliffs throughout the Northern Hemisphere.

Western Wallflower

Erysimum asperum

SIZE:
4-14 in. tall; flower ¾ in. wide.

WHAT TO LOOK FOR:
flowers bright yellow in dense clusters, with spicy fragrance; leaves straplike, occasionally toothed.

HABITAT:
prairies, bluffs, dry places.

IN BLOOM:
Apr.-Aug.

Fringepods *Thysanocarpus*

Like many in the mustard family, fringepods are hard to recognize by their flowers. But when fruits begin forming from the bottom of the flowering stalk, there is no mistaking them. In some species the lacy effect of the seedpods is heightened by small holes between the coglike rays.

FRUIT

Fringepod

Thysanocarpus curvipes

SIZE: 8-20 in. tall; fruit ¼ in. wide; flower minute.

WHAT TO LOOK FOR: fruits brownish, with gearlike green pattern; flowers tiny, greenish to white.

HABITAT: dry mountain grasslands, sagebrush, open oak woods.

IN BLOOM: Mar.-June.

Whitlow Grasses *Draba*

In old England, a whitlow was an inflammation under or around the fingernails or toenails. The sharply acidic juices of the whitlow grasses were said to be a remedy for the affliction, although it is unlikely they did much good. Like some others of the mustard family, these plants are known as winter annuals because they sprout in the fall, survive the winter, and begin to grow again in early spring.

Whitlow Grass

Draba verna

SIZE: 3-12 in. tall; flower ¼ in. wide.

WHAT TO LOOK FOR: flowers white, with yellow centers and 4 deeply notched petals; leaves spatula-shaped, clustered at base.

HABITAT: dry grasslands.

IN BLOOM: Mar.-June.

111

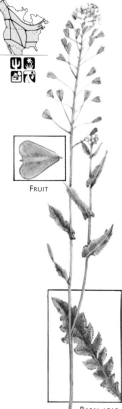

FRUIT

BASAL LEAF

Shepherd's Purses *Capsella*

The little white flowers that are tightly clustered atop the stems of these weedy plants begin to form fruit from the bottom up. As each seedpod forms, its stalk elongates and the stem above it continues to grow. When the plant has gone completely to seed, it looks like a coat tree with small heart-shaped purses or pouches on its arms.

Shepherd's Purse

Capsella bursa-pastoris

SIZE:
3-20 in. tall; fruit to ¼ in. long; flower minute.

WHAT TO LOOK FOR:
fruits heart-shaped; flowers cream-colored, clustered atop straight stem; much-divided leaves at base.

HABITAT:
fields, lawns, disturbed areas.

IN BLOOM:
Feb.-Dec.

Watercresses *Nasturtium*

Watercress grows almost everywhere in the world that freshwater runs, and its leaves and stems are prized for salads and fresh greens wherever it grows. It must be washed carefully before being eaten; it can survive in polluted water, and its leaves are a favored browsing place for tiny snails and water insects.

Bittercresses *Cardamine*

Only the older bittercress leaves are bitter enough to be truly unpalatable. The young leaves of most species are so sharply flavored that they rival Watercress as a pungent salad green. The bulbous rootstock of Springcress can be grated and mixed with vinegar to make a substitute for horseradish.

Springcress

Cardamine bulbosa

SIZE:
4-20 in. tall; flower about ½ in. wide.

WHAT TO LOOK FOR:
flowers white, loosely clustered at top of slender stem; leaves lance-shaped along stem, rounded at base.

HABITAT:
moist woods, wet meadows, shallow freshwater.

IN BLOOM:
Mar.-June.

◀Watercress

Nasturtium officinale

SIZE:
to 10 ft. long; flower ¼ in. wide.

WHAT TO LOOK FOR:
stems matted in water, creeping on bank; leaves shiny, divided into many leaflets; flowers white, in clusters.

HABITAT:
cold water; banks of springs and streams.

IN BLOOM:
Mar.-Nov.

Manzanitas *Arctostaphylos*

Among this group of evergreen shrubs the low-growing Bearberry is unique. It occurs in northern Europe and Asia as well as in colder areas of North America, where its berries are more valuable as winter food for birds and deer than for bears.

Cranberries *Vaccinium*

Wild cranberries—so named because their flower resembles the head of a crane—were among the first native foods that the Pilgrims learned to relish, and soon became one of the first North American crops grown commercially for export.

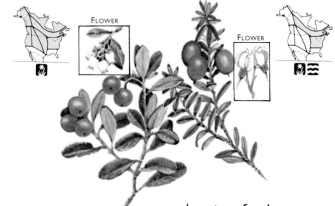

FLOWER

FLOWER

Bearberry

Arctostaphylos uva-ursi

SIZE:
stem to 10 ft. long;
flower about ¼ in. wide.

WHAT TO LOOK FOR:
leaves glossy; flowers white to pink, urn-shaped; red to purple berries last all winter.

HABITAT:
dry, sandy soils.

IN BLOOM:
Apr.-June.

American Cranberry

Vaccinium macrocarpon

SIZE:
8-12 in. high; flower ½ in. wide.

WHAT TO LOOK FOR:
stems wiry, trailing; leaves small, oval, leathery; flowers pink, with swept-back petals; berries red, about ¾ in. long.

HABITAT:
bogs; moist, sandy meadows.

IN BLOOM:
June-Oct.

Trailing Arbutuses *Epigaea*

North America's single species of trailing arbutus is the state flower of Massachusetts. (The only other species is native to Japan.) Its fragrant spring flowers are so tempting that picking them is forbidden by law in many parts of its range.

Mayflower

Epigaea repens

SIZE:
stem to 5 ft. long;
flower ¼-½ in. wide.

WHAT TO LOOK FOR:
leaves in pairs; stems trailing on ground; flowers pink and white, trumpet-shaped.

HABITAT:
sandy or peaty woods, clearings.

IN BLOOM:
Mar.-July.

Wintergreens *Gaultheria*

The evergreen leaves of wintergreens were the original source of wintergreen oil, also found in the inner bark of some birches. Because a ton of wintergreen leaves is required to produce a pound of oil, commercial producers now rely on birch twigs and synthetic compounds for this familiar flavoring.

Checkerberry

Gaultheria procumbens

SIZE:
2-6 in. tall; flower ¼ in. wide.

WHAT TO LOOK FOR:
flowers white, nodding; leaves leathery, oval; berries red; plant aromatic.

HABITAT: sandy woods, clearings.

IN BLOOM: July-Aug.

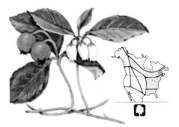

Cassiopes *Cassiope*

Most of these dwarf shrubs are native to high northern mountains around the globe, and others grow in the Arctic. With one exception—*Cassiope stelleriana* of the American Northwest—they bear tiny leaves that overlap like shingles to protect against the drying effect of the wind.

White Heather

Cassiope mertensiana

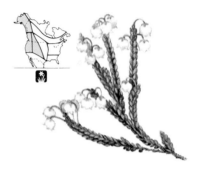

SIZE:
2-10 in. tall; flower about ¼ in. wide.

WHAT TO LOOK FOR:
flowers white, nodding; leaves scalelike.

HABITAT:
tundra; moist, stony soils.

IN BLOOM:
July-Aug.

Mountain Heathers *Phyllodoce*

Like Europe's true Heather (*Calluna vulgaris*), these high-altitude beauties of the tundra and northern mountain ranges are low, mat-forming shrubs whose dense covering of fine foliage forms a textured backdrop for clustered masses of bell-like blossoms.

Mountain Heather

Phyllodoce breweri

SIZE:
4-12 in. high; flower ½ in. wide.

WHAT TO LOOK FOR:
flowers pink, bowl-shaped, clustered at ends of stems; leaves needlelike, with blunt tips.

HABITAT:
tundra; open, moist, rocky soil.

IN BLOOM:
July-Aug.

Pipsissewas *Chimaphila*

The Cree Indians called these plants *pipsisikweu,* which means "it-breaks-into-small-pieces," because they believed the leaves were effective in breaking down kidney stones and gallstones. Pipsissewa tonic was still a popular home remedy in the early part of this century, but today this leaf extract is used merely to flavor candy and soft drinks. In Colonial times, the leathery leaves were also used to make a poultice to apply to bruises and skin irritations.

Pipsissewa

Chimaphila umbellata

SIZE:
3-10 in. tall; flower ¾ in. wide.

WHAT TO LOOK FOR:
flowers white to pink, fragrant, nodding, in clusters atop stems; leaves evergreen, toothed, broad near tips, borne in whorls.

HABITAT:
dry woods, often in acid soil.

IN BLOOM:
July-Aug.

Spotted Wintergreen

Chimaphila maculata

SIZE:
4-10 in. tall; flower ¾ in. wide.

WHAT TO LOOK FOR:
flowers white to pink, nodding, fragrant; leaves evergreen, striped white along midvein, in whorls.

HABITAT:
dry woods.

IN BLOOM:
May-Aug.

Shinleafs *Pyrola*

These small plants carpet the floors of coniferous forests throughout North America, their stalks of waxy, fragrant flowers rising from rosettes of glossy, evergreen leaves. Shinleafs differ from most flowers in that their anthers (the pollen-bearing tips of the male organs) do not split lengthwise to release pollen. Instead, the pollen comes out through a small pore at the end of each anther.

Shinleaf

Pyrola elliptica

SIZE:
4-12 in. tall; flower ¾ in. wide.

WHAT TO LOOK FOR:
flowers white, waxy, nodding, along slender stalk; leaves shiny green, oval, clustered at base of plant.

HABITAT:
dry to moist woods, usually in acid soil.

IN BLOOM:
June-Aug.

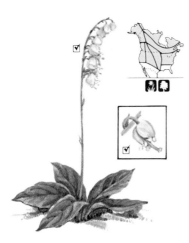

One-sided Pyrola

Pyrola secunda

SIZE:
2-8 in. tall; flower ¼ in. wide.

WHAT TO LOOK FOR:
flowers greenish yellow, along one side of arching stalk; leaves oval or rounded, in clusters at base.

HABITAT:
moist to dry woods, clearings, tundra.

IN BLOOM:
June-Aug.

One-flowered Wintergreens *Moneses*

There is only one species in this group, which is sometimes included among the shinleafs. Each delicate plant produces a single small and surprisingly fragrant flower, borne on a slender stalk above a few evergreen leaves. Although these flowers grow in many places, they were never abundant and are now becoming rare, even in the northern coniferous woods and bogs.

One-flowered Wintergreen

Moneses uniflora

SIZE:
1-6 in. tall; flower about ¾ in. wide.

WHAT TO LOOK FOR:
flowers white, nodding, fragrant; leaves round, leathery, clustered at base of plant.

HABITAT:
cool, mossy forests.

IN BLOOM:
June-Aug.

Indian Pipes *Monotropa*

The Indian Pipes are unusual among flowering plants (as opposed to mushrooms and other fungi, which they somewhat resemble) in that they contain no chlorophyll. They do not manufacture their own food by photosynthesis, depending instead on small wood-rotting fungi in the soil to free nutrients for their use.

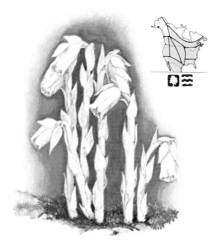

Indian Pipe

Monotropa uniflora

SIZE:
2-12 in. tall; flower ½-¾ in. wide.

WHAT TO LOOK FOR:
plants waxy white, scaly, often pink- or purple-tinged; flowers white, solitary, nodding, cup-shaped.

HABITAT:
rich, acid soil in woods and bogs.

IN BLOOM:
May-Sept.

Pinesap

Monotropa hypopithys

SIZE:
4-16 in. tall; flower ¼-½ in. wide.

WHAT TO LOOK FOR:
plants yellow to red, fleshy, scaly; flowers yellow, often highlighted with red, in nodding clusters.

HABITAT:
open woods.

IN BLOOM:
June-Oct.

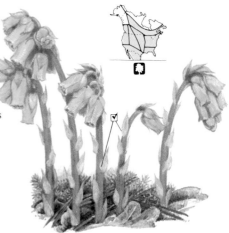

Wandflowers *Galax*

The single species of wandflower is one of the few plants for which a town—Galax, Virginia—has been named. Its round, glossy evergreen leaves are a familiar sight in the forests of the southern Appalachians, where they often form continuous ground covers beneath such woodland plants as Mountain Laurel. Wandflowers now grow in the wild as far north as Massachusetts, having escaped from gardens where they are cultivated for their distinctive flower spikes.

Wandflower

Galax rotundifolia

SIZE:
3-24 in. tall; flower about ¼ in. wide.

WHAT TO LOOK FOR:
leaves heart-shaped, shiny, dark green (bronze in fall and winter), in clusters near ground; flowers small, white, at top of wandlike stalk.

HABITAT:
rich woods and streambanks in mountain areas.

IN BLOOM:
May-July.

Snow Plants *Sarcodes*

Red is invisible to bees and most other pollinating insects, but it attracts carrion insects. The Snow Plant, which looks like a chunk of meat left on the ground, is believed to be pollinated by beetles and other such carrion eaters. Snow plants were once thought to be root parasites, but in fact, like the Indian Pipes, they subsist on nutrients freed by fungi from decaying matter in the soil.

Snow Plant

Sarcodes sanguinea

SIZE: 4-12 in. tall; flower ½-¾ in. long.

WHAT TO LOOK FOR: plants bright red, fleshy; leafless but with leaflike red scales to 4 in. long; flowers urn-shaped.

HABITAT: deep humus in forests.

IN BLOOM: May-June.

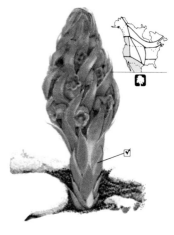

Douglasias *Douglasia*

These humble plants, whose small flowers are so profuse that they all but blot out the leaves, share a distinction with the lordly Douglas-firs growing in the same parts of the Pacific Northwest. Both are named for the Scottish explorer David Douglas, who found them while on a plant-hunting expedition from Oregon to Hudson Bay. The Mountain Douglasia is one of several species popular among rock gardeners.

Mountain Douglasia

Douglasia montana

SIZE: 1-3 in. tall; flower ¼-½ in. wide.

WHAT TO LOOK FOR: flowers pink, in clusters at stem tips; leaves tiny, narrow, forming tufted mats.

HABITAT: dry, rocky soil; mountaintops.

IN BLOOM: May-July.

Shooting Stars *Dodecatheon*

Legend has it that wherever a star falls to earth these flowers appear with their swept-back petals. The plants are quite versatile, flourishing in sunny grasslands and shady woods. The Sierra Shooting Star (*Dodecatheon jeffreyi*) thrives from the mountains of Alaska to California's Sierra Nevada. Like most kinds of Shooting Stars, it is able to produce seeds by self-pollination, thus assuring species survival even where insects are scarce.

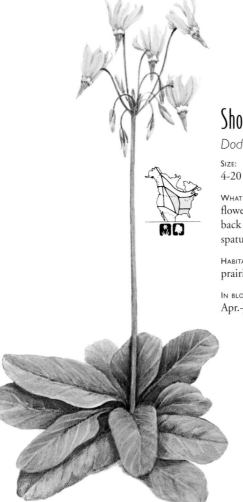

Shooting Star

Dodecatheon meadia

SIZE:
4-20 in. tall; flower ¾-1 in. wide.

WHAT TO LOOK FOR:
flower petals white to pink, swept back like trailing flames; leaves spatula-shaped, at base of stalk.

HABITAT:
prairies, meadows, open woods.

IN BLOOM:
Apr.-June.

Primroses *Primula*

These denizens of mountain slopes, northern streambanks, and other cool, moist places take their name from the Latin word for "first." Wherever they grow, they are likely to be among the earliest bloomers. Their small, brilliant flowers appear in clusters atop naked stalks that rise from rosettes of leaves. Each bloom's yellow center attracts bees and other pollinators to the nectar within. Humans are not always similarly attracted: the lovely Mountain Primrose, for example, has a foul odor.

Mountain Primrose

Primula parryi

SIZE:
4-16 in. tall; flower ½-1 in. wide.

WHAT TO LOOK FOR:
flowers rose-purple, with yellow centers; leaves fleshy, clustered at base of stalk.

HABITAT:
high mountain meadows, streambanks.

IN BLOOM:
June-Aug.

Bird's-eye Primrose

Primula mistassinica

SIZE:
1-6 in. tall; flower ¼-½ in. wide.

WHAT TO LOOK FOR:
flowers pink or lilac, with yellow centers;
leaves clustered at base of stalk.

HABITAT:
moist cliffs, meadows.

IN BLOOM:
Apr.-Aug.

Sierra Primrose

Primula suffrutescens

SIZE:
1-4 in. tall; flower ¼-½ in. wide.

WHAT TO LOOK FOR:
flowers pink or purple, with yellow centers;
leaves in tufts at base of downy stalks.

HABITAT:
cliffs, ledges.

IN BLOOM:
July-Aug.

Loosestrifes *Lysimachia*

"If thy yoked oxen show contention, give them loose-strife," admonished the ancient Greek physician Dioscorides. "Do ye the same," he added, "for quarrelsome lovers." Although their tranquilizing powers are not documented, these plants were until recent times widely used as a nerve tonic for both man and beast. Lysimachus, a legendary Sicilian king, is said to have noted this trait while being chased by a bull. The monarch desperately thrust a sprig of loosestrife at the maddened animal and the bull was instantly pacified—released from its strife.

Tufted Loosestrife

Lysimachia thyrsiflora

SIZE:
6-30 in. tall; flower ⅛-¼ in. wide.

WHAT TO LOOK FOR:
flowers yellow, in globelike clusters arising from leaf bases; leaves in pairs.

HABITAT:
swamps, wet woods, marshes.

IN BLOOM:
May-July.

Swamp Candles

Lysimachia terrestris

SIZE: 6-30 in. tall; flower ½-¾ in. wide.

WHAT TO LOOK FOR: flowers bright yellow with red centers, in dense plumes atop stem; leaves in pairs.

HABITAT: marshes, wet roadsides, lakeshores.

IN BLOOM: June-Aug.

Whorled Loosestrife

Lysimachia quadrifolia

SIZE: 8-24 in. tall; flower ½ in. wide.

WHAT TO LOOK FOR: leaves in whorls of 4-6; flowers yellow with red centers, each on threadlike stalk from leaf base.

HABITAT: open woods, wet meadows. **IN BLOOM:** May-Aug.

Moneywort
Lysimachia nummularia

SIZE: stem to 5 ft. long; flower ¾-1¼ in. wide.

WHAT TO LOOK FOR: stems prostrate, creeping; leaves in pairs, rounded; flowers yellow, scattered, growing from leaf bases.

HABITAT: wet woods, swamps, meadows.

IN BLOOM: June-Aug.

Pimpernels *Anagallis*

The Scarlet Pimpernel is a European native that is now widespread in North America and around the world. In England it is known as the Poor Man's Weather Glass because of its great sensitivity to atmospheric change. Not only do its blossoms close at the first hint of approaching dusk and fail to open on overcast days, but—in response to rising humidity—they close when stormy weather threatens.

Scarlet Pimpernel
Anagallis arvensis

SIZE: stem 1-10 in. long; flower ¼-½ in. wide.

WHAT TO LOOK FOR: flowers red or orange (occasionally blue or white), shaped like shallow bowls; leaves oval, in pairs along slender, spreading stems.

HABITAT: roadsides, waste places, dry meadows.

IN BLOOM: Mar.-Aug.

Featherfoils *Hottonia*

When conditions are right, the seeds of these water plants sprout in late summer and grow underwater throughout fall and winter. In spring, buoyed by air-filled cells, the hollow stems surface and bloom, surrounded by a submerged wreath of feathery leaves. Conditions are seldom right, however, and so the plants may bloom profusely one season, then disappear for several years before blooming again.

Featherfoil

Hottonia inflata

SIZE: 3-12 in. tall; flower ⅛-¼ in. wide.

WHAT TO LOOK FOR: stems protruding above water; flowers white, clustered at stem joints; leaves below surface, feathery.

HABITAT: still freshwater.

IN BLOOM: Apr.-June.

Sea Milkworts *Glaux*

Although it lives where water is abundant, this seaside plant (the only sea milkwort species in the world) is similar in many ways to some desert succulents. The common denominator is the ability of the small, fleshy leaves to withstand the drying effect of salt. The root membranes supply added protection by regulating the movement of water, thus allowing the plants to grow even where water is quite salty.

Sea Milkwort

Glaux maritima

SIZE: 1-12 in. long; flower ⅛ in. wide.

WHAT TO LOOK FOR: flowers white, pink, or purple, borne singly at leaf bases; leaves oblong, in pairs along gray-green, sprawling stems.

HABITAT: beaches, salt marshes.

IN BLOOM: May-July.

Stonecrops *Sedum*

Stonecrops can survive in arid locales—including deserts, rocky shores, tundra, and dry spots in otherwise congenial climates—because their fleshy leaves store water. In addition, the pores of their leaves follow an unusual schedule of opening and closing, one that is the reverse of the general rule: they open at night to admit the carbon dioxide needed for growth, then close during the day to prevent water loss. So effective is this system of conservation that many species are known as live-forevers: the leaves stay fresh long after the plants have been picked.

Orpine
Sedum telephium

SIZE:
10-22 in. tall; flower ¼-½ in. wide.

WHAT TO LOOK FOR:
flowers yellow-green or reddish lavender, in dense cluster atop stem; leaves fleshy, toothed, oval.

HABITAT:
fields, meadows.

IN BLOOM:
July-Sept.

Roseroot
Sedum rosea

SIZE:
1-12 in. tall; flower ¼-½ in. wide.

WHAT TO LOOK FOR:
stems matted, turning up at ends; flowers red-purple, clustered at stem tips; leaves fleshy, oval.

HABITAT:
tundra, mountains, rocky coasts.

IN BLOOM:
July-Sept.

Wall Pepper

Sedum acre

SIZE:
1-3 in. tall; flower ⅓-½ in. wide.

WHAT TO LOOK FOR:
stems creeping, matted; leaves succulent, evergreen; flowers yellow, star-shaped, in small clusters atop short stalks.

HABITAT:
rocks, walls, dry clearings.

IN BLOOM:
June-July.

Ditch Stonecrops *Penthorum*

Though they look a great deal like stonecrops and belong to the same botanical family, the ditch stonecrops are not succulent. They are wetland plants that usually grow in ditches and other low spots where water collects. Of the group's three species, the one shown here is the only North American native; the others originated in Asia.

Ditch Stonecrop

Penthorum sedoides

SIZE:
6-36 in. tall; flower ¼-½ in. wide.

WHAT TO LOOK FOR:
flowers greenish with creamy white tips, densely borne on leafless stalks; leaves lance-shaped, along upright stem.

HABITAT:
marshes, ditches, streambanks.

IN BLOOM: June-Oct.

Dudleyas *Dudleya*

These western plants are closely related to the stonecrops (many species in each group are known as live-forevers) and thrive in the same arid conditions. The most obvious difference is the way the flowers are borne. Those of the dudleyas appear on stalks that arise from among a cluster of leaves, while the stonecrops' are borne at the ends of leafy stems.

Canyon Dudleya

Dudleya cymosa

SIZE: 4-8 in. tall; flower ¼-½ in. wide.

WHAT TO LOOK FOR: flowers yellow to bright red, bell-shaped, clustered atop nearly leafless stalks; leaves broad, oblong, densely clustered at base of plant.

HABITAT: rocky cliffs, sagebrush, open woods.

IN BLOOM: Mar.-July.

Starflowers *Trientalis*

Many flowers are starlike in form, but these fragile shade-lovers have a special right to their name: the astral effect of their blossoms is repeated in an underlying collar of pointed leaves. Like many other spring bloomers, the starflowers store nutrients through the winter in fleshy underground tubers. Because of these tubers, one pink-flowered western species, *Trientalis latifolia,* is commonly known as Indian Potato.

Starflower

Trientalis borealis

SIZE: 2-8 in. tall; flower ⅓-½ in. wide.

WHAT TO LOOK FOR: flowers white, 7-petaled, rising on hairlike stalks above cluster of lance-shaped, pointed leaves.

HABITAT: rich woods, clearings, bogs.

IN BLOOM: May-Aug.

Bishop's Caps *Mitella*

These plants are among the proofs that Asia and North America were once one landmass, for bishop's caps are native to both. The Barestem Bishop's Cap (*Mitella nuda*), for example, grows both in eastern Asia and in the American West. The bishop's caps are named for their miter-shaped seedpods (the plants are also called miterworts). Other names, such as fringe cups and fairy cups, refer to the tiny flowers, as intricate as snowflakes.

SEEDPOD

Bishop's Cap

Mitella diphylla

Size:

8-18 in. tall; flower ⅛-¼ in. wide.

WHAT TO LOOK FOR:
flowers creamy white, fringed, scattered along slender spike; leaves lobed, toothed, clustered at base (1 pair on stem); seedpods 2-beaked, miterlike.

HABITAT:
rich woods.

IN BLOOM:
Apr.-June.

False Miterworts *Tiarella*

Like the bishop's caps they resemble, these shade-loving plants are found on both sides of the Pacific. Because their leaves were brewed into medicinal tea for treating fevers, they were once commonly known as coolworts. In Japan they are called *zuda-yakushu* ("asthma helpers").

Allegheny Foamflower

Tiarella cordifolia

SIZE: 4-12 in. tall; flower ¼ in. wide.

WHAT TO LOOK FOR: flowers white with long stamens, forming fuzzy spikes; leaves maplelike, hairy, at base of plant.

HABITAT: moist woods, shady cliffs.

IN BLOOM: Apr.-June.

Saxifrages *Saxifraga*

The saxifrages come in two types: those like the Early Saxifrage, which grow in rocky, seemingly barren places, and those few like the popular garden-grown Strawberry Geranium (*Saxifraga stolonifera*), which need rich, moist soil. Each long-lasting flower remains open until its 10 to 15 pollen-bearing stamens have matured, one at a time. Each stamen bends toward the center of the flower before releasing its pollen, and then straightens, making room for the next.

Early Saxifrage

Saxifraga virginiensis

SIZE: 2-16 in. tall; flower ¼ in. wide.

WHAT TO LOOK FOR: flowers white, in clusters atop hairy stalk; leaves at base of plant, leathery, hairy.

HABITAT: rocky cliffs, hillsides.

IN BLOOM: Apr.-June.

Ivesias *Ivesia*

Most of the 20 species in this group are limited to the Sierra Nevada of California. Gordon's Ivesia is the most striking exception; it grows as far north as Washington's Cascade mountains and eastward into the Rockies of Colorado and Montana.

Gordon's Ivesia

Ivesia gordoni

SIZE: 2-10 in. tall; flower ⅛-¼ in. wide.

WHAT TO LOOK FOR: flowers yellow, starlike, clustered atop wiry stems; leaves fernlike, mostly at base of plant.

HABITAT: mountain slopes, ridges, riverbanks.

IN BLOOM: June-Aug.

FRINGED GRASS
OF PARNASSUS

Grasses of Parnassus *Parnassia*

Parnassus is a mountain in Greece where these plants do not grow. Moreover, they in no way resemble grass. Their name resulted from several confusions over the centuries, having to do with translating the word for "green plant" from Greek to Latin to English and back again. Most species look much alike, but the Fringed Grass of Parnassus (*Parnassia fimbriata*) of western mountain ranges has petals edged with lacy frills.

Grass of Parnassus

Parnassia glauca

SIZE: 4-25 in. tall; flower ¾-1¼ in. wide.

WHAT TO LOOK FOR: flowers white, with green stripes; leaves leathery, heart-shaped to round, at base of plant (1 leaf clasps stem).

HABITAT: wet meadows, ditches, bogs.

IN BLOOM: July-Oct.

Meadowsweets *Filipendula*

Only one species of this group, the spectacular Queen of the Prairie, is native to North America. Other species, including the shorter Queen of the Meadow (*Filipendula ulmaria*), were imported from Europe or Asia.

Queen of the Prairie
Filipendula rubra

SIZE:
2-6 ft. tall; flower ¼ in. wide.

WHAT TO LOOK FOR:
flowers pink, in flat-topped clusters on tall stalks; leaves large, toothed, deeply divided.

HABITAT:
moist prairies, meadows, marshes.

IN BLOOM:
June-Aug.

Strawberries *Fragaria*

"Doubtless God could have made a better berry," wrote Izaak Walton, "but doubtless God never did." In fact, the juicy strawberry is not a berry at all, but the pulpy center of the flower, and each of its apparent seeds is actually a complete one-seeded fruit.

Wild Strawberry
Fragaria virginiana

SIZE:
2-10 in. tall; flower ½-¾ in. wide.

WHAT TO LOOK FOR:
leaflets hairy, in 3's; white flowers and red "berries" clustered among leaves.

HABITAT:
meadows, clearings.

IN BLOOM:
Apr.-July.

Spireas *Spiraea*

These shrubby plants are closely related to the meadow-sweets, and are often known by the same name. Native wild spireas, such as the Steeplebush, though less showy than the larger garden species from Asia, are often used for landscaping.

Steeplebush

Spiraea tomentosa

Size: 2-4 ft. tall; flower ⅛-¼ in. wide.

What to look for: flowers pink, in dense steeple-shaped clusters at ends of branches; leaves oblong, toothed, with woolly undersides.

Habitat: wet fields, meadows. In bloom: July-Sept.

Burnets *Sanguisorba*

It is a botanical truism that petalless flowers are pollinated by the wind; but as the burnets demonstrate, such truisms are not always true. Bees, butterflies, and other insects are attracted by the colored sepals, the long-stalked stamens, and the fragrance of the flowers. Several Eurasian species now grow in North America.

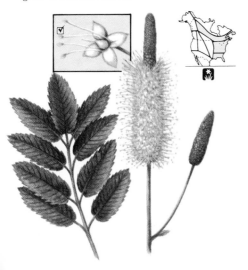

American Burnet

Sanguisorba canadensis

Size: 2-6 ft. tall; flower ⅛-¼ in. wide.

What to look for: flowers white with long stamens, in dense, fuzzy spikes; leaves divided into many toothed leaflets.

Habitat: moist open ground.

In bloom: June-Oct.

Cinquefoils *Potentilla*

The name cinquefoil means "five-leaf." Indeed, the leaves of many species, such as Fivefingers, are divided into 5 leaflets, but in others the number may vary from 3 to 15 or more. Of the world's more than 300 cinquefoil species, about one-third grow in North America, in habitats ranging from swamplands to dry rocky fields. Like many weeds that invade barren areas where others of their own kind are scarce, most cinquefoils bear flowers that can produce viable seeds with or without fertilization.

Marsh Cinquefoil
Potentilla palustris

SIZE:
4-24 in. tall; flower ¾-1 in. wide.

WHAT TO LOOK FOR:
flowers crimson, star-shaped, scattered on slender stems; leaflets toothed, in groups of 5-7.

HABITAT:
wet meadows, swamps, marshes.

IN BLOOM:
June-Aug.

Fivefingers
Potentilla simplex

SIZE:
stem to 3 ft. long; flower ¼-½ in. wide.

WHAT TO LOOK FOR:
flowers yellow with blunt petals, borne singly on slender stalks along trailing stems; leaflets toothed, in groups of 5.

HABITAT:
dry open woods, meadows, roadsides.

IN BLOOM:
Apr.-June.

Tall Cinquefoil

Potentilla arguta

SIZE:
1-3 ft. tall; flower ½-¾ in. wide.

WHAT TO LOOK FOR:
flowers creamy white with yellow centers, borne in loose clusters atop branching stems; leaves divided into 7-11 oval, toothed leaflets.

HABITAT:
dry open woods, prairies.

IN BLOOM:
June-Aug.

Silverweed

Potentilla anserina

SIZE:
stem to 5 ft. long; flower ½-1 in. wide.

WHAT TOO LOOK FOR:
flowers yellow with oval petals, borne singly on slender stalks along trailing stems; leaves divided into 7-15 leaflets; leaflets toothed, hairy, silvery underneath.

HABITAT:
moist open sand, beaches, salt marshes.

IN BLOOM:
May-Sept.

Prairie Mimosas *Desmanthus*

Like the true mimosas for which they are named, these shrubby plants bear leaves that are twice-divided; each leaf is divided into several long stalks, each of which bears a double row of small leaflets. The fluffy flower clusters are made up of 40 to 50 tiny flowers, each with five long stamens.

Prairie Mimosa

Desmanthus illinoensis

SIZE: 2-6 ft. tall; flower cluster ½ in. wide.

WHAT TO LOOK FOR: flowers minute, white, in powder-puff clusters; leaves twice-divided into many tiny leaflets; seedpods clustered.

HABITAT: prairies, pastures, riverbanks.

IN BLOOM: May-Sept.

Sensitive Briers *Schrankia*

Each of these plants' leaflets is supported by a small, water-filled swelling at the base. When these are jarred, loss of osmotic pressure causes the water to leave the cells, and the leaflets fold up. So sensitive are these organs that they respond to vibrations carried from one interlacing branch to another.

Cat's Claw

Schrankia nuttallii

SIZE: stem to 4 ft. long; flower cluster ¾-1 in. wide.

WHAT TO LOOK FOR: flowers minute, pink, in powder-puff clusters; leaves divided into many tiny leaflets; stems sprawling, covered with hooked thorns.

HABITAT: dry prairies. IN BLOOM: May-Sept.

Avens _Geum_

When the flowers of avens produce fruit, each tiny, nutlike seed retains the style (the stalklike extension of the seed-producing organ). In some woodland species, such as the eastern Redroot (_Geum canadense_), these styles have hooks and adhere to the fur of animals, who thus help to disperse the seeds. In others, such as the avens known as Prairie Smoke, the styles form feathery sails that are caught and carried by the wind.

Prairie Smoke
Geum triflorum

SIZE:
4-16 in. tall; flower ¼-½ in. wide.

WHAT TO LOOK FOR:
flowers red-purple, urn-shaped, nodding; fruits with long feathery tails; leaves much divided, toothed, lobed.

HABITAT:
dry prairies, limestone gravel, lakeshores.

IN BLOOM: Apr.-Aug.

FRUIT

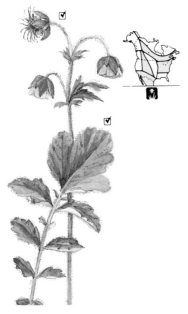

Purple Avens
Geum rivale

SIZE:
1-4 ft. tall; flower ½ in. wide.

WHAT TO LOOK FOR:
flowers brownish purple, nodding atop hairy stalks; fruits like soft burrs; leaves hairy, toothed; leaves at base much divided, with large leaflet at tip; leaves on stem 3-fingered.

HABITAT:
wet meadows, bogs.

IN BLOOM: May-Aug.

Sennas *Cassia*

Sennas have been used medicinally since ancient times. The dried leaves of Wild Senna yield an effective laxative, and in the old days they were often gathered from the wild and sold to apothecaries. Commercial markets, however, prefer the more potent Golden Shower (*Cassia fistula*), imported from India.

Partridge Pea

Cassia fasciculata

SIZE:
6-30 in. tall; flower ¼-1½ in. wide.

WHAT TO LOOK FOR:
flowers bright yellow with brown centers; leaflets narrow, 6-18 pairs on each stalk; seedpods small, flat.

HABITAT:
meadows, fields, prairies.

IN BLOOM:
July-Sept.

Wild Senna

Cassia marilandica

SIZE:
3-6 ft. tall; flower ¼-1 in. wide.

WHAT TO LOOK FOR:
flowers bright yellow with brown centers; leaflets oval, 4-8 pairs on each stalk; seedpods flat, segmented.

HABITAT:
roadsides, thickets, prairies, wet woods.

IN BLOOM:
July-Aug.

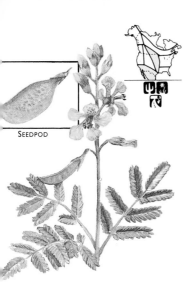

SEEDPOD

Hog Potatoes *Hoffmanseggia*

The tuberlike swellings on the roots are edible and nutritious, though hardly tasty. To the Indians of the Southwest, the plants were valuable as emergency rations because they grow where other food is scarce.

Hog Potato

Hoffmanseggia densiflora

SIZE: 5-16 in. tall; flower ½ in. wide.

WHAT TO LOOK FOR: flowers yellow and orange, in erect spikes; leaves fernlike, mostly at base of plant; seedpods flat, about 1 in. long.

HABITAT: dry grasslands, scrublands; deserts.

IN BLOOM: Apr.-Sept.

Leadplants *Amorpha*

All plants need nitrogen to grow, but they cannot take it directly from the air. It must be "fixed"—converted to a water-soluble compound—before plant roots can use it. Legumes such as leadplants have special nodules in their roots that house nitrogen-fixing bacteria. It is this trait that makes them important cover crops. When they die back or are plowed under after a season's growth, the nitrogen stored in their tissues enriches the soil.

Fragrant Leadplant

Amorpha nana

SIZE: 1-3 ft. tall; flower ⅛-¼ in. long.

WHAT TO LOOK FOR: flowers purple with long yellow stamens, in dense slender spikes; leaves divided into small oval leaflets.

HABITAT: dry prairies. IN BLOOM: June-July.

Wild Peas *Lathyrus*

Wild peas, or vetchlings, are closely related to the vetches. (Botanists tell them apart by the placement of small hairs inside the flowers.) Many species are grown as fodder or cover crops or—like the Sweet Pea (*Lathyrus odoratus*)—for floral beauty. The crimson Pride of California (*Lathyrus splendens*) is outstanding among the Pacific Coast's many wild peas.

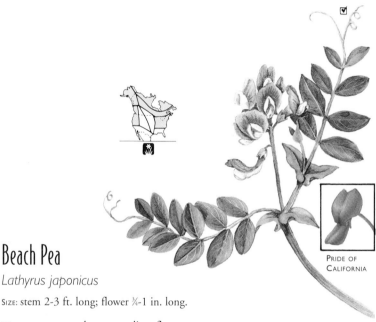

PRIDE OF
CALIFORNIA

Beach Pea

Lathyrus japonicus

SIZE: stem 2-3 ft. long; flower ¾-1 in. long.

WHAT TO LOOK FOR: plants sprawling; flowers red-purple (maturing to blue and white), in clusters; leaves divided, tendriled.

HABITAT: open beaches, dunes.

IN BLOOM: June-Aug.

Vetches *Vicia*

An Old World vetch, the Broad Bean (*Vicia faba*), is one of the earliest plants known to have been cultivated by man and is still grown as a winter vegetable. The Cow Vetch is also widely cultivated, though generally for use as fodder rather than for human consumption. When grown as a cover crop, it is plowed under in the fall to enrich the soil.

Cow Vetch

Vicia cracca

SIZE: stem to 6 ft. long; flower ¼-½ in. long.

WHAT TO LOOK FOR: stems climbing or sprawling; flowers violet to blue, in dense, one-sided spikes; leaves divided, ending in 2 tendrils.

HABITAT: fields, grasslands.

IN BLOOM: May-Aug.

Locoweeds *Oxytropis*

YELLOW LOCOWEED

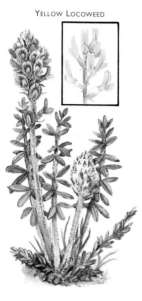

Ranchers may call any of several poisonous plants locoweeds, but the name properly belongs to this group and to various milk vetches that contain the same addictive, slow-acting poison. Animals seldom eat locoweed unless drought or overgrazing forces them to; then they may become habituated and search for more, even when tastier forage is available. Yellow Locoweed (*Oxytropis campestris*) is widespread in Canada and the northern United States.

Showy Locoweed

Oxytropis splendens

SIZE: 4-14 in. tall; flower ½ in. long.

WHAT TO LOOK FOR: flowers pink to blue, in dense spikes; plants covered with silky white hairs; leaflets in whorls along stalk.

HABITAT: dry prairies, meadows, mountain slopes.

IN BLOOM: June-Aug.

Locoweed

Astragalus purshii

SIZE: stem to 8 in. long; flower ½-1 in. long.

WHAT TO LOOK FOR: plants low, spreading; leaflets downy; flowers pink, purple, or yellowish.

HABITAT: grassy plains to dry mountain slopes.

IN BLOOM: Apr.-Aug.

Milk Vetches *Astragalus*

Milk vetches are close relatives of the locoweeds. Many species contain the same poisonous substance, locoine, and some are known by the same name. The slow poison causes visual impairment, weakness, loss of muscular control, and eventually death in cattle, horses, and other range animals. It even kills the bees that pollinate the plants. In addition, the seeds of the plants contain a quick-acting poison called abrin.

Milk Vetch

Astragalus canadensis

SIZE:
1-4 ft. tall; flower ½-⅔ in. long.

WHAT TO LOOK FOR:
flowers boat-shaped, creamy white to greenish yellow, in dense spikes; leaves divided, fernlike.

HABITAT:
open woods, thickets, shores.

IN BLOOM: June-Aug.

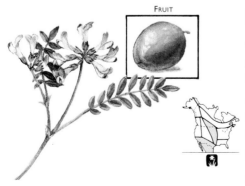

FRUIT

Ground Plum

Astragalus crassicarpus

SIZE: stem to 2 ft. long; flower ¾ in. long.

WHAT TO LOOK FOR: plants sprawling; flowers purple and white; fruits plumlike, ¾-1 in. across.

HABITAT: dry prairies, desert grasslands.

IN BLOOM: Mar.-July.

Hoary Peas *Tephrosia*

Toxic to mammals, these legumes are often called goat's rues. Yet many birds eat the seeds; the plants came to be called turkey peas. The tough rootstocks earned the names devil's shoestring and catgut. Used by Indians to poison fish, the roots are a source of the insecticide rotenone.

Goat's Rue

Tephrosia virginiana

SIZE: 6-30 in. tall; flower ½-¾ in. long.

WHAT TO LOOK FOR: flowers pink to purple with yellow upper lips, borne in dense clusters; leaves divided into narrow leaflets, covered with silky silver hairs.

HABITAT: dry open woods, fields, prairies (often in sand).

IN BLOOM: May-Aug.

Licorices *Glycyrrhiza*

The rhizomes, or rootlike underground stems, of these plants yield the popular flavoring for candy and medicines. ("Licorice" is a corruption of the Latin name *Glycyrrhiza*, which means "sweet root.") An Old World species, *Glycyrrhiza glabra*, is the commercial source, but the rhizomes of Wild Licorice were dried and chewed by Indians.

Wild Licorice

Glycyrrhiza lepidota

SIZE: 8-40 in. tall; flower about ½ in. long.

WHAT TO LOOK FOR: flowers white to yellow, in dense spikes; leaves divided into lance-shaped leaflets; seedpods prickly, clustered.

HABITAT: prairies, meadows, streambanks.

IN BLOOM: May-Aug.

SEEDPODS

Crown Vetches *Coronilla*

Only one species of this group of shrubby Old World legumes has become widespread in North America. It was imported from Europe to serve as a ground cover, and its pink flowers and lush foliage are now a familiar sight along highway embankments in the East.

Crown Vetch

Coronilla varia

SIZE:
8-40 in. tall; flower about ½ in. wide.

WHAT TO LOOK FOR:
flowers pink, in dense clusters on sprawling stems; leaves divided into many oval leaflets.

HABITAT:
fields, roadsides, banks.

IN BLOOM:
May-Sept.

Trefoils *Lotus*

The ancient Greeks called many plants "lotus," including trees, shrubs, water plants, and perhaps some members of this group. Most North American species grow only in the Far West. The Birdfoot Trefoil is a European import that has spread across the continent.

Birdfoot Trefoil

Lotus corniculatus

SIZE:
6-24 in. tall; flower about ½ in. wide.

WHAT TO LOOK FOR:
flowers yellow to orange, in clusters; plants erect or sprawling; leaflets in 5's (3 at tip of stalk, 2 at base).

HABITAT:
roadsides, meadows, fields.

IN BLOOM:
June-Sept.

Coralbeans *Erythrina*

These plants are unusual among legumes, for their flowers lack the jutting keel petals that generally serve as landing platforms for bees. Coral beans are pollinated instead by birds. The New World species are adapted for hummingbirds, which hover in the air before the long, tubular blossoms. In Africa, where there are no hummingbirds, the lower petals of the coralbean flower form a kind of perch for sunbirds.

False Lupines *Thermopsis*

Lupines and false lupines look very much alike, although few lupines bear yellow flowers. The easiest way to tell the difference between false lupines and yellow-flowered species of true lupines is to count the leaflets. Those of the false lupines are arranged in groups of three; the number varies among the true lupines, but it is always larger than three.

Rattleboxes *Crotalaria*

The mature seeds of the rattleboxes, which rattle inside their dry pods when disturbed, are said to make a tasty coffee substitute if boiled long enough. Eaten raw, however, they are deadly.

Cardinal Spear

Golden Pea

DRY SEEDPOD

Rattlebox

◀Cardinal Spear

Erythrina herbacea

SIZE: 2-5 ft. tall; flower 1½-2 in. long.

WHAT TO LOOK FOR: flowers bright red, tubular, in spectacular spikes; leaflets in 3's, shaped like arrowheads.

HABITAT: pine forests, sandlands, thickets.

IN BLOOM: Apr.-June.

◀Golden Pea

Thermopsis montana

SIZE: 1-4 ft. tall; flower ½-¾ in. wide.

WHAT TO LOOK FOR: flowers yellow, in showy wands; leaflets broad, rounded, in 3's, on wiry stalks arising from between 2 leaflike appendages.

HABITAT: wet meadows, slopes, open sites in mountains.

IN BLOOM: May-July.

◀Rattlebox

Crotalaria sagittalis

SIZE: 6-16 in. tall; flower ¼ in. wide.

WHAT TO LOOK FOR: flowers yellow, on slender stalks arising from leaf base; fruits green to brown seedpods, rattling when dry.

HABITAT: dry fields, prairies, waste places.

IN BLOOM: June-Sept.

Groundnuts *Apios*

One year, when Henry David Thoreau's potato crop failed, he dug groundnuts in the woods and roasted them, as the Pilgrims had learned to do from the Indians long before. He found them nourishing and took pleasure in their nutty flavor.

Groundnut

Apios americana

SIZE: stem to 4 ft. long; flower about ½ in. wide.

WHAT TO LOOK FOR: flowers purplish brown with upper lip turned back, in dense clusters; leaflets lance shaped; plants sprawling or climbing.

HABITAT: thickets, wooded edges of fields, roadsides.

IN BLOOM: July-Sept.

Butterfly Peas *Clitoria*

Only one species of this group of tropical legumes is widespread in North America. (Another, *Clitoria fragrans*, grows in the Florida sandlands.) The flowers often turn upside down at maturity, making a landing platform for pollinating insects.

Butterfly Pea

Clitoria mariana

SIZE: stem to 6 ft. long; flower 1½-2 in. wide.

WHAT TO LOOK FOR: flowers lavender-pink; leaflets in 3's; stems sprawling or climbing.

HABITAT: dry open woods, riverbanks, sandy clearings.

IN BLOOM: June-Aug.

False Indigoes *Baptisia*

The colonists found many uses for these bushy plants, from brushing away horseflies while plowing (hence the names Horsefly Weed and Shoofly) to treating malaria. The commonest use, however, was as a substitute for the blue dye that has since ancient times been extracted for commercial purposes from the roots of the Asian Indigo (*Indigofera tinctoria*). The false indigoes are members of the legume, or pea, family, as are all the plants on pages 140 to 163.

Wild Indigo
Baptisia tinctoria

SIZE: 1-3 ft. tall; flower about ½ in. long.

WHAT TO LOOK FOR: flowers yellow, in long clusters among branching stems; leaflets in 3's, blue-green.

HABITAT: dry open woods, clearings, grasslands.

IN BLOOM: May-Sept.

Prairie False Indigo
Baptisia leucantha

SIZE: 3-6 ft. tall; flower ¾-1 in. long.

WHAT TO LOOK FOR: flowers white, in long wands; leaflets in 3's, gray-green, fleshy.

HABITAT: moist prairies; clearings, roadsides.

IN BLOOM: May-July.

Lupines *Lupinus*

Most of the more than 200 lupine species are found in the southwestern states and on the Pacific Coast, where their hard, round seeds are valuable food for quail and other game birds. A few grow in the South and Midwest, but only the Blue Lupine is widespread in the Northeast. (These boundaries are becoming less distinct as a result of the cultivation of lupines in gardens.) Several species contain an alkaloid that is toxic to cattle and other grazing animals, but the effects are serious only when the leaves make up a large proportion of the animals' diet or when the extremely poisonous seeds are eaten. The Texas Bluebonnet is the state flower of Texas.

Texas Bluebonnet

Lupinus subcarnosus

SIZE:
6-24 in. tall; flower about ½ in. long.

WHAT TO LOOK FOR:
flowers blue with white centers, in wandlike spikes; leaflets like spokes.

HABITAT:
dry prairies chiefly in Texas.

IN BLOOM:
Apr.-June.

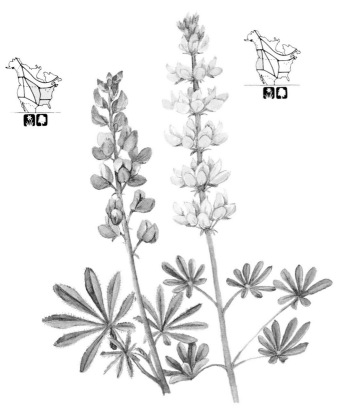

Blue Lupine

Lupinus perennis

SIZE:
8-24 in. tall; flower ½ in. long.

WHAT TO LOOK FOR:
flowers blue-purple, in upright spikes;
leaflets like spokes.

HABITAT:
dry, open woods; fields; pinelands.

IN BLOOM:
Apr.-July.

Yellow Lupine

Lupinus luteolus

SIZE:
12-32 in. tall; flower about ½ in. long.

WHAT TO LOOK FOR:
flowers pale yellow, in slender spikes;
leaflets like spokes.

HABITAT: pine and oak forests; dry,
grassy slopes.

IN BLOOM:
May-Aug.

Clovers *Trifolium*

The three-part clover leaf is a recurrent motif in folklore and popular imagery, its use ranging from the Irish Shamrock purportedly chosen by St. Patrick as a symbol of the Trinity to the complex intersections of modern highways. Clover plants are beneficial in many ways: as forage for range animals; as soil-improving cover crops; as a source of honey; and as free food relished by campers and hikers. Roots, stems, leaves, and flowers are all edible, but should be soaked in salted water or cooked briefly to make them more digestible. Red Clover is the state flower of Vermont.

Crimson Clover

Trifolium incarnatum

SIZE:
6-34 in. tall; flowerhead 1-2½ in. long.

WHAT TO LOOK FOR:
flowers crimson, in dense conical heads; leaflets large, dark green, in 3's.

HABITAT:
meadows, fields.

IN BLOOM:
Apr.-July.

Red Clover

Trifolium pratense

SIZE:
2-24 in. tall; flowerhead 1 in. long.

WHAT TO LOOK FOR:
flowers rose-pink, in dense heads;
leaflets pointed, in 3's.

HABITAT:
meadows, waste places, streets.

IN BLOOM:
Mar.-Sept.

Rabbit's-foot Clover

Trifolium arvense

SIZE:
4-18 in. tall; flowerhead ½-1 in. long.

WHAT TO LOOK FOR:
flowers white, nearly hidden by pinkish
to silvery-tan wool that covers dense
heads; leaflets narrow, in 3's.

HABITAT:
dry fields, grassy banks.

IN BLOOM:
May-Oct.

White Clover

Trifolium repens

SIZE:
1-15 in. tall;
flowerhead 1 in. long.

WHAT TO LOOK FOR:
flowers white with pink
bases, in dense heads; leaflets
heart-shaped, in 3's.

HABITAT:
lawns, grasslands, fields.

IN BLOOM:
Mar.-Oct.

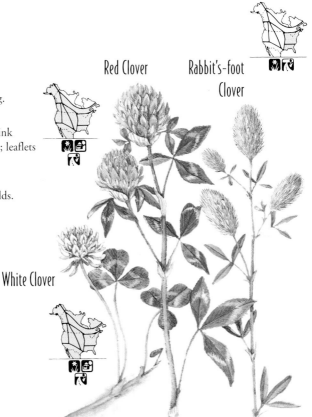

Red Clover

Rabbit's-foot
Clover

White Clover

Sweet Clovers *Melilotus*

Like most of the clovers (*Trifolium*) common in lawns and meadows, the sweet clovers were originally imported from the Old World and have long since spread across North America. White Sweet Clover and the somewhat shorter Yellow Sweet Clover (*Melilotus officinalis*) are grown as cover crops, bee plants, and forage. The fragrance of sweet clover hay is a cherished memory of many a country childhood.

White Sweet Clover
Melilotus alba

SIZE:
1-8 ft. tall; flower to ¼ in. long.

WHAT TO LOOK FOR:
flowers white, borne in profuse spikes among leaves and at tips of branches; plants bushy; leaflets small, toothed, in 3's.

HABITAT:
fields, meadows, waste places.

IN BLOOM:
Apr.-Oct.

YELLOW
SWEET CLOVER

Prairie Clovers *Petalostemum*

Many of the prairie clovers are confined to high plains in western states and provinces. The Purple Prairie Clover and the very similar White Prairie Clover (*Petalostemum candidum*) are more widespread. Like their western cousins, they can survive periods of drought because their deep root systems draw in water far below the surface.

Purple Prairie Clover

Petalostemum purpureum

SIZE:
8-24 in. tall; flowerhead ½-2 in. long.

WHAT TO LOOK FOR:
flowers rose-purple, borne in conical heads (flowering begins at bottom and proceeds upward in a ring around the head); leaflets narrow, in 3's.

HABITAT:
prairies.

IN BLOOM:
June-Sept.

WHITE
PRAIRIE
CLOVER

Tick Trefoils *Desmodium*

These legumes are named for their segmented seedpods, the notorious beggar's ticks. Each detachable segment contains one seed and is covered with tiny barbed hairs, which cling tenaciously to clothing, shoelaces, animal fur, and other textured surfaces. Thus the seeds are carried away from the parent plant, lessening the competition between members of the same species.

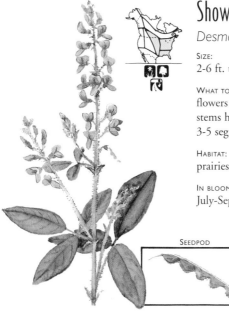

Showy Tick Trefoil

Desmodium canadense

SIZE:
2-6 ft. tall; flower about ½ in. long.

WHAT TO LOOK FOR:
flowers rose-pink to bluish, borne in tall clusters; stems hairy; leaflets long, oval, in 3's; seedpods in 3-5 segments, prickly.

HABITAT:
prairies, edges of woods, clearings, fields.

IN BLOOM:
July-Sept.

SEEDPOD

Bush Clovers *Lespedeza*

About 20 kinds of bush clover grow wild in North America, including 4 or 5 from abroad (the numbers are uncertain because the species hybridize quite easily). Important plants for pasturage and hay, they are among the best crops for improving the nitrogen content of dry soil. The seeds of some species are a primary food for quail.

Wisterias *Wisteria*

This group's two native varieties, American Wisteria and the very similar Kentucky Wisteria are now considered to be one species. They are neither as showy nor as winter-hardy as the popular garden species imported from the Orient. Like the imports, the native wisterias are vigorous twining vines whose woody stems may, over the years, grow to be several inches thick.

American Wisteria

Wisteria frutescens

SIZE: vine to 50 ft. high; flower ¼-¾ in. long.

WHAT TO LOOK FOR: flowers blue-purple, in dense, drooping clusters; leaves dark green (rose-colored when young), divided into oblong, pointed leaflets.

HABITAT: thickets, bottomlands, moist woods, riverbanks.

IN BLOOM: Mar.-May.

◄Round-headed Bush Clover

Lespedeza capitata

SIZE:
1-4 ft. tall; flower ¼-½ in. long.

WHAT TO LOOK FOR:
plants silvery, hairy; leaflets in 3's, densely clustered; flowers creamy with reddish to brown markings, in bristly clusters.

HABITAT:
dry open fields, clearings, prairies.

IN BLOOM:
July-Sept.

Rosary Peas *Abrus*

Scarlet tipped with black, the glossy seeds of these woody tropical vines have long been used for rosary beads and decorative jewelry. They are, however, extremely poisonous; less than one seed, chewed and swallowed, can kill an adult, and toddlers have died merely from sucking on a seed. The single North American species grows only in Florida.

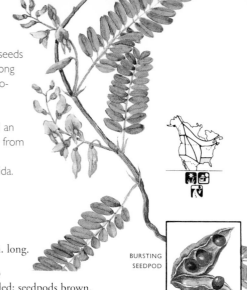

Crab's Eye

Abrus precatorius

SIZE: vine to 10 ft. high; flower ½-¾ in. long.

WHAT TO LOOK FOR: flowers rose-pink to purple, in clusters; leaves much divided; seedpods brown, clustered, bursting to reveal red and black seeds.

HABITAT: woods, thickets, roadsides.

IN BLOOM: Mar.-July.

BURSTING
SEEDPOD

Medicks *Medicago*

Several species in this group of Old World legumes, imported to North America as crop plants, now grow wild all across the continent. Alfalfa was one of the earliest domesticated plants (the name comes from the Arabic for "best fodder"). Flourishing in well-drained nonacidic soils, it is still among the world's most important forage and soil-improving cover crops.

Kudzus *Pueraria*

The fast-growing Kudzu was imported from Japan in 1911 to control erosion and restore nitrogen-depleted soil. The edible rootstocks and tough bark fibers were added benefits, and the leaves supplied fodder and chicken feed. But in the warm, wet climate of the Southeast, the Kudzu ran rampant, overgrowing forests, fields, and buildings at the rate of 100 feet a year and more. Today, the kudzu invasion is a serious problem throughout the region.

Kudzu

Pueraria lobata

SIZE: vine to 75 ft. high; flower ¾-1 in. long.

WHAT TO LOOK FOR: plants climbing and sprawling; leaflets oval, pointed, in 3's; flowers red-purple, grape-scented, in long spikes.

HABITAT: fencerows, woods; overrunning old buildings.

IN BLOOM: Aug.-Sept.

ABANDONED HOUSE
OVERRUN BY KUDZU

◄Alfalfa

Medicago sativa

SIZE:
1-3 ft. tall; flower ½ in. long.

WHAT TO LOOK FOR:
plants erect or sprawling; flowers purple to yellowish, in loose heads; fruits corkscrewlike; leaflets in 3's.

HABITAT:
fields, waste ground.

IN BLOOM:
May-Oct.

Willow Herbs *Epilobium*

These members of the evening primrose family take their name from their willow-like leaves and watery habitat. Several species are known as fireweeds, for they are often the first plants to grow on land that has been devastated by fire. They serve to stabilize the soil and start a new cycle of plant succession.

Fireweed

Epilobium angustifolium

SIZE:
2-6 ft. tall; flower ¾-1½ in. wide.

WHAT TO LOOK FOR:
flowers rose-pink, clustered along tall stalks; seedpods slender, opening to reveal white, fluffy down; leaves lance-shaped.

HABITAT:
burns, clearings, open land.

IN BLOOM:
July-Sept.

SEEDPOD

California Fuchsias *Zauschneria*

Like most bright red, tubular flowers, the blossoms of these West Coast natives are pollinated largely by hummingbirds. The Hummingbird Trumpet grows in several seemingly inhospitable habitats, including desert lowlands and high, barren ridges. It often looks different in different places. The leaves of plants in deserts, for example, are small and woolly compared with those at high elevations.

Hummingbird Trumpet

Zauschneria californica

SIZE:
4-38 in. tall; flower 1-1½ in. long.

WHAT TO LOOK FOR:
flowers bright red to red-orange, funnel-shaped, loosely borne along leafy spikes; leaves lance-shaped, gray-green, downy.

HABITAT:
sagebrush, chaparral, cliffs, rocky streambeds.

IN BLOOM:
Aug.-Oct.

Clarkias *Clarkia*

The clarkias are particularly interesting to botanists who study plant evolution because of the comparative speed with which species are being shaped by a process called catastrophic selection. The ancestral type from which present-day clarkias descended was a moisture-loving plant. Yet many of its offspring grow in the foothills of the Sierra Nevada, where recurrent droughts alternate with wet periods. During the dry spells, some species cannot compete with grasses and are eliminated from entire localities. But new forms, able to hold their own against the competition, have developed and spread into dry areas over the years.

Deerhorn

Clarkia pulchella

SIZE:
4-20 in. tall; flower 1-2 in. wide.

WHAT TO LOOK FOR:
flowers pink to rose-purple, with 4 elaborately lobed petals; leaves straplike.

HABITAT:
mountain grasslands, dry plains.

IN BLOOM:
June-July.

Farewell-to-spring

Clarkia amoena

SIZE:
1-3 ft. tall; flower 1½-2½ in. wide.

WHAT TO LOOK FOR:
flowers showy, pink and white (often blotched with red);
leaves straplike; plants erect or sprawling.

HABITAT:
coastal scrublands, forest edges (oak, redwood), chaparral.

IN BLOOM:
June-Aug.

Winecup Clarkia

Clarkia purpurea

SIZE:
4-24 in. tall; flower 1-2 in. wide.

WHAT TO LOOK FOR:
flowers purple, lavender, or reddish
(often with darker blotches); leaves
oval to lance-shaped.

HABITAT:
dry open woods, scrublands.

IN BLOOM:
Apr.-July.

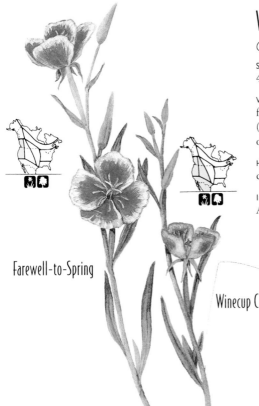

Farewell-to-Spring

Winecup Clarkia

Evening Primroses *Oenothera*

Botanists and naturalists prefer the logic of Latin nomenclature over the expressiveness of common names in identifying plants. This group is an argument in their favor. To call these plants evening primroses is to suggest that they are primroses that bloom late in the day. This is doubly deceptive. They are unrelated to primroses (*Primula*) and have little in common with them beyond the fact that some species in each group smell the same. Moreover, although the flowers of many evening primroses open in late afternoon and stay open overnight, others bloom in the morning and fade by midafternoon (some of the latter are often known as sundrops).

Prairie Evening Primrose

Oenothera albicaulis

SIZE:
8-24 in. tall; flower 1-3 in. wide.

WHAT TO LOOK FOR:
flowers white (turning to pink), with 4 heart-shaped petals; lower leaves roughly spoon-shaped, upper ones deeply cut.

HABITAT:
dry prairies, plains.

IN BLOOM:
May-July (evening).

Texas Buttercup

Oenothera triloba

SIZE:
2-10 in. tall; flower ¾-1½ in. wide.

WHAT TO LOOK FOR:
flowers yellow, on leafless stalks; leaves
bunched on ground, dandelionlike.

HABITAT:
moist prairies, clearings.

IN BLOOM:
Feb.-July (evening).

Missouri Primrose

Oenothera missouriensis

SIZE:
6-20 in. tall; flower 2-4 in. wide.

WHAT TO LOOK FOR:
flowers yellow, showy, borne singly on stalks
above leaves; leaves lance-shaped to straplike.

HABITAT:
dry prairies, rocky open slopes.

IN BLOOM:
May-Sept. (evening).

Common Evening Primrose

Oenothera biennis

SIZE: 1-6 ft. tall; flower 1-2 in. wide.

WHAT TO LOOK FOR: flowers yellow, in branched spikes atop hairy, reddish stems; leaves in pairs, lance-shaped.

HABITAT: fields, waste places.

IN BLOOM: June-Oct. (evening).

Showy Evening Primrose

Oenothera speciosa

SIZE: 8-30 in. tall; flower 2-3½ in. wide.

WHAT TO LOOK FOR: flowers pink to white; leaves lance-shaped to straplike; plants erect or sprawling.

HABITAT: fields, prairies, dry grasslands.

IN BLOOM: Apr.-July (daytime).

Purple Loosestrifes *Lythrum*

North America has several native species of this group, but none is as large, as aggressive, or as spectacular as the imported European species shown here. Dense growths of its waving purple flower spikes have become a familiar sight throughout southeastern Canada, the northeastern states, and into the Midwest.

Spiked Loosestrife

Lythrum salicaria

SIZE:
2-5 ft. tall; flower ½-¾ in. wide.

WHAT TO LOOK FOR:
flowers rose to deep magenta, in long, dense wands; leaves lance-shaped, in groups of 2-3 along stout stems.

HABITAT:
marshes, pond edges, wet meadows, ditches.

IN BLOOM:
June-Sept.

Dogwoods *Cornus*

At first glance, it seems odd that the low-growing Bunchberry is included among this group of upright woody plants. However, a closer look at the showy, petallike bracts that set off the flower clusters, and at the whorls of lustrous leaves that grow beneath them, reveals the close kinship.

FRUITS

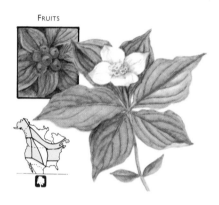

Bunchberry
Cornus canadensis

SIZE:
3-8 in. tall; flowerhead ¾-1½ in. wide.

WHAT TO LOOK FOR:
flowerheads made of tight greenish clusters of flowers and 4 white petallike bracts; whorl of leaves below flowerhead; fruits red, berrylike, clustered.

HABITAT:
rich woods, thickets, bogs.

IN BLOOM:
May-July.

Mistletoes *Phoradendron*

When Oklahoma chose Mistletoe as its flower in 1893, it was joining in a tradition as old as mythology itself. Since earliest antiquity these parasitic evergreens and their European counterparts (*Viscum*)—the golden bough of lore and legend—have symbolized mankind's shared aspirations and darkest fears.

Mistletoe

Phoradendron leucarpum

SIZE:
6-30 in. tall; berry ⅛-¼ in. wide; flower minute.

WHAT TO LOOK FOR:
plants in rounded clumps on tree branches; leaves leathery, spoon-shaped; flowers greenish; berries white.

HABITAT:
tree branches.

IN BLOOM:
May-July.

Meadow Beauties *Rhexia*

These aptly named flowers resemble evening primroses in that they have four large petals surrounding a showy cluster of eight long yellow stamens. However, they lack the evening primroses' characteristic cross-shaped stigma (the tip of the pistil, or female organ). Another way to tell them apart is by the meadow beauties' fruits, described by Thoreau as "perfect little cream pitchers."

Pale Meadow Beauty

Rhexia mariana

SIZE:
8-25 in. tall; flower ¾-1½ in. wide.

WHAT TO LOOK FOR:
flowers lavender to white, with sicklelike stamens; plant hairy; fruits urnlike, sticky.

HABITAT:
fields, meadows, pinelands.

IN BLOOM:
June-Sept.

Deergrass

Rhexia virginica

SIZE:
4-36 in. tall; flower ¾-1¼ in. wide.

WHAT TO LOOK FOR:
flowers bright pink to maroon, with down-curled stamens; fruits urnlike, sticky; stems square, with 4 long ridges.

HABITAT:
wet, sandy meadows; bogs; open pinelands.

IN BLOOM:
July-Sept.

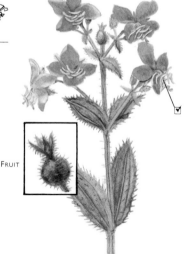

FRUIT

Bittersweets *Celastrus*

The bittersweet's main attraction is its bright, fleshy fruits. Because these are regularly gathered and sold for decorations, the plants are becoming scarce in many areas. Only one species is native to North America, although the extremely aggressive Oriental Bittersweet (*Celastrus orbiculatus*), imported for gardens, now grows wild in the Northeast.

Climbing Bittersweet
Celastrus scandens

SIZE:
vine to 50 ft. high; flower ⅛ in. wide.

WHAT TO LOOK FOR:
stems twining or sprawling; leaves leathery, oblong; flowers greenish, in clusters; fruits orange-yellow (capsules split to reveal pulpy, red to orange seeds).

HABITAT:
thickets, woods, riverbanks, fields.

IN BLOOM:
May-June.

Poison Sumacs *Toxicodendron*

These notorious pests are close relatives of true sumacs (*Rhus*), and many botanists include them among that group. True sumacs lack the toxic oil. Until fairly recently, the widespread Poison Ivy was thought to be two distinct species: "Poison Ivy," a vine with pointed leaflets; and "Poison Oak," a shrubby plant with oaklike leaflets. But when cuttings from the same plant were grown in different locations, both forms were produced. Those in moist, shady forests became poison ivy vines; those in dry, sunny places grew into poison oak plants. In the Far West there is a completely different species that is known as the Poison Oak. Usually shrubby, it too is variable in leaf shape and growth form.

Poison Ivy

"POISON OAK"
FORM IN FALL

Poison Oak

Toxicodendron diversiloba

SIZE: 1-9 ft. tall; flower ⅛-¼ in. wide.

WHAT TO LOOK FOR: plants shrubby (occasionally viny); leaflets in 3's (center leaflet long-stalked), reddish green, lobed; flowers greenish white, clustered; berries white, clustered.

HABITAT: woods, thickets, scrub, chaparral.

IN BLOOM: Apr.-June.

Pachysandras *Pachysandra*

The native Allegheny Spurge is evergreen in the Southeast, but in northern areas it dies back each winter. Japanese Spurge (*Pachysandra terminalis*) is a spreading evergreen that was imported as a garden ground cover. Although the leaves of both species resemble those of true spurges (*Euphorbia*), the plants lack the milky sap that marks that group.

Allegheny Spurge
Pachysandra procumbens

SIZE:
6-12 in. tall; flower ¼ in. long.

WHAT TO LOOK FOR:
leaves mottled, in umbrellalike clusters; flowers greenish white, in dense thumb-shaped spikes.

HABITAT:
deep woods, clearings.

IN BLOOM:
Mar.-May.

◄Poison Ivy (Poison Oak)
Toxicodendron radicans

SIZE:
vine to 100 ft. high; flower ⅛ in. wide.

WHAT TO LOOK FOR:
vine or shrub; leaflets in 3's (center one long-stalked), glossy green (summer) or bright red (fall), variable in shape (can be toothed, smooth-edged, or deeply lobed); flowers greenish, loosely clustered; berries white, clustered (fall and winter).

HABITAT:
woods, fields, thickets, fencerows.

IN BLOOM:
May-July.

Spurges *Euphorbia*

Included among the world's nearly 1,700 spurge species are the familiar Christmas Poinsettia (*Euphorbia pulcherrima*), from the tropical forests of Mexico and Central America, and the Crown of Thorns (*Euphorbia milii*), from arid Madagascar plateaus. Many spiny succulents native to the deserts of Africa and Asia are also in this group, though they can be hard to tell apart from American cacti. Most spurges contain a bitter, milky sap that is irritating to the skin on contact and poisonous if eaten. Some, including the beautiful Snow-on-the-mountain, are so toxic that bees who visit their flowers often produce poisonous honey.

Cypress Spurge

Euphorbia cyparissias

SIZE: 8-30 in. tall; flowerhead ¼-½ in. wide.

WHAT TO LOOK FOR: flowerheads in flat-topped clusters, showy, made of tiny true flowers between 2 yellow bracts; leaves needlelike.

HABITAT: meadows, lawns, fields.

IN BLOOM: Mar.-Sept.

FLOWERHEAD

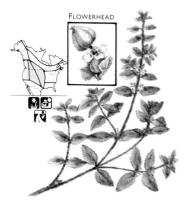

FLOWERHEAD

Milk Purslane

Euphorbia supina

SIZE: to 3 ft. long; flowerhead minute.

WHAT TO LOOK FOR: stems sprawling, matted; leaves green, with purple mottling; flowerheads clustered at leaf bases.

HABITAT: sand, gravel, fields, waste places.

IN BLOOM: May-Sept.

Snow-on-the-mountain

Euphorbia marginata

SIZE:
6-36 in. tall; flowerheads minute.

WHAT TO LOOK FOR:
flowerheads greenish, surrounded by white bracts; leaves light green, with white margins.

HABITAT:
prairies, plains, waste places, fields.

IN BLOOM:
June-Oct.

Wild Poinsettia

Euphorbia heterophylla

SIZE:
6-36 in. tall; flowerhead ¼ in. wide.

WHAT TO LOOK FOR:
flowerheads greenish, in flat clusters amid red bracts; leaves marked with red (near flowers).

HABITAT:
damp sandy clearings.

IN BLOOM:
June-Sept.

Woodbines *Parthenocissus*

These cousins of the grapes climb in two ways: by twining tendrils, and by modified roots equipped with adhesive pads that cling to walls and other surfaces. Poisonous to humans, the fruits of Virginia Creeper are an important fall and winter food for many songbirds and other wildlife. The group includes Boston Ivy (*Parthenocissus tricuspidata*), which, despite its name, was imported from Asia.

Virginia Creeper

Parthenocissus quinquefolia

SIZE: vine to 150 ft. high; fruit ½ in. wide.

WHAT TO LOOK FOR: stems climbing or sprawling; leaves divided into 3 or 5 stalked leaflets, green (summer) or red (fall); flowers tiny, greenish, clustered; fruits dark blue.

HABITAT: rich woods, riverbanks, thickets, field edges.

IN BLOOM: June-Aug.

Spurge Nettles *Cnidoscolus*

The leaves, stems, and even the flowers of these members of the spurge family are covered with stinging hairs similar to those on the true nettles (*Urtica*). Each hair is like a little hypodermic needle, with an acid irritant stored in its swollen base. The combined injections from many hairs can cause painful swelling and rash.

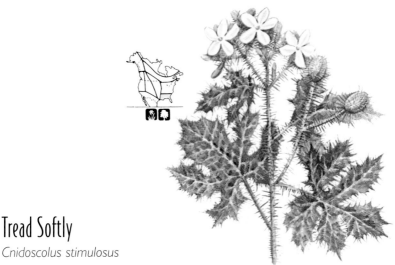

Tread Softly

Cnidoscolus stimulosus

Size: 1-4 ft. tall; flower about 1 in. wide.

What to look for: male flowers white to creamy, trumpet-shaped, in clusters with small, greenish female flowers; leaves deeply cut, lobed, mottled; plants covered with stinging hairs.

Habitat: dunes, hammocks, pinelands, coastal plains.

In bloom: Feb.-Nov.

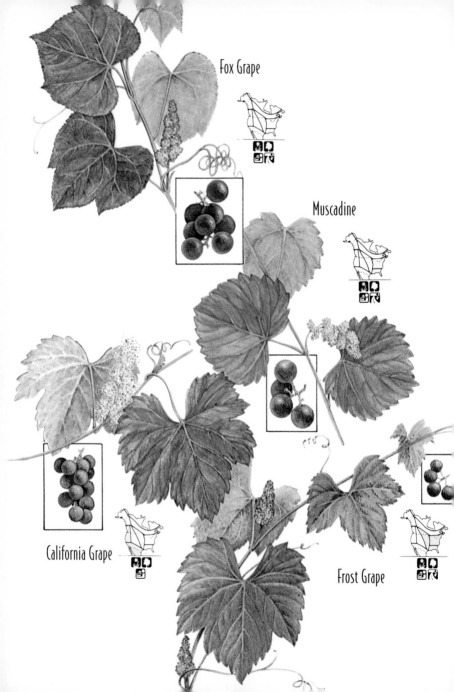

Fox Grape

Muscadine

California Grape

Frost Grape

Grapes *Vitis*

When the ancients wrote of "The Vine," they meant the European Wine Grape (*Vitis vinifera*), grown for food and drink in the earliest centers of Western civilization and still the source of most European wines. This long history nearly came to an end in the late 19th century, when a root louse, accidentally introduced from the New World, devastated Europe's vineyards. Today almost all surviving *Vitis vinifera* vines are grafted onto the rootstocks of various North American natives, which are resistant to this pest. A wild grape vine may live for well over a century.

Fox Grape
Vitis labrusca

SIZE: vine to 60 ft. high; fruit ½-¾ in. wide.

WHAT TO LOOK FOR: stems climbing or trailing; leaves woolly below, with 3 shallow lobes; flowers tiny, greenish, clustered; fruits dark red to black.

HABITAT: thickets, field edges, clearings, woods.

IN BLOOM: May-July.

Muscadine (Scuppernong)
Vitis rotundifolia

SIZE: vine to 30 ft. high; fruit ½-¾ in. wide.

WHAT TO LOOK FOR: stems climbing or trailing; leaves broad, toothed; flowers tiny, greenish, clustered; fruits blue-black (muscadine) to blue-green (scuppernong).

HABITAT: fencerows, thickets, sandy coastal scrub.

IN BLOOM: May-June.

California Grape
Vitis californica

SIZE: vine to 40 ft. high; fruit ¼-½ in. wide.

WHAT TO LOOK FOR: stems climbing; leaves lobed, toothed, fuzzy below; flowers tiny, greenish, clustered; fruits purple, with white sheen.

HABITAT: woods, streambanks, canyons.

IN BLOOM: May-June.

Frost Grape
Vitis riparia

SIZE: vine to 100 ft. high; fruit ¼-½ in. wide.

WHAT TO LOOK FOR: stems climbing; leaves 3-lobed, toothed; flowers tiny, greenish, clustered; fruits black, with whitish sheen.

HABITAT: rich woods, riverbanks, thickets.

IN BLOOM: May-July.

Geraniums *Geranium*

Several geranium species are also known as cranesbills because of the shape of their seedpods. These pods are so constructed that they spread the plant's seeds in a rather violent fashion. As a pod dries, its outer surface contracts, gradually building up tension until it bursts at the seams. Each of its five sections springs upward, and the spoonlike bases catapult seeds as far as 22 feet. The geranium commonly grown in gardens and flowerpots belongs to a closely related group (*Pelargonium*).

Wild Geranium

Geranium maculatum

SIZE:
1-3 ft. tall; flower 1-1½ in. wide.

WHAT TO LOOK FOR:
flowers 5-petaled, purple to rose, loosely clustered above paired leaves; leaves deeply lobed, toothed; fruits beaklike.

HABITAT:
clearings, open woods.

IN BLOOM:
Apr.-June.

Cranesbill

Geranium richardsonii

SIZE: 1-3 ft. tall; flower ¾-1 in. wide.

WHAT TO LOOK FOR: flowers in pairs, 5-petaled, white to pink with purple veins; leaves deeply lobed, each lobe roughly diamond-shaped; stems hairy; fruits beaklike.

HABITAT: mountain meadows, canyons, moist pinelands.

IN BLOOM: May-Aug.

Herb Robert

Geranium robertianum

SIZE: 4-24 in. tall; flower ¼-½ in. wide.

WHAT TO LOOK FOR: flowers pink to purplish, 5-petaled, profuse; leaves divided into lobed leaflets; stems hairy, sticky; fruits beaklike.

HABITAT: banks, ditches, woods, clearings.

IN BLOOM: May-Oct.

Touch-me-nots *Impatiens*

This group's hostile-sounding name is not inspired by thorns, spines, stinging hairs, or toxic oils. On the contrary, the juice of Jewelweed—and of the similar Pale Jewelweed (*Impatiens pallida*) found in the East and Midwest—contains a soothing fungicide that makes it an effective treatment for athlete's foot. It also helps ease the burning of nettle stings and inflammation from Poison Ivy. (Happily, Jewelweeds often grow in the same places as these problem plants.) The name touch-me-not comes from the explosive fruits: the swollen capsules burst at a touch to disperse the seeds.

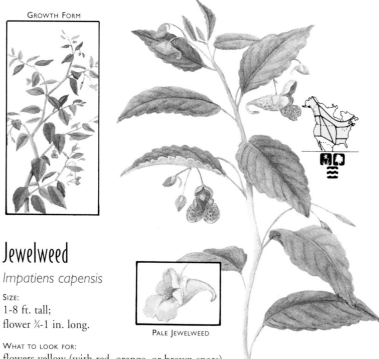

GROWTH FORM

Jewelweed

Impatiens capensis

SIZE:
1-8 ft. tall;
flower ¾-1 in. long.

WHAT TO LOOK FOR:
flowers yellow (with red, orange, or brown spots), horn-shaped, on slender stalks; plant bushy, with succulent stems.

HABITAT:
swampy woods, streambeds, clearings.

IN BLOOM: June-Sept.

PALE JEWELWEED

Flax *Linum*

Common Flax is one of the plants upon which civilization was built. Prehistoric Swiss lake dwellers made rope and fishnet from its fibrous stems and ate its oily seeds. It was made into fabric to wrap Egyptian mummies and to clothe ancient Chinese nobles. The Romans called it *linum*, from which developed such words as line, linen, lingerie, lint, and linseed oil (the basic constituent of linoleum). The American Indians used several native North American species, such as Yellow Wild Flax (*Linum virginianum*) of the East and Midwest, for many of the same purposes.

YELLOW WILD FLAX

Common Flax
Linum usitatissimum

SIZE:
1-3 ft. tall; flower ¾-1 in. wide.

WHAT TO LOOK FOR:
flowers blue in loose, flat-topped clusters atop slender, branching stems; leaves lance-shaped.

HABITAT:
fields, waste places, along railways.

IN BLOOM:
Feb.-Sept.

Wood Sorrels *Oxalis*

Several plants with pleasantly sour foliage are known as sorrel (from the old German for "sour"), and in fact, the wood sorrels are called sour grasses or sour clovers in many places. Popular salad ingredients for centuries, they were also used by old-time herbalists to treat various stomach ailments and to cure scurvy (they are rich in vitamin C). It is now known, however, that eating too much oxalic acid, the chemical responsible for the sourness, tends to inhibit the body's absorption of calcium. The special flavor of wood sorrel should thus be enjoyed only occasionally.

Yellow Wood Sorrel

Oxalis stricta

SIZE:
1-8 in. tall; flower ¼-½ in. wide.

WHAT TO LOOK FOR:
plants spreading, freely branched; flowers yellow; leaflets in 3's, heart-shaped, closed at night; fruits like little candlesticks on bent stalks.

HABITAT:
open woods, fields, clearings, lawns, waste places.

IN BLOOM:
Mar.-Nov.

Violet Wood Sorrel

Oxalis violacea

SIZE:
1-6 in. tall; flower ½-¾ in. wide.

WHAT TO LOOK FOR:
flowers purple, on slender stalks; leaflets in 3's, heart-shaped, purplish below.

HABITAT:
open woods, clearings, thickets, prairies.

IN BLOOM:
Apr.-Oct.

Common Wood Sorrel

Oxalis montana

SIZE:
1-6 in. tall; flower ¾ in. wide.

WHAT TO LOOK FOR:
flowers white with purplish stripes, on slender stalks; leaflets in 3's, heart-shaped, closed at night.

HABITAT:
rich woods, swampy lowlands.

IN BLOOM:
May-Aug.

Milkworts *Polygala*

The ancients fed milkworts to dairy cattle, goats, and nursing mothers to increase the flow of milk. There is no evidence that the practice did any good, but it went on for centuries and gave the plants the name by which they are still known. The group includes trees, shrubs, and small plants that grow on every continent except Antarctica, in surroundings ranging from deserts to rain forests. Although it is difficult at a glance to see the kinship between the bizarre blossoms of Gaywings and the cloverlike flower-heads of Field Milkwort, the problem is simply one of perspective. The flowers of both species, like those of all milkworts, have three petals that form a tube and are flanked by two petal-colored sepals (the wings of Gaywings). These blossoms feature an intricate pollination system activated when an insect lands on the fringed bottom petal.

Gaywings
Polygala paucifolia

Size: 1-6 in. tall; flower ½-1 in. long.

What to look for: flowers pink to purple, fringed, with 2 large wings; leaves egg-shaped, clustered near flowers.

Habitat: rich woods.

In bloom: May-July.

Field Milkwort
Polygala sanguinea

Size: 2-16 in. tall; flower ¼ in. long.

What to look for: flowers rose-purple to pink with 2 wings, in dense heads atop branching stems; leaves straplike.

Habitat: moist meadows, fields, ditches, bogs.

In bloom: June-Oct.

Orange Milkwort

Polygala lutea

SIZE:
6-12 in. tall; flower ¼ in. long.

WHAT TO LOOK FOR:
flowers orange (turning yellow) with 2 pointed wings, in dense heads atop branching stems; leaves spoon-shaped.

HABITAT:
moist sand, peat bogs, meadows, ditches.

IN BLOOM:
Apr.-Oct.

Orange
Milkwort

Seneca
Snakeroot

Seneca Snakeroot

Polygala senega

SIZE:
4-20 in. tall; flower ⅛-¼ in. long.

WHAT TO LOOK FOR:
flowers white with 2 spreading wings, in dense spike atop straight stem; leaves lance-shaped.

HABITAT:
dry woods, meadows, prairies.

IN BLOOM:
May-July.

Yellow Jessamines *Gelsemium*

South Carolina's state flower, the Carolina Jessamine, is a common sight along roadsides throughout the southeastern United States. Its vivid yellow flowers, though fragrant and beautiful, are dangerous—children sucking out the nectar have been poisoned. The flowers, and all other parts of the plant, contain a lethal alkaloid similar to strychnine.

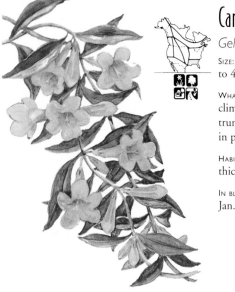

Carolina Jessamine

Gelsemium sempervirens

SIZE:
to 40 ft. high; flower 1 in. wide.

WHAT TO LOOK FOR:
climbing, tangled vine; flowers yellow, trumpetlike, with 5 flaring lobes; leaves in pairs, lance-shaped to oval.

HABITAT:
thickets, hammocks, forest edges.

IN BLOOM:
Jan.-May.

Aralias *Aralia*

Like many members of the ginseng family, North America's aralias are prized for their aromatic roots. Those of the Wild Sarsaparilla served the Indians as emergency rations and were brewed by settlers into root beer and medicinal tea. The roots of American Spikenard produce a less pungent beverage, but it was even more highly regarded as a treatment for coughs, backaches, and other ailments. California Spikenard (*Aralia californica*), found along the Pacific Coast, is somewhat larger than American Spikenard and bears up to three times as many flowers in each of its spherical clusters.

BERRIES

Wild Sarsaparilla

Aralia nudicaulis

SIZE: 5-16 in. tall;
flower ⅛ in. wide.

WHAT TO LOOK FOR: single leaf divided
into 3 groups of 5 toothed leaflets;
flowers creamy, in 3 spherical clusters
on branched, leafless stalk; berries
dark purple.

HABITAT: woods. IN BLOOM: May-July.

American Spikenard

Aralia racemosa

SIZE:
2-10 ft. tall; flower ⅛ in. wide.

WHAT TO LOOK FOR:
leaves divided into many oval leaflets; flowers greenish, in round clusters on branched
stalks; berries dark red to purple.

HABITAT:
rich woods, clearings.

IN BLOOM:
June-Aug.

Rhatanies *Krameria*

Rhatany root, the powdered astringent that was a common stock-in-trade of apothecaries well into the 20th century, is made from a South American species of this group. The same extract is also used for tanning leather and flavoring port wine. North America's species—most of which are known as prairie burs because of their spiny fruits—have also been used medicinally, as well as for tanning and dyeing.

FRUIT

Prairie Bur

Krameria lanceolata

SIZE: to 6 ft. long; flower ½-¾ in. wide.

WHAT TO LOOK FOR: stems hairy, trailing; flowers crimson to rose, starlike; leaves small, lance-shaped to straplike, tipped with tiny prickles; fruits spiny, covered with white down.

HABITAT: prairies, deserts, hillsides, open woods.

IN BLOOM: Apr.-Aug.

Harbingers of Spring *Erigenia*

On the floor of the eastern deciduous forests where this plant grows (there is only one species), sunshine is a brief phenomenon of spring and must be quickly taken advantage of. Nourished by food energy stored in the bulbous corm, the Harbinger of Spring's flower stalk arises and blossoms long before leaf buds swell on most trees—in fact, its fruit often begins to form before its own leaves have unfurled.

Wormroots *Spigelia*

The difference between poison and medicine is often a matter of how much is used, and how carefully. Spigeline, the toxic alkaloid extracted from the roots of these plants, is a case in point. The Indians used it in small doses to expel tapeworms and roundworms, and they taught their techniques to colonists. Soon the plants were being shipped in bales to Europe for pharmaceutical processing.

Indian Pink

Spigelia marilandica

SIZE:
1-2 ft. tall; flower 1-2 in. long.

WHAT TO LOOK FOR:
flowers red, tubular, with 5 yellow, pointed lobes, in clusters atop erect stem; leaves in pairs, oval.

HABITAT:
woods, thickets, clearings.

IN BLOOM:
Apr.-June.

◄ Harbinger of Spring

Erigenia bulbosa

SIZE: 2-10 in. tall; flower ¼ in. wide.

WHAT TO LOOK FOR: flowers white, in loose clusters atop stalk with 1 small, divided leaf; leaves at base divided into 2-3 leaflets, usually developing after flowers.

HABITAT: rich woods.

IN BLOOM: Feb.-May.

Ginsengs *Panax*

The Chinese call these plants *jen-shen* ("manlike") because of the branching root of the Asian species, *Panax pseudoginseng*. For the same reason, Indians called American Ginseng *garantoquen,* which also means "manlike." Wondrous medicinal and aphrodisiac powers have been ascribed to both species, although modern medicine has yet to verify such claims. Nonetheless, the roots of American Ginseng have been so assiduously collected that it is listed as a threatened species in 31 states. Dwarf Ginseng's round tubers never inspired similar folklore, but they were valued as food by Indians and woodsmen.

American Ginseng

Panax quinquefolius

SIZE:
8-24 in. tall;
flower ⅛ in. wide.

WHAT TO LOOK FOR:
3 leaves, each divided into 5 toothed leaflets, atop straight stalk; flowers white, in spherical cluster; berries red, clustered.

HABITAT:
deep woods.

IN BLOOM:
June-July.

BERRIES

ROOT

Dwarf Ginseng

Panax trifolius

SIZE:
1-8 in. tall; flower ⅛ in. wide.

WHAT TO LOOK FOR:
3 leaves, each divided into 3-5 leaflets, atop straight stalk; flowers white, in spherical cluster.

HABITAT:
rich woods, thickets.

IN BLOOM:
Apr.-May.

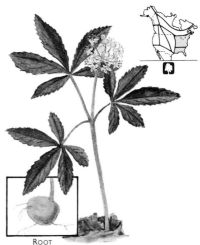

ROOT

Zizias *Zizia*

The flowers of zizias, like those of most of the carrot family, are borne in umbels—clusters with branches that radiate from a central point like the ribs of an umbrella. Golden Alexanders is the commonest eastern species. Heartleaf Alexanders (*Zizia aptera*), commoner in the Midwest, can be recognized by the heart-shaped leaves that arise on separate stalks from the base of its stem.

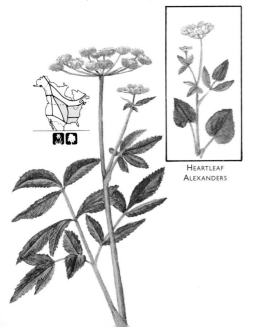

HEARTLEAF
ALEXANDERS

Golden Alexanders

Zizia aurea

SIZE:
1-3 ft. tall; flower ⅛-¼ in. wide.

WHAT TO LOOK FOR:
flowers yellow, in flat-topped compound umbels; leaflets in 2's or 3's, toothed.

HABITAT:
moist open woods, meadows, thickets, shores.

IN BLOOM:
Apr.-June.

Carrots *Daucus*

The garden carrot is a large-rooted variety (*sativa*) of Queen Anne's Lace. The wild variety's roots are also edible, but there is danger of confusing it with any of several poisonous plants, such as Poison Hemlock and Water Hemlock (*Cicuta maculata*). Look for the dark flower that is usually found in the center of the lacy, white umbel of Queen Anne's Lace.

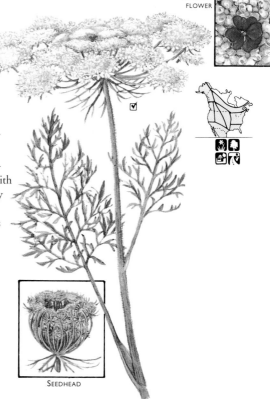

CENTRAL FLOWER

Queen Anne's Lace
Daucus carota

SIZE:
1-5 ft. tall; flower ⅛ in. wide.

WHAT TO LOOK FOR:
flowers creamy white, in flat-topped compound umbels with feathery green collars (usually with single dark flower in center); leaves fernlike; stems hairy; fruits spiny, in dried seedheads like birds' nests.

HABITAT:
fields, meadows, roadsides, open woods.

IN BLOOM:
May-Oct.

SEEDHEAD

Cow Parsnips *Heracleum*

When the radiating branches of an umbel end in smaller umbels, the cluster is called a compound umbel. It is the commonest flower form among members of the carrot family, and is displayed by cow parsnips and several of the plants shown on pages 197 to 202. The flowers are usually wide open and shallow, so that the nectar and pollen are easily reached by the short tongues of beetles and flies.

Cow Parsnip

Heracleum lanatum

SIZE:
2-10 ft. tall; flower ⅛-¼ in. wide.

WHAT TO LOOK FOR:
flowers white, in flat-topped compound umbels; leaflets in 3's, large, deeply lobed, toothed; sheaths at leaf bases; plants hairy.

HABITAT:
meadows, pastures, marshes.

IN BLOOM:
Apr.-Sept.

FLOWER
CLOSE-UP

Eryngoes *Eryngium*

The eryngoes are exceptional among the carrot family on several counts. They are one of the few groups with spiny leaves. Their flowers are borne in dense heads rather than the usual umbels, and each flower forms a tube whose nectar can be reached only by such long-tongued insects as bees and butterflies. The roots of Rattlesnake Master were once reputed to cure snakebite.

Rattlesnake Master

Eryngium yuccifolium

Size: 2-5 ft. tall; flower ⅛ in. wide.

What to look for: flowers white, in dense bristly heads; leaves long, spiny, strap-shaped.

Habitat: prairies, thickets, open woods.

In bloom: July-Aug.

Pennyworts *Hydrocotyle*

The pennyworts can be recognized by their small, rounded leaves. There are more than 50 species worldwide, including nearly a dozen in North America. The Water Pennywort grows along both coasts and in swampy areas near Lake Michigan. A similar species, *Hydrocotyle verticillata,* bears several umbels in tiers on each stalk.

Water Pennywort

Hydrocotyle umbellata

Size: 1-14 in. tall; flower ⅛ in. wide.

What to look for: plants creeping; leaves round, on stalks attached to center; flowers white, in spherical umbels.

Habitat: wet banks, beaches, marshes, swamps.

In bloom: June-Sept.

Poison Hemlocks *Conium*

One poison hemlock species grows in South Africa; the only other is a European weed, which is now found throughout much of North America. All parts of the plant are deadly; it was the source of the poison used to execute Socrates and other Athenian dissidents of the time.

Poison Hemlock

Conium maculatum

SIZE:
2-9 ft. tall; flower ⅛-¼ in. wide.

WHAT TO LOOK FOR:
flowers white, in many flat-topped umbels; leaves parsleylike.

HABITAT:
wet fields, meadows, ditches.

IN BLOOM:
June-Sept.

Angelicas *Angelica*

This group includes the garden Angelica (*Angelica archangelica*), whose leaves were once believed to be a cure-all for contagious diseases and whose stems are traditionally candied to decorate Christmas cakes in France. The celerylike leafstalks of wild species are also edible. Other members of the carrot family supply such foodstuffs as anise, caraway, celery, dill, fennel, lovage, and parsley.

Great Angelica

Angelica atropurpurea

SIZE:
1-9 ft. tall; flower ¼ in. wide.

WHAT TO LOOK FOR:
flowers greenish white, in compound umbels; leaves divided into many toothed leaflets; sheaths at leaf bases; stems purple.

HABITAT:
thickets, bottomlands, swamps, meadows.

IN BLOOM:
June-Oct.

Columboes *Frasera*

These plants may be known by several names in the course of their growth cycle. At first, when they produce clusters of long leaves much prized by browsing animals, they are often called elkweeds. When the tall stems arise—often in the following year—they take a pyramidal form that inspires the name monument plants. Deertongue—named for the shape of its leaves—and a similar eastern species, *Frasera caroliniensis,* are also known as Green Gentians.

Deertongue

Frasera speciosa

Size:
2-7 ft. tall; flower 1-1½ in. wide.

What to look for:
flowers pale green with tiny spots, 4-petaled, borne on long stalks from leaf bases; leaves straplike, clustered at base and along stem.

Habitat:
desert scrub, prairies, open pine forests.

In bloom:
June-Aug.

Gentians *Gentiana*

Pollinating insects are attracted to gentians by the fragrant nectar in the vaselike flowers—a substance so enticing that bees force open the petals of Bottle Gentians to reach it. Because many flying insects avoid dark places, they would be hesitant to enter the blue flowers of most gentians were it not for translucent white patches that admit light to the bottom of the blossoms. Species with light colors, such as the Yellow Gentian (*Gentiana flavida*) of the East and Midwest, need no such devices. Gentians are late bloomers. Those of tundra and mountaintops are sometimes still in blossom when the snows come, and finish their flowering cycle in the spring.

YELLOW GENTIAN

Bottle Gentian

Gentiana andrewsii

SIZE:
1-3 ft. tall; flower 1¼-2 in. long.

WHAT TO LOOK FOR:
flowers blue to purple, closed (petal tips folded together), in clusters at bases of upper leaves; leaves in pairs of 4's, oval to lance-shaped.

HABITAT:
moist meadows, fields, thickets, ditches.

IN BLOOM:
Aug.-Oct.

Fringed Gentian
Gentianopsis crinita

Size:
1-3 ft. tall; flower 1½-2½ in. long.

What to look for:
flowers blue, tubular, with 4 flaring fringed petals; leaves in pairs, oval to lance-shaped.

Habitat:
moist meadows, streambanks, forest edges.

In bloom:
Aug.-Nov.

Purple-tipped Gentian
Gentiana algida

Size:
2-8 in. tall; flower 1½ in. long.

What to look for:
flowers creamy white with purple markings at petal tips; leaves straplike, clustered at base of plant and scattered in pairs along stems.

Habitat:
high mountain meadows, rocky slopes, tundra.

In bloom:
June-Aug.

Downy Gentian

Gentiana puberulenta

SIZE:
8-20 in. tall; flower 1½-2 in. long.

WHAT TO LOOK FOR:
flowers deep blue, with 5 pointed petals, clustered atop downy stems; leaves in pairs, lance-shaped, stiff, rough-edged.

HABITAT:
dry prairies.

IN BLOOM:
Sept.-Oct.

Explorer's Gentian

Gentiana calycosa

SIZE:
6-12 in. tall; flower 1-1½ in. long.

WHAT TO LOOK FOR:
flowers blue to purplish, funnel-shaped, with 5 rounded lobes separated by small forked fringes; leaves in pairs, rounded.

HABITAT:
moist mountain meadows, streambanks, conifer forests.

IN BLOOM:
July-Sept.

Prairie Gentians *Eustoma*

Two of this group's three species grow in warmer parts of North America; the third is native to the tropics of Central and South America. Though Bluebells is mainly a western species, it may occasionally be found along the Gulf Coast. The Catchfly Gentian (*Eustoma exaltatum*), with flowers of rose, purple, or white, ranges from the desert mountains of southern California to the hammocks and coastal sands of Florida. The leaves of both species have a waxy bloom that can be rubbed off with the fingertips.

Bluebells

Eustoma grandiflorum

SIZE:
8-26 in. tall; flower 1½-3 in. wide.

WHAT TO LOOK FOR:
flowers blue to purplish (or yellow with purple tinges), cuplike; leaves in pairs, oval, bases clasping stem.

HABITAT:
moist prairies, fields, pond edges.

IN BLOOM:
June-Sept.

Buckbeans *Menyanthes*

The world's only buckbean species is a distinctive plant, easily identified by its clusters of thickly bearded white flowers and its leathery three-part leaves. Both rise on stalks above the surface of bogs and shallow ponds. Although many botanists include the Buckbean in the gentian family, many others place it in a family all its own. It is known by a variety of names, such as Bogbean, Bognut, Marsh Clover, Moorflower, and Water Shamrock.

Buckbean

Menyanthes trifoliata

SIZE: 4-12 in. tall; flower ½-1 in. wide.

WHAT TO LOOK FOR: flowers white, starlike, hairy, clustered atop leafless stalks; leaflets in 3's, leathery, oblong.

HABITAT: swamps, marshes, forest bogs, ditches, shallow water.

IN BLOOM: Apr.-Sept.

Centauries *Centaurium*

According to Greek myth, Chiron, the wisest and most benevolent of the centaurs, was skilled in the use of medicinal plants and passed on much of his skill to various Greek heroes. He is said to have treated wounds with the bitter, antiseptic juice of these plants, and so they came to be named after him. Most centaury species found in the eastern states are European imports, but several attractive species are native to the Far West.

Bluestars *Amsonia*

These southern plants look very much like the dogbanes, and their stems are filled with the same kind of milky sap. The form and color of their flowers set them apart, however. There are no dogbanes with blue flowers (although the bluestars are often known as blue dogbanes), and the petals of these plants are narrower and more widely spread than those of dogbanes, forming the five-pointed stars that give them their name.

Bluestar

Amsonia tabernaemontana

SIZE:
1-3 ft. tall; flower ½-¾ in. wide.

WHAT TO LOOK FOR:
flowers pale blue with yellow centers, starlike, clustered atop erect stems; leaves oval to lance-shaped.

HABITAT:
bottomlands, streambanks, moist woods, clearings.

IN BLOOM:
Mar.-May.

◄Rosita

Centaurium calycosum

SIZE: 4-24 in. tall; flower ¼-½ in. wide.

WHAT TO LOOK FOR: flowers funnel-shaped, 5-petaled, pink with white throats; leaves in pairs, lance-shaped to oblong.

HABITAT: moist meadows, streambanks, salt marshes.

IN BLOOM: Apr.-June.

Marsh Pinks *Sabatia*

This diverse group has about 20 species, all found in the southeastern states. Some grow in the West Indies as well, many are found as far north as New England, and a few range west to Kansas. Those species that grow in bogs, swamps, and other watery sites are generally known as marsh pinks; others are usually called rose pinks.

Prairie Rose Pink

Sabatia campestris

SIZE:
4-14 in. tall; flower 1-1½ in. wide.

WHAT TO LOOK FOR:
flowers rose with yellow centers, 5-petaled, with pointed green sepals between petals; leaves in pairs, oval.

HABITAT:
prairies, fields, meadows.

IN BLOOM:
July-Sept.

Rose Pink

Sabatia angularis

SIZE:
1-3 ft. tall; flower 1-1½ in. wide.

WHAT TO LOOK FOR:
flowers pink with yellow centers, 5-petaled; leaves in pairs, egg-shaped, upper ones clasping stems; stems square, with sharp lengthwise ridges.

HABITAT:
open woods, meadows, fields, prairies.

IN BLOOM:
July-Sept.

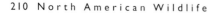

Large Marsh Pink

Sabatia dodecandra

SIZE: 1-2 ft. tall; flower 1-2½ in. wide.

WHAT TO LOOK FOR: flowers pink or white with yellow centers, 8- to 13-petaled; leaves in pairs, lance-shaped to oblong.

HABITAT: salt marshes, brackish ponds, saline meadows.

IN BLOOM: July-Sept.

Periwinkles *Vinca*

Early European settlers brought with them two species of these spreading shade-lovers, which they grew for both medicinal and ornamental purposes. It was said that chewing periwinkle leaves would stop bleeding and that wrapping a stem around the leg would ease a muscle cramp. The Greater Periwinkle (*Vinca major*), with flowers up to 2 inches across, is larger than Running Myrtle, but is much less hardy.

Running Myrtle

Vinca minor

SIZE: 1-6 in. tall; flower ½-1 in. wide.

WHAT TO LOOK FOR: flowers blue-violet, with 5 wedge-shaped petals; leaves in pairs, dark green, glossy, oval; stems trailing, rooting, with upright branches.

HABITAT: wooded slopes, lawns, roadsides, fields.

IN BLOOM: Feb.-Aug.

Rubber Vines *Echites*

These tropical lianas (woody vines), with their latexlike sap, belong to the infamous dogbane family. Like most plants in the family, they are poisonous. The Devil's Potato, one of three species that grow along the Florida coast and in the Keys, is named for its large, tuberous, toxic root.

Devil's Potato

Echites umbellata

SIZE: to 20 ft. long; flower 2-2½ in. long.

WHAT TO LOOK FOR: stems trailing, intertwined; flowers white to greenish, tubular, with 5 twisted, frilled petals; leaves in pairs, egg-shaped.

HABITAT: coastal hammocks, swamps.

IN BLOOM: all year.

Spreading Dogbane

Apocynum androsaemifolium

SIZE:
1-4 ft. tall; flower ¼ in. wide.

WHAT TO LOOK FOR:
flowers light pink, bell-shaped, in loose clusters scattered on low-branching stems; leaves in pairs, oval to egg-shaped.

HABITAT:
dry fields, thickets, slopes.

IN BLOOM:
June-Sept.

Dogbanes *Apocynum*

The Indians used the long, strong fibers from the stems of dogbanes to make twine, rope, fishing nets, and even clothing. To obtain the fibers, they treated the stems in much the same way that flax is treated: first the stems were retted, or allowed to soak in water until the soft tissues rotted; then they were beaten to separate the fibers, which were rinsed and combed clean. Most dogbanes, including the two species shown here, are poisonous to livestock, but because of their latexlike sap, few animals willingly eat them.

Indian Hemp

Apocynum cannabinum

SIZE:
3-5 ft. tall; flower ⅛ in. wide.

WHAT TO LOOK FOR:
flowers greenish white, urn-shaped, in open clusters on erect branching plant; leaves in pairs, oval to lance-shaped.

HABITAT:
fields, marshes, deserts, meadows, thickets, waste places.

IN BLOOM:
June-Sept.

Milkweeds *Asclepias*

MILKWEED FLOWER

There is a legend of the Old West about a runty outlaw who drank rattlesnake venom every morning so he could kill a big man by spitting in his eye. Milkweeds furnish similar venom for Monarch butterflies. The leaves are poisonous to most animals, but Monarch caterpillars and a few others eat nothing else. As a result, they—and the butterflies they become—are themselves toxic to potential predators. The crownlike flowers of milkweeds are cunning traps for insect pollinators, second in their intricacy only to the orchids. Each blossom has five nectar cups with smooth, incurved horns growing from them. When an insect lands, its foot slips on a horn and goes into a slit between two cups. If the insect is not strong enough to pull its leg out, it dies there. If it is strong enough, it comes away carrying two bags of pollen, called pollinia, like saddlebags. At the next flower, its foot slips again; this time, as it picks up more pollinia, it deposits the first two beside the cups, where the pollen develops to fertilize future seeds.

Common Milkweed

Asclepias syriaca

SIZE:
2-6 ft. tall; flower ½ in. wide.

WHAT TO LOOK FOR:
flowers pink to lavender, star-shaped, in dense rounded clusters at top of straight stem; leaves in pairs, broad, oval; sap milky; seedpods warty, filled with downy fluff.

HABITAT:
fields, meadows.

IN BLOOM:
June-Aug.

SEEDPOD

Butterfly Weed

Asclepias tuberosa

SIZE: 1-3 ft. tall; flower ¼-½ in. wide.

WHAT TO LOOK FOR: flowers bright orange, star-shaped, in dense, flat-topped clusters at top of erect or sprawling stem; leaves alternate; sap not milky.

HABITAT: sandy fields, prairies, dry pinelands.

IN BLOOM: June-Sept.

Swamp Milkweed

Asclepias incarnata

SIZE: 1-5 ft. tall; flower ¼-½ in. wide.

WHAT TO LOOK FOR: flowers deep pink to rose, star-shaped, in dense clusters at top of straight stem; leaves in pairs, narrow, lance-shaped; sap milky.

HABITAT: marshes, swamps, wet meadows.

IN BLOOM: May-Sept.

Sand Milkweed

Asclepias amplexicaulis

SIZE:
2-3 ft. tall; flower ½ in. wide.

WHAT TO LOOK FOR:
flowers purple to greenish, star-shaped, in dense spherical clusters atop straight stem; leaves in pairs, with wavy edges; sap milky.

HABITAT:
dry fields, sandy prairies.

IN BLOOM:
May-Aug.

Whorled Milkweed

Asclepias verticillata

SIZE:
1-3 ft. tall; flower ¼ in. wide.

WHAT TO LOOK FOR:
flowers white, star-shaped, in dense rounded clusters along slender stem; leaves in whorls, narrow; sap milky.

HABITAT:
dry slopes, fields, open woods.

IN BLOOM:
May-Oct. (north); all year (south).

Green Milkweed

Asclepias cryptoceras

<small>SIZE:</small> stem to 1 ft. long; flower ½-1 in. wide.

<small>WHAT TO LOOK FOR:</small> flowers greenish yellow with reddish crownlike centers, star-shaped, hornless, in clusters at ends of sprawling stems; leaves in pairs, rounded, grayish green; sap milky.

<small>HABITAT:</small> sandy or gravelly slopes, dry plains, open pinelands, sagebrush scrublands, deserts.

<small>IN BLOOM:</small> Apr.-June.

Desert Milkweed

Asclepias erosa

<small>SIZE:</small>
2-4 ft. tall; flower ¼-½ in. wide.

<small>WHAT TO LOOK FOR:</small>
flowers greenish yellow, star-shaped, in dense rounded clusters at top of erect stem; leaves in pairs; sap milky.

<small>HABITAT:</small>
deserts, dry scrublands.

<small>IN BLOOM:</small>
Apr.-Oct.

Buffalo Bur

Black Nightshade

Horse Nettle

Nightshades *Solanum*

This contradictory group gives us potatoes and eggplants as well as many poisonous plants. In fact, the contradiction often exists within a single species. Some parts of the Potato (*Solanum tuberosum*), for example, are poisonous; and although the ripe berries of the Black Nightshade are used for pies and jams, the leaves and unripened berries are deadly. The Bittersweet Nightshade—so called because the taste of its root and berries changes in the mouth of one foolish enough to chew them—is sometimes known as the Deadly Nightshade, a name that properly belongs to an even more toxic European relative, *Atropa belladonna*. The Horse Nettle and the Buffalo Bur also contain poisons, but their thorns discourage consumption by livestock and humans.

Buffalo Bur
Solanum rostratum

SIZE: 8-28 in. tall; flower 1 in. wide.

WHAT TO LOOK FOR: flowers yellow, broadly star-shaped; leaves deeply lobed, prickly; fruits spiny.

HABITAT: fields, prairies, dry pastures, waste places.

IN BLOOM: Apr.-Oct.

Black Nightshade
Solanum americanum

SIZE: 1-3 ft. tall; flower ¼-½ in. wide.

WHAT TO LOOK FOR: flowers star-shaped, with 5 white petals backswept from yellow "nose"; leaves oval to lance-shaped; berries green, turning black.

HABITAT: fields, meadows, waste places.

IN BLOOM: Mar.-Nov.

Horse Nettle
Solanum carolinense

SIZE: 1-3 ft. tall; flower ¾-1 in wide.

WHAT TO LOOK FOR: flowers white to violet, star-shaped; stems and oaklike leaves spiny; berries yellow.

HABITAT: fields, meadows, waste places.

IN BLOOM: May-Oct.

Bittersweet Nightshade

Ground Cherries *Physalis*

Each fleshy fruit of these plants is enclosed in a lanternlike husk. When green, the berries, like the young leaves, are poisonous. But when the berries are fully ripe, they are edible and sweet—a favorite trail snack of many hikers. Some species, known as Strawberry Tomatoes, are grown for food. The ornamental Chinese Lantern Plant (*Physalis alkekengi*) is cultivated for its bright red husks.

Virginia Ground Cherry

Physalis virginiana

SIZE: 1-3 ft. tall; flower ¾-1 in. wide.

WHAT TO LOOK FOR: flowers yellow with purplish blotches in center; fruits papery, 5-sided, lantern-shaped, containing fleshy berry.

HABITAT: fields, prairies, open woods, waste places.

IN BLOOM: May-Aug.

Bittersweet Nightshade

Solanum dulcamara

SIZE: 1-8 ft. high; flower ½ in. wide.

WHAT TO LOOK FOR: stems climbing or sprawling; flowers star-shaped, with 5 purple petals backswept from pointed yellow "nose"; leaves spade-shaped, usually with 2 pointed lobes at base; berries green, turning red when ripe.

HABITAT: open woods, fields, thickets, swamps.

IN BLOOM: Apr.-Sept.

FRUIT

Ground Cherries *Leucophysalis*

These ground cherries differ from the *Physalis* ground cherries in that their fruits have no papery husks. Despite the shared name, the berries of both groups are more like little tomatoes than cherries. Tomatoes grown in gardens (*Lycopersicon*) also belong to the nightshade family, as do all the plants shown on pages 218 to 222; and their unripe fruits are also poisonous if eaten raw.

White-flowered Ground Cherry

Leucophysalis grandiflora

SIZE: 1-3 ft. tall; flower 1¼-2 in. wide.

WHAT TO LOOK FOR: flowers white, saucerlike, with 5 points; leaves oval to lance-shaped; stems sticky, hairy.

HABITAT: open woods, sandy clearings.

IN BLOOM: June-Aug.

Thornapples *Datura*

British troops were sent to Jamestown in 1676 to suppress a rebellion. Short of rations, they cooked the foliage of the plant that has ever after been known familiarly as Jimsonweed. The result was described by Robert Beverley in his *History and Present State of Virginia* (1705). "They turn'd natural fools upon it for several days. One would blow up a feather in the air; another would dart straws at it with much fury; and another stark naked was sitting up in a corner like a monkey, grinning and making mows at them." After 11 days, they "return'd to themselves again, not remembering any thing that had pass'd." Had the British not cooked the leaves, few would have survived, for the potent hallucinogens produced by thornapple plants are extremely toxic. Another species, the Indian Apple, or Sacred Datura (*Datura meteloides*), with flowers up to 10 inches long, was used by the Indians of the Southwest for a variety of rituals.

Jimsonweed

Datura stramonium

SIZE: 1-7 ft. tall; flower 3-4 in. long.

WHAT TO LOOK FOR: flowers white to lavender, trumpetlike; leaves oval, pointed, coarsely toothed; fruit spiny.

HABITAT: fields, clearings, waste places.

IN BLOOM: June-Oct.

INDIAN APPLE

Bindweeds *Convolvulus*

Less spectacular but even more troublesome than the morning glories, these pernicious weeds overgrow many crops. The Field Bindweed is particularly difficult to control. Tearing up its roots with a plow or hoe does not kill the plant, but scatters fragments that often grow into many new individuals.

Field Bindweed
Convolvulus arvensis

SIZE:
to 15 ft. high; flower ½-¾ in. wide.

WHAT TO LOOK FOR:
flowers trumpet-shaped, white (often with purple to lavender lines on back); leaves arrow-shaped; stems tangled, climbing or sprawling.

HABITAT:
hedgerows, thickets, fields.

IN BLOOM:
May-Oct.

Hedge Bindweed
Calystegia sepium

SIZE:
to 15 ft. high; flower 1½-2 in. wide.

WHAT TO LOOK FOR:
flowers trumpet-shaped, white to pinkish; leaves triangular to arrow-shaped; stems creeping or climbing.

HABITAT:
hedges, thickets, waste places, marshes.

IN BLOOM:
Apr.-Sept.

Morning Glories *Ipomoea*

To appreciate the imagery in this group's name, you have only to see the colorful and fragrant blossoms, which open soon after dawn and close a few hours later. Unfortunately, the technical name, from the Greek for "wormlike," is equally apt. The viny stems wind their way up the stalks of other plants, and the large leaves rob them of sunlight. Such crops as corn, cotton, and soybeans may be seriously affected. Several morning glory species are valued for their edible tubers, including the Sweet Potato (*Ipomoea batatas*). The giant tuber of the Wild Potato Vine, also known as Man of the Earth, weighs up to 30 pounds, and was an important food for Indians and settlers.

Bush Morning Glory
Ipomoea leptophylla

Size: 2-4 ft. long; flower 2-2½ in. wide.

What to look for: stems sprawling, bushy; flowers trumpet-shaped, rose to purple; leaves straplike.

Habitat: dry prairies, sandy fields.

In bloom: May-July.

Wild Potato Vine
Ipomoea pandurata

Size: to 20 ft. long; flower 2-3 in. wide.

What to look for: stems trailing or climbing; flowers trumpet-shaped, white with pink centers; leaves heart- or fiddle-shaped.

Habitat: dry fields, plains, thickets, open woods.

In bloom: May-Sept.

Ivyleaf Morning Glory

Ipomoea hederacea

SIZE:
to 10 ft. high; flower 1-1½ in. wide.

WHAT TO LOOK FOR:
stems twining; flowers trumpet-shaped with 5 pointed petals, sky-blue (turning rose-purple); leaves hairy, deeply lobed.

HABITAT:
fencerows, fields, waste places.

IN BLOOM:
June-Nov.

Common Morning Glory

Ipomoea purpurea

SIZE:
to 10 ft. high; flower 1½-2 in. wide.

WHAT TO LOOK FOR:
stems twining; flowers trumpet-shaped, blue, purple, pink, or white; leaves heart-shaped.

HABITAT:
fencerows, fields, waste places.

IN BLOOM:
June-Oct.

Dodders *Cuscuta*

Unlike the rest of the morning glory family, the dodders are true parasites, drawing their sustenance directly from the host plants. The seeds take root in the ground, and the young shoots rotate until they come in contact with something climbable. If it turns out to be a suitable host, the dodder sinks parasitic roots (called haustoria) into its stem and begins drawing nourishment through them. Soon its own connection with the soil withers away.

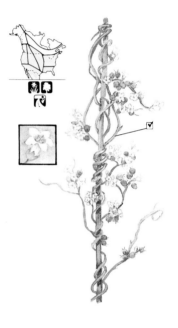

Dodder

Cuscuta cephalanthii

SIZE: to 10 ft. high; flower ⅛ in. wide.

WHAT TO LOOK FOR: stems creamy-orange, twining on shrubs and other plants; flowers bell-shaped, white, in dense clusters.

HABITAT: moist thickets, marshes.

IN BLOOM: July-Oct.

Starglories *Quamoclit*

These tropical vines are sold in North America as garden annuals, often under the name Red Morning Glory. They have turned out to be surprisingly hardy and have spread to the wild in many places. One broad-leaved species, *Quamoclit coccinea,* is found as far north as Michigan and New England.

Moonflowers *Calonyction*

The moonflowers could easily be called evening glories because—although they are members of the morning glory family—their large, extremely fragrant blossoms open only at night. Like most night-bloomers, they are pollinated by moths that are attracted by the glowing whiteness and strong scent of the flowers.

Moonflower

Calonyction aculeatum

SIZE: to 30 ft. high; flower 4-5 in. wide.

WHAT TO LOOK FOR: flowers saucer-shaped at tip of slender tube, white, fragrant; leaves oval to heart-shaped; vine climbing or trailing.

HABITAT: hammocks, burned fields, waste places, thickets.

IN BLOOM: all year.

Cypress Vine

Quamoclit pennata

SIZE: to 15 ft. high; flower 1½ in. long.

WHAT TO LOOK FOR: flowers tubular with star-shaped flare, bright red; leaves featherlike; stem slender, twining.

HABITAT: fields, waste places.

IN BLOOM: July-Oct.

Phlox *Phlox*

Open almost any popular seed catalog and you are likely to find a colorful display of phlox, often under the name Sweet William. They are popular because they produce a vivid and long-lasting display for a minimum of effort. Botanists describe the flowers as salverform— "tray-shaped"—because of the flat surface formed by the five petals at the end of the narrow tube. All of the group's roughly 60 species are native to North America (*Phlox sibirica* is found in both Alaska and Siberia). Although no species are native to Hawaii or New England, garden-grown plants have spread to the wild in both places, and so phlox are found in all 50 states, as well as Mexico and much of Canada.

Mountain Phlox
Phlox diffusa

SIZE: 4-12 in. tall; flower ½-¾ in. wide.

WHAT TO LOOK FOR: flowers pale lilac to white, with 5 broad petals at end of slender tube; leaves needle-like along spreading stems; plant mound-forming.

HABITAT: alpine meadows, rocky slopes, open woods.

IN BLOOM: May-Aug.

Creeping Phlox
Phlox stolonifera

SIZE: 4-16 in. tall; flower 1 in. wide.

WHAT TO LOOK FOR: flowers violet to purple, with 5 oval petals at end of slender tube; stems creeping, with flowers clustered at tips of erect, hairy branches; leaves in pairs, spoon-shaped.

HABITAT: moist woods.

IN BLOOM: Apr.-May.

Blue Phlox
Phlox divaricata

SIZE:
6-20 in. tall; flower ¾-1¼ in. wide.

WHAT TO LOOK FOR:
flowers light blue, with 5 petals (often notched) at end of slender tube, in clusters atop sticky stem; leaves in pairs, lance-shaped.

HABITAT:
rich woods, clearings, fields, bluffs.

IN BLOOM:
Apr.-June.

Canyon Phlox
Phlox nana

SIZE:
4-12 in. tall; flower 1 in. wide.

WHAT TO LOOK FOR:
flowers purple, pink, or white, with 5 broad petals at end of short tube; leaves in pairs, straplike, sticky, hairy.

HABITAT:
rocky slopes, chaparral, deserts.

IN BLOOM:
May-June.

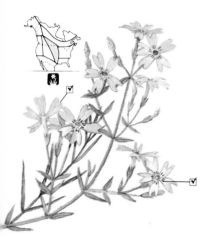

Cleft Phlox

Phlox bifida

SIZE:
4-12 in. tall; flower ¾ in. wide.

WHAT TO LOOK FOR:
flowers pale purple, with 5 forked petals at end of slender tube and 2 spots at base of each petal; leaves in pairs, stiff.

HABITAT:
dry prairies, sandy ledges.

IN BLOOM:
Apr.-May.

Downy Phlox

Phlox pilosa

SIZE:
1-2 ft. tall; flower ¾ in. wide.

WHAT TO LOOK FOR:
flowers rose-pink to violet, with 5 wedgelike petals at end of slender tube, in clusters atop downy stems; leaves in pairs, lance-shaped, hairy.

HABITAT:
sandy prairies, open woods.

IN BLOOM:
May-July.

Langloisias *Langloisia*

When the brief rainy season arrives in the deserts of California, these small plants spring suddenly into existence, bearing flowers that seem all out of proportion to the size of the plants. They are gone when the rains cease. Some species range southward into Mexico and others grow as far north as Oregon and Idaho.

Lilac Sunbonnets

Langloisia punctata

SIZE: 1-6 in. tall; flower ¾-1 in. wide.

WHAT TO LOOK FOR: flowers pale lilac with purple spots, bowl-shaped; leaves triangular, with spiny lobes; plants tuft- or mat-forming.

HABITAT: rocky slopes, open pine scrub (Mojave Desert).

IN BLOOM: Apr.-June.

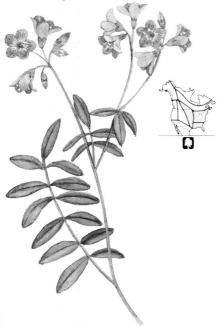

Jacob's Ladders *Polemonium*

The long compound leaves with rung-like leaflets that give this group its name are most obvious in such large, upright species as Greek Valerian. The small leaflets of the blue-flowered Sky Pilot (*Polemonium viscosum*) are so tightly crowded that they form fuzzy tubes rather than ladders.

Greek Valerian

Polemonium reptans

SIZE: 6-18 in. tall; flower ½-¾ in. wide.

WHAT TO LOOK FOR: flowers blue, bell-shaped, in loose clusters; leaves ladder-like, divided into 5-15 leaflets.

HABITAT: rich woods. IN BLOOM: Apr.-June.

Gilias *Ipomopsis*

The richly varied gilias make up one of those plant groups in which botanists can watch evolution in action. Its many species and subspecies, all native to the New World, produce new varieties and hybrids with notable frequency. The result is a process of trial and error whereby the group as a whole survives in a changing world and—because it adapts more quickly than most plants—continually expands its range into new habitats.

Pale Trumpets
Ipomopsis longiflora

SIZE: 1-2 ft. tall; flower ½-¾ in. wide.

WHAT TO LOOK FOR: flowers pale blue to white, trumpet-shaped, with 5-pointed flare; leaves threadlike; plants bushy.

HABITAT: dry plains, sandy slopes.

IN BLOOM: June-Aug.

Standing Cypress
Ipomopsis rubra

SIZE: 2-6 ft. tall; flower ½ in. wide.

WHAT TO LOOK FOR: flowers red, trumpet-shaped, with 5-pointed flare, in plumelike cluster at top of leafy stem; leaves threadlike.

HABITAT: sandy fields, pastures, riverbanks, waste places.

IN BLOOM: May-Aug.

Navarretias *Navarretia*

Early settlers in the western states, like pioneers everywhere, found little need to speak about plants that were neither useful, troublesome, nor spectacular. Botanists of the day, however, were quick to study and to name the members of the new flora. As a result, many such innocuous charmers as the navarretias have only the Latinized names that the botanists gave them. The foul-smelling Skunkweed (*Navarretia squarrosa*) is an exception.

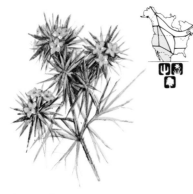

Navarretia

Navarretia breweri

SIZE: ½-4 in. tall; flower ⅛ in. wide.

WHAT TO LOOK FOR: stems brownish, hairy, much branched, covered with hairlike spiky leaves; flowers yellow, star-shaped, profuse.

HABITAT: deserts to moist valleys, mountain slopes, mesas, pinyon forests.

IN BLOOM: June-Aug.

Linanthuses *Linanthus*

Included for many years among the gilias, these plants are now regarded as a separate group, set apart by the odd form of their paired leaves. Each leaf is so deeply divided that a pair of leaves often looks like a grassy tuft sprouting along the stem. Most of the group's nearly 40 species are native to California, several ranging south to Mexico and north into the Cascade mountains. A few are found as far east as Colorado and the Northern Plains.

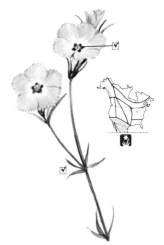

Ground Pink

Linanthus dianthiflorus

SIZE: 1-8 in. tall; flower ¾-1 in. wide.

WHAT TO LOOK FOR: flowers pink with dark centers, bowl-shaped, with 5 sharply toothed petals; leaves in pairs, hairlike.

HABITAT: sandy grasslands, chaparral, sagebrush areas. IN BLOOM: Feb.-Apr.

Scorpionweeds *Phacelia*

Southern California is the home of the vast majority of this group's more than 200 species, although almost every part of North America, from the Yukon to the Florida coast, has at least one native species. The hallmark of the group is a cluster of young flowers, coiled like a scorpion's tail, at the end of a stem. The flowers are all borne on one side of this cluster. In most species the coil straightens somewhat as the blossoms mature; in others, each flower's stalk grows so long that the clustered appearance is all but lost. Nearly all scorpionweeds are valued as bee plants. They tend to blanket areas where few other plants grow, and their flowers yield a flavorsome honey.

Purple Fringe

Phacelia sericea

SIZE: 4-16 in. tall; flower ⅛ in. wide.

WHAT TO LOOK FOR: flowers purple with long stamens, in many dense coils forming a single cylindrical cluster; leaves covered with silvery, silky hairs.

HABITAT: mountain woods, brush, rocky slopes.

IN BLOOM: June-July.

Stinging Scorpionweed

Phacelia malvifolia

SIZE: 8-40 in. tall; flower ¼ in. wide.

WHAT TO LOOK FOR: flowers dull white, clustered along one side of curled stem tips; leaves maple-like; plants covered with stinging hairs.

HABITAT: moist woods, coastal scrublands.

IN BLOOM: Apr.-July.

Miami Mist

Phacelia purshii

<small>SIZE:</small> 6-16 in. tall; flower ½ in. wide.

<small>WHAT TO LOOK FOR:</small> flowers pale blue, with 5 fringed petals, in loose clusters at ends of stems; leaves divided into straplike sections.

<small>HABITAT:</small> moist woods, clearings, fields.

<small>IN BLOOM:</small> Apr.-June.

Waterleaves *Hydrophyllum*

A blotchy, light green pattern gives a look of fine watermarked stationery to the foliage of many waterleaf species. This may be the reason for the group's name, or it may have been inspired by the juicy leaves of several species, including the Virginia Waterleaf. The leaves are edible raw or cooked, giving rise to such additional names as John's Cabbage, Iroquois Greens, and Shawnee Salad.

Virginia Waterleaf

Hydrophyllum virginianum

<small>SIZE:</small>
1-3 ft. tall; flower ¼ in. wide.

<small>WHAT TO LOOK FOR:</small>
flowers white to purple, bell-shaped, with long hairlike stamens, densely clustered; leaves mottled, divided into toothed leaflets.

<small>HABITAT:</small>
moist woods, clearings, thickets.

<small>IN BLOOM:</small>
May-Aug.

Namas *Nama*

In the informal lexicon of botanists and other nature lovers, a belly plant is one that is so tiny that the best way to find it, and the only way to study it, is from the prone position. In time of drought, these inhabitants of western deserts, plains, and mountain canyons are single-flowered belly plants. But in a rainy year, most species put forth many stems, spreading into luxuriant leafy mats and covering themselves with a profusion of colorful blossoms.

Nama

Nama aretioides

SIZE: ½-4 in. tall; flower ¼-¾ in. wide.

WHAT TO LOOK FOR: flowers red to purple with pale starlike centers, funnel-shaped, with 5 rounded petals; leaves narrow, spoon-shaped.

HABITAT: sandy washes, sagebrush areas, open pine woods.

IN BLOOM: May-June.

Sandfoods *Ammobroma*

The world's only Sandfood species looks like nothing so much as a tennis ball half-buried in the sand, covered with tiny purple flowers. But this fuzzy gray growth, which merely hints at what lies beneath, is the top of a long underground stem that is attached to the deep root of a woody desert plant. Since the Sandfood contains no chlorophyll, it does not manufacture its own food. Instead, it draws sustenance from the root of a host plant through its own parasitic roots.

Sandfood

Ammobroma sonorae

SIZE: 1-2 in. tall; 2-5 in. wide; flower ⅛ in. wide or less.

WHAT TO LOOK FOR: flowers purple, in rings on fuzzy gray mound; stem scaly, gray, subterranean, 2-5 ft. long.

HABITAT: Colorado Desert. IN BLOOM: Mar.-Apr.

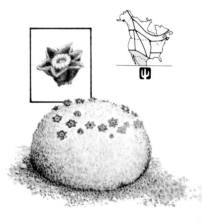

Nemophilas *Nemophila*

Several nemophila species are known as Baby Blue-eyes, although the one usually offered under that name in garden catalogs is the California Baby Blue-eyes (*Nemophila menziesii*), which grows wild in moist valleys and on hillsides of California and southern Oregon. Most nemophila species are low, sprawling plants that grow in sun or partial shade (those in full sun tend to bear flowers of a deeper hue).

Fivespot
Nemophila maculata

SIZE: 5-25 in. long; flower ¾-1¾ in. wide.

WHAT TO LOOK FOR: stems sprawling; flowers white with purple blotch on each petal tip, bowl-shaped; leaves deeply lobed.

HABITAT: meadows, open woods.

IN BLOOM: Apr.-July.

Baby Blue-eyes
Nemophila phacelioides

SIZE: 2-18 in. tall; flower ¾-1¼ in. wide.

WHAT TO LOOK FOR: flowers blue to purple, bowl-shaped, borne singly on slender stalks or clustered at stem tips; leaves hairy, divided into 9-11 lobed leaflets.

HABITAT: prairies, open woods.

IN BLOOM: Mar.-May.

Viper's Buglosses *Echium*

Because the fruit of these handsome European weeds and shrubs seems to resemble a viper's head, the ancients considered the plants a cure—even a preventive—for snakebite. The second part of the name, bugloss, is from the Greek for "ox tongue." Whether it was inspired by the rough-textured leaves or by the open-mouthed flowers with their protruding red stamens is open to conjecture.

Blueweed

Echium vulgare

SIZE: 12-30 in. tall; flower ½-¾ in. long.

WHAT TO LOOK FOR: flowers blue with long red stamens, borne in one-sided coiled wands along upper part of bristly stem; leaves oblong to lance-shaped, hairy.

HABITAT: fields, waste places. IN BLOOM: June-Sept.

Gromwells *Lithospermum*

The roots of the Hoary Puccoon yield a yellow dye. Other gromwell species that give red or purple dyes are also known as puccoons—an Indian word for any herbal source of dye. The name gromwell from the Old French *gromil* refers to the hard white nutlets. Because of these stonelike fruits, the plants were prescribed by many herbalists as a cure for kidney stones.

Hoary Puccoon

Lithospermum canescens

SIZE: 4-20 in. tall; flower ½ in. wide.

WHAT TO LOOK FOR: flowers orange to yellow, in flat wands with coiled tips; leaves lance-shaped; plant densely covered with gray hairs.

HABITAT: sandy prairies, fields; open woods. IN BLOOM: Apr.-June.

Bluebells *Mertensia*

Virginia Bluebells, the best-known member of this group, was named at a time when the English still referred to Massachusetts as North Virginia. Among the many western species are the Tall Bluebells (*Mertensia paniculata*) of the Northern Plains and Pacific Northwest, and the tiny Alpine Bluebells (*Mertensia alpina*) of the high Rockies.

Virginia Bluebells

Mertensia virginica

SIZE: 8-28 in. tall; flower ¾-1 in. long.

WHAT TO LOOK FOR: flowers blue (buds pink), trumpet-shaped, hanging from arched clusters at tips of stems; leaves broad, oval, smooth, covered with whitish film.

HABITAT: moist woods, meadows, bottomlands, thickets.

IN BLOOM: Mar.-May.

Forget-me-nots *Myosotis*

Alaskans chose the forget-me-not as their state flower because it is "emblematic of the quality of constancy, the dominant trait of the intrepid pioneers" who settled the territory. The delicate waterside plants have similar names in many languages (in Japan, for example, they are called *wasurena gusa,* or "do-not-forget herbs"). The name is usually justified by a legend about a lover tragically lost.

Forget-me-not

Myosotis scorpioides

SIZE: 4-24 in. tall; flower ¼ in. wide.

WHAT TO LOOK FOR: flowers sky-blue with yellow centers, in flat wands with coiled tips; stems erect or sprawling; leaves oblong, hairy.

HABITAT: streambanks, ditches, marshes.

IN BLOOM: May-Sept.

Hound's Tongues *Cynoglossum*

The hound's tongues (named for their broad leaves) are found in temperate zones all around the world. Many species are also known as beggar's lice because of their small, four-seeded fruits. These burs are covered with barbed prickles, which adhere to clothing and fur.

FRUIT

Hound's Tongue

Cynoglossum officinale

SIZE: 1-3 ft. tall; flower ¼-½ in. wide.

WHAT TO LOOK FOR: flowers red to maroon, in arching wands; leaves oblong to lance-shaped, clustered at base and scattered along stem; plant branched, downy; fruits star-shaped, prickly, with 4 seeds.

HABITAT: fields, waste places, pastures.

IN BLOOM: May-Aug.

Heliotropes *Heliotropium*

The vast majority of this group's nearly 250 species are tropical; the Garden Heliotrope (*Heliotropium arborescens*), valued for the vanillalike fragrance of its purple flowers, is native to Peru. The salt-loving Seaside Heliotrope also originated in South America, but has spread around the world. Inland it is called "Quail Plant" for the birds that feed on its fruits.

Seaside Heliotrope

Heliotropium curassavicum

SIZE: 4-20 in. long; flower ¼ in wide.

WHAT TO LOOK FOR: stems spreading; flowers white with yellow in throat (often with purple spots), funnel shaped, in curled spikes; leaves spoon-shaped, succulent.

HABITAT: salty deserts, alkaline plains, seashores.   IN BLOOM: Mar.-Oct.

Fiddlenecks *Amsinckia*

The tightly coiled flower clusters for which this group is named are typical of most of the borage family. The buds are borne along one side of the coiled stalk, which unfurls as the flowers open. Fiddlenecks are native to western deserts and dry plains, where they are valued for forage (in Arizona they are called *saccato gordo,* from the Spanish for "fat grass"). Several species have recently spread to the East.

Fiddleneck

Amsinckia tessellata

Size: 8-25 in. tall; flower ½ in. long.

What to look for: flowers orange, tubular, in coiled or twisted spikes; leaves narrow, lance-shaped; plants covered with stiff hairs.

Habitat: sandy plains, desert scrub, open woods.

In bloom: Mar.-June.

White Forget-me-nots *Cryptantha*

This group's name is misleading: some true forget-me-nots (*Myosotis*) bear white flowers, and at least one of these hairy western plants, *Cryptantha flava,* has yellow blossoms. Most of the group's 100-odd species, however, bear small white flowers and are so alike that botanists turn to obscure technical differences to tell them apart.

Sulphur-throated Forget-me-not

Cryptantha flavoculata

Size: 4-14 in. tall; flower ⅛ in. wide.

What to look for: flowers white with yellow throats, in dense curling spikes; leaves narrow, spatula-shaped, covered with silky hairs.

Habitat: deserts, dry open woods, sagebrush areas.

In bloom: May-July.

Vervains *Verbena*

Although modern medicine has yet to discover any medicinal use for the vervains, they have had an honored place in folk medicine through the ages. Ancient Greeks, Persians, and Romans, Celtic Druids, and American Indians all revered them as sacred. They were later held to be proof against witchcraft and curses of all kinds, and came to be prescribed by European herbalists and Indian medicine men alike to treat jaundice, dropsy, and various ailments of the stomach, kidneys, and bladder.

Hoary Vervain

Verbena stricta

SIZE: 1-4 ft. tall; flower ¼ in. wide.

WHAT TO LOOK FOR: flowers lavender to deep blue, in rings around spikes; leaves in pairs, toothed; plants covered with white hairs.

HABITAT: prairies, fields, waste places.

IN BLOOM: June-Sept.

Rose Vervain

Verbena canadensis

SIZE: 1-2 ft. tall; flower ½ in. wide.

WHAT TO LOOK FOR: stems bushy, often sprawling; flowers blue to lavender (turning pink with age), in dense clusters at ends of stems; leaves in pairs, deeply lobed, toothed.

HABITAT: dry prairies, fields, open woods, thickets, hillsides.

IN BLOOM: Feb.-Oct.

Savories *Satureja*

"Hot lavender, mints, savory, marjoram: /...these are flowers/Of middle summer, and I think they are given/To men of middle age." The midsummer blossoms listed by Shakespeare in these lines from *The Winter's Tale* belong to the mint family. Like most of the family, the savories have been used for centuries to season food and to treat such midlife complaints as heartburn and indigestion.

Yerba Buena
Satureja douglasii

SIZE: to 2 ft. long; flower ½ in. long.

WHAT TO LOOK FOR: flowers white to purplish, borne singly at leaf bases, leaves oval to heart-shaped, in pairs along trailing, square stems.

HABITAT: shady woods, scrub.

IN BLOOM: Apr.-Sept

Plantains *Plantago*

The weedy persistence that makes plantains the despair of gardeners and lawn tenders is a virtue in the eyes of those who cook and eat the very young leaves, rich in iron and vitamins A and C. A new leafy whorl appears a day or two after the plant is cut to the ground.

Common Plantain
Plantago major

SIZE: 2-20 in. tall; flower ⅛ in. wide.

WHAT TO LOOK FOR: flowers greenish white, in dense spikes arising from center of leafy rosette; leaves broad, oval, with prominent ribs, long stalks.

HABITAT: fields, meadows, lawns, sidewalks, road-sides, waste places.

IN BLOOM: Apr.-Oct.

Mints *Mentha*

This group's only native North American species, the Field Mint, is easily recognized because its flowers are borne in many clusters along the stem rather than at the tips. Other widespread species, most of which were brought from Europe by early colonists, are harder to tell apart, largely because they hybridize quite freely. Peppermint, for example, is believed to be a cross between Spearmint and Water Mint (*Mentha aquatica*). The pungent oils that give mint leaves their distinctive flavors are said to repel several insect pests, including some caterpillars, beetles, ants, and mosquitoes.

Spearmint

Mentha spicata

SIZE:
4-36 in. tall; flower ⅛ in. wide.

WHAT TO LOOK FOR:
flowers pink to pale violet, borne in dense bunches along slender spikes; leaves lance-shaped, toothed, in pairs along square stem.

HABITAT:
moist fields, meadows, swamps, ditches, streambanks.

IN BLOOM:
June-Oct.

Peppermint
Mentha piperita

SIZE: 1-3 ft. tall; flower ⅛ in. wide.

WHAT TO LOOK FOR: flowers purple to lavender, borne in dense clusters and wands at tops of stems; leaves oblong to lance-shaped, toothed, in pairs along branching, square stems.

HABITAT: moist fields, meadows, ditches, streambanks.

IN BLOOM: June-Oct.

Field Mint
Mentha arvensis

SIZE: 6-36 in. tall; flower ⅛ in. wide.

WHAT TO LOOK FOR: flowers white to pale lavender, in dense clusters at leaf bases; leaves lance-shaped, toothed, in pairs along square stem.

HABITAT: wet fields, woods, ditches, shores, streambanks.

IN BLOOM: July-Sept.

Mountain Mints *Pycnanthemum*

Despite the name by which the group is known, only a few species are commonly found in the mountains. The great majority, including the Virginia Mountain Mint, are lowland plants that thrive in woods and prairies.

Virginia Mountain Mint

Pycnanthemum virginianum

SIZE: 8-30 in. tall; flower ⅛ in. wide.

WHAT TO LOOK FOR: flowers white with purple spots, in dense heads; leaves straplike to lance-shaped, in pairs along square stems.

HABITAT: moist prairies, meadows, thickets, open woods, streambanks.

IN BLOOM: July-Sept.

Selfheals *Prunella*

Heal-all has been used by many peoples to clean open sores and fresh wounds, but its ancient reputation as a wonder drug was due to the yawning shape of its flowers. According to the Doctrine of Signatures, believed by many 17th-century physicians, these gulletlike blossoms were a divine sign that the plant was meant to cure diseases of the mouth and throat.

Heal-all

Prunella vulgaris

SIZE: 2-28 in. tall; flower ½ in. long.

WHAT TO LOOK FOR: plants erect or matted; flowers violet to pink or white, in dense clusters; leaves lance-shaped, in pairs on square stems.

HABITAT: fields, woods, waste places, streambanks.

IN BLOOM: Apr.-Nov.

Germanders *Teucrium*

The flowers of most members of the mint family—the four-petaled mints (*Mentha*) are themselves exceptions—are like open mouths with two distinct lips. In the germanders, the lower lip is a large landing platform for bees and the upper is small and cleft, resembling two front teeth.

American Germander

Teucrium canadense

SIZE: 1-4 ft. tall; flower ½-¾ in. long.

WHAT TO LOOK FOR: flowers pink to lavender, with large lower lip, in dense spike atop square stem; leaves in pairs, oblong to lance-shaped, toothed.

HABITAT: moist woods, thickets, streambanks, shores, waste places. IN BLOOM: June-Sept.

Betonies *Stachys*

The betonies are also known as hedge nettles because their hairy leaves are reminiscent of nettles. Unlike nettles, however, betonies have no stinging hairs; in fact, the leaves of the Woundwort were used for centuries to bandage open wounds, staunching the flow of blood and easing the pain.

Woundwort

Stachys palustris

SIZE: 1-3 ft. tall; flower ½-¾ in. long.

WHAT TO LOOK FOR: flowers magenta, mottled with purple, tubular with lobed lower lip, in leafy clusters near top of square stem; leaves in pairs, lance-shaped, toothed.

HABITAT: moist meadows, grassy marshes, shores, ditches. IN BLOOM: June-Sept.

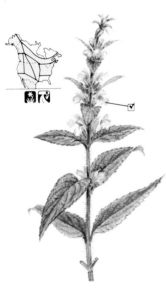

Catmints _Nepeta_

The catmints' well-known effect on cats seems to be a strange side effect of an oil whose main value is defensive. It is repellent, sometimes even toxic, to many leaf-eating insects. Catnip is a European native that was imported by the colonists, who brewed the leaves into a bracing tea.

Catnip

Nepeta cataria

SIZE: 6-36 in. tall; flower ½ in. long.

WHAT TO LOOK FOR: flowers pale violet to white, purple-dotted, in crowded clusters at ends of stem and branches; leaves in pairs, scalloped, heart-shaped; plant velvety, musty-smelling.

HABITAT: waste places, fields.

IN BLOOM: June-Oct.

Deadnettles _Lamium_

The deadnettles' hairy leaves may look like nettle leaves, but they lack the sting. Most of the group, including Henbit, are cool-weather weeds; they die back in the heat of summer only to regrow, flower again, and produce a new crop of seedlings. These persist through winter to blossom and set seed the following spring. The seeds of Henbit are eaten by many birds, including hens.

Henbit

Lamium amplexicaule

SIZE: 4-12 in. tall; flower ½-¾ in. long.

WHAT TO LOOK FOR: flowers pink to purple, in whorls near ends of stems; stems square, upright or sprawling, branched; leaves in pairs, scalloped (upper leaves clasp stem).

HABITAT: fields, waste places. IN BLOOM: Mar.-Nov.

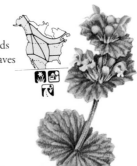

Monardellas *Monardella*

Most species of this group grow only in California, some in a single range of mountains or a limited part of the Mojave Desert. Various species are occasionally known by such names as Mountain Pennyroyal, Desert Pennyroyal, and Coyote Mint, but none of these names seems to have become firmly affixed to any one species.

Mountain Monardella

Monardella odoratissima

SIZE: 6-14 in. tall; flower ½ in. wide.

WHAT TO LOOK FOR: flowers pale rose to purple, star-shaped, borne in dense heads; stem square, branching, often woody; leaves in pairs, lance-shaped.

HABITAT: dry slopes. IN BLOOM: May-Sept.

Bugleweeds *Ajuga*

The bugleweeds were brought to North America by the colonists, who grew them for such medicinal uses as the herbalist Nicholas Culpeper described in 1653: "Many times such as give themselves much to drinking are troubled with strange fancies, strange sights in the night time, and some with voices….These I have known cured by taking only two spoonfuls of the syrup of this herb after supper two hours, when you go to bed."

Carpet Bugleweed

Ajuga reptans

SIZE: 4-12 in. tall; flower ½-¾ in. long.

WHAT TO LOOK FOR: plants mat-forming; flowers blue, in leafy spikes atop square stems that arise from spreading runners; leaves in pairs, oval.

HABITAT: fields, waste places.

IN BLOOM: May-July.

False Dragonheads *Physostegia*

Plant breeders have produced several garden varieties of these showy members of the mint family, whose snapdragon-onlike flowers range from white to pink, red, and many shades of purple. Like many wild species, they are often known as obedience or obedient plants because their flowers—whether moved backward, forward, or sideways—will hold the position in which they are left.

Skullcaps *Scutellaria*

Ancient Asians, Europeans, and American Indians all believed that these plants could cure hysteria, convulsions, and all manner of nervous disorders. Small wonder that modern research has found an effective antispasmodic, scutellaine, in the flower extract. Despite its name and time-honored reputation, however, the Mad Dog Skullcap (*Scutellaria laterifolia*) does not cure rabies in man or beast.

Obedience

Downy Skullcap

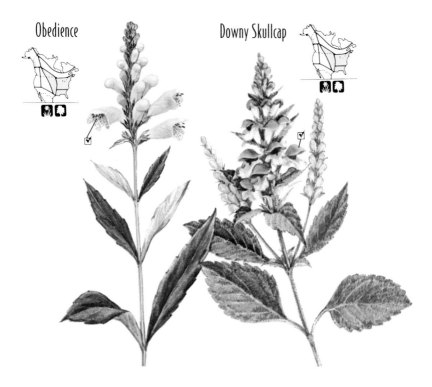

Ground Ivies *Glechoma*

Gill-over-the-ground, the only species of this Eurasian group to become established in the New World, was once widely used in France to brew beer (the French word *guiller* means "to ferment beer"). In England, gill tea was drunk by house painters to combat "painter's colic," caused by the lead in their paint—the leaves are rich in vitamin C, which is used to counteract lead poisoning.

Gill-over-the-ground

Glechoma hederacea

SIZE:
to 3 ft. long; flower ½-¾ in. long.

WHAT TO LOOK FOR:
flowers blue, in small clusters at leaf bases; leaves scalloped, heart-shaped, in pairs; stems square, creeping.

HABITAT:
fields, moist woods, waste places.

IN BLOOM:
Apr.-June.

◄Obedience

Physostegia virginiana

SIZE: 1-4 ft. tall; flower ¾-1 in. long.

WHAT TO LOOK FOR: flowers pink to rose, spotted, in spikes atop square stem; leaves in pairs, lance-shaped, toothed.

HABITAT: moist open woods, thickets, streambanks, prairies.

IN BLOOM: July-Sept.

◄Downy Skullcap

Scutellaria incana

SIZE: 1-4 ft. tall; flower ¾-1 in. long.

WHAT TO LOOK FOR: flowers blue, with drooping lower lip and hoodlike upper lip, in several wands at top of square stem; leaves oval, long-stalked, scalloped; plant covered with downy hair.

HABITAT: upland woods, meadows, thickets.

IN BLOOM: June-Aug.

Dittanies *Cunila*

Most of the group's 16 species are found in Mexico and South America. The leaves of the North American Stonemint were brewed by Indians and settlers into a tea, which they used as a stimulant in treating fevers and the effects of snakebite.

Stonemint
Cunila origanoides

Size: 6-18 in. tall; flower ¼-½ in. long.

What to look for: flowers rose-purple to white, in dense clusters around square stem at leaf bases; leaves in pairs, oval to triangular, toothed.

Habitat: dry, open woods; clearings; thickets.

In bloom: July-Oct.

Horehounds *Marrubium*

Although old-fashioned horehound candy, once a standard household remedy for coughs and sore throats, is still available, it is no longer easy to find. The Old World herbs from which it is made have been used for centuries to treat bronchitis and other congestive complaints; a decoction of the leaves acts as a mild expectorant.

Common Horehound
Marrubium vulgare

Size: 1-2 ft. tall; flower ¼ in. long.

What to look for: flowers white, in dense clusters around square stem at base of leaves; leaves in pairs, oval, scalloped; plant covered with white, woolly hair.

Habitat: fields, waste places.

In bloom: May-Sept.

Blue Curls *Trichostema*

These delicately branched plants, with their distinctively curled, blue-stalked stamens, are easily recognized during their flowering season. In early summer, when they are not in bloom, look for the sticky, hairy leaves that emit a balsam-like odor when bruised. The odor of one western species is so strong that it is known as Vinegarweed (*Trichostema lanceolatum*).

Blue Curls

Trichostema dichotomum

SIZE:
4-28 in. tall; flower ½-¾ in. long.

WHAT TO LOOK FOR:
flowers blue, with arching blue stamens, borne at tips of square stems; leaves in pairs, oval to straplike; plant much branched, covered with sticky hairs.

HABITAT:
dry fields, open woods, sandy clearings.

IN BLOOM: Aug.-Oct.

Motherworts *Leonurus*

"There is no better herb to take melancholy vapours from the heart and to strengthen it," wrote Nicholas Culpeper, the 17th-century herbalist. "It makes mothers joyful and settles the womb, therefore it is called Motherwort." Early colonists brought this highly lauded plant to North America, along with many other members of the mint family, to grow in their herb gardens for medicinal and culinary uses.

Motherwort
Leonurus cardiaca

SIZE: 2-5 ft. tall; flower ¼-½ in. long.

WHAT TO LOOK FOR: flowers pink, purple, or white, with fuzzy upper lip, borne in spiny clusters around square stem at base of leaves; leaves long-stalked, deeply lobed, toothed.

HABITAT: fields, waste places, fencerows.

IN BLOOM: June-Sept.

GROWTH FORM

Bladder Sages *Salazaria*

The Bladder Sage, also known as the Paper Bag Bush, is an oddity among the mint family: though most mints are herbs, dying back each year, this one is a shrub with woody, prickly stems that endure. Odd, too, are its flowers, with their papery bases, and its inflated pods.

Horse Balms *Collinsonia*

Like the horsemints, the horse balms were named not for any equine preference for eating them but because they look like larger, coarser versions of another plant (in this case, the European balms).

Horse Balm

Collinsonia canadensis

SIZE: 2-4 ft. tall; flower ½ in. long.

WHAT TO LOOK FOR: flowers yellow, tubular, with fringed lower lip, in branching clusters at top of square stem; leaves in pairs, oblong, toothed.

HABITAT: rich, moist woods.

IN BLOOM: July-Sept.

◄ Bladder Sage

Salazaria mexicana

SIZE: 2-4 ft. tall;
flower ½-¾ in. long.

WHAT TO LOOK FOR: flowers extending from papery base, tubular, with purple lower lip and tan upper lip; fruits swollen, papery; leaves small, in pairs along square, branching stems.

HABITAT: deserts, dry washes, scrublands.

IN BLOOM: Mar.-June.

Horsemints *Monarda*

When, after the Boston Tea Party, American colonists boycotted imported tea, they had to use native plants as substitutes. A favorite beverage, brewed from the leaves of the Bee Balm, had long been used medicinally by several Indian peoples (the plant is still sometimes called Oswego Tea). Bee Balm is one of the few horsemints seldom visited by bees; its scarlet blossoms are usually pollinated by hummingbirds.

Bee Balm

Monarda didyma

SIZE:
2-5 ft. tall; flower 1¼-1¾ in. long.

WHAT TO LOOK FOR:
flowers scarlet, with arching lower lip, in dense heads at tips of square stems; leaves in pairs, oval to triangular.

HABITAT:
moist woods, thickets, streambanks.

IN BLOOM:
June-Aug.

Spotted Horsemint

Monarda punctata

SIZE:
1-3 ft. tall; flower ¾-1 in. long.

WHAT TO LOOK FOR:
flowers yellow with purple spots, in dense clusters around square stem, surrounded by leafy lilac bracts; leaves in pairs.

HABITAT:
dry fields, prairies, sand dunes.

IN BLOOM:
July-Oct.

Wild Bergamot

Monarda fistulosa

SIZE:
2-5 ft. tall; flower ¾-1¼ in. long.

WHAT TO LOOK FOR:
flowers lavender, with drooping lower lip, in dense heads at tips of square stems; leaves in pairs, lance-shaped.

HABITAT:
dry fields, prairies, thickets, roadsides.

IN BLOOM:
June-Sept.

Sages *Salvia*

Most kinds of sage are superb honey plants, well adapted for pollination by bees. When a bee's tongue strikes a small plate within a freshly opened flower, a pair of hinged stamens pivots down to coat the insect's back with pollen. When the bee visits an older flower, some pollen is removed by a precisely placed stigma. (Red-flowered species, such as the Tropical Sage, are similarly adapted to hummingbird pollination.)

Cancerweed

Salvia lyrata

SIZE: 1-2 ft. tall; flower ¾-1¼ in. long.

WHAT TO LOOK FOR: flowers blue-purple, tubular, with large lower lip, borne in whorls along square stem; leaves mostly at base of plant, deeply lobed.

HABITAT: dry, open woods; clearings; sandy meadows; fields.

IN BLOOM: Apr.-July.

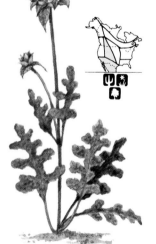

Chia

Salvia columbariae

SIZE: 4-25 in. tall; flower ½-¾ in. long.

WHAT TO LOOK FOR: flowers blue to purple, tubular, in dense clusters amid spiny bracts; leaves mostly at base of square stem, crinkly, lobed.

HABITAT: deserts, dry scrublands, chaparral, open woods.

IN BLOOM: Mar.-June.

Tropical Sage
Salvia coccinea

SIZE:
1-3 ft. tall; flower 1 in. long.

WHAT TO LOOK FOR:
flowers scarlet, with drooping lower lip, in whorls along square stem; leaves in pairs, triangular to heart-shaped.

HABITAT:
open woods, sandy hammocks, waste places.

IN BLOOM:
Feb.-Nov.

Blue Sage
Salvia azurea

SIZE:
2-5 ft. tall; flower ½-1 in. long.

WHAT TO LOOK FOR:
flowers blue, tubular, with drooping lower lip, borne in wandlike cluster along square stem; leaves in pairs, lance-shaped.

HABITAT:
dry plains, prairies, sandy pinelands.

IN BLOOM:
May-Oct.

Gerardias *Agalinis*

The gerardias are part-time, or facultative, parasites (as are Indian paintbrushes, yellow rattles,
and a few other members of the snapdragon
family). Perfectly able to survive on their own,
they will take nourishment from the roots of
other plants if the opportunity arises. Their pink
or crimson flowers open in the morning and
last only half a day, falling off by afternoon if
brushed too hard by a butterfly's wing.

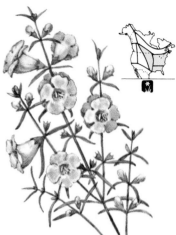

Purple Gerardia

Agalinis purpurea

SIZE: 1-4 ft. tall; flower ½-1½ in. wide.

WHAT TO LOOK FOR: flowers rose-pink, funnel-shaped, with 5 flaring petals,
borne on slender stalks from bases of upper leaves; leaves in pairs, straplike.

HABITAT: moist fields, thickets, meadows, shores.

IN BLOOM: Aug.-Oct.

Blue-eyed Marys *Collinsia*

Most of this group's 20 species are limited to
the Pacific states. Many are known as Chinese
houses because their flowers, arranged in a
series of tight whorls along the stem, give the
impression of a pagoda's ascending roofs.
Although the flowers seem to have only four
petals, there is actually a fifth in the center of
the lower lip, folded lengthwise over the
pollen-bearing stamens.

Indian Paintbrushes *Castilleja*

The tubular flowers of the Indian paintbrushes, clustered among brightly colored bracts (modified leaves), offer no landing place for bees or other pollinators; the plants therefore depend on hovering insects and hummingbirds for cross-fertilization. The pistil and the pollen-bearing stamens arch downward from the tip of the flower's upper lip, or galea, to touch the heads of these nectar-seeking creatures as they thrust their tongues or bills into the blossom. The red-flowered Wyoming Paintbrush (*Castilleja linariaefolia*) is that state's flower.

Giant Red Paintbrush
Castilleja miniata

SIZE: 1-3 ft. tall; flower ¾-1¼ in. long.

WHAT TO LOOK FOR: flowers greenish with red tips, in dense clusters with red bracts atop straight stems; leaves straplike.

HABITAT: mountain meadows, coniferous forests, streambanks, ledges.

IN BLOOM: May-Sept.

◄Blue-eyed Mary
Collinsia verna

SIZE: 6-20 in. tall; flower ½-¾ in. wide.

WHAT TO LOOK FOR: flowers white (upper lip) and blue (lower lip), in loose whorls around top of stem; leaves in pairs, oval; stems erect or sprawling.

HABITAT: moist woods, thickets, bottomlands.

IN BLOOM: Apr.-June.

Downy Paintbrush

Castilleja sessiliflora

SIZE:
4-16 in. tall; flower 1½-2¼ in. long.

WHAT TO LOOK FOR:
flowers sulphur-yellow to pinkish, in dense clusters with small green bracts atop straight stems; leaves deeply lobed; plant covered with soft hairs.

HABITAT:
dry prairies, plains.

IN BLOOM:
May-July.

Scarlet Paintbrush

Castilleja coccinea

SIZE:
4-24 in. tall; flower ¾-1 in. long.

WHAT TO LOOK FOR:
flowers greenish or red, in dense cluster with showy scarlet bracts atop straight stem; leaves deeply lobed along stem, straplike at base.

HABITAT:
moist prairies, meadows, fields.

IN BLOOM:
May-July.

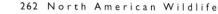

Purple Paintbrush

Castilleja purpurea

SIZE: 8-13 in. tall;
flower 1-1½ in. long.

WHAT TO LOOK FOR: flowers red-purple
or greenish yellow, in dense clusters
with purple to orange bracts at tips
of branches; leaves straplike to lance-
shaped, covered with soft hairs.

HABITAT: sandy prairies, fields.

IN BLOOM: Mar.-May.

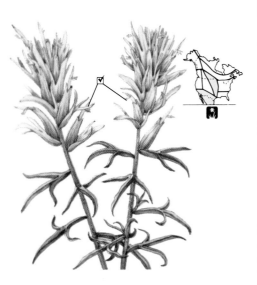

Yellow Rattles *Rhinanthus*

The dry, seed-filled pod for which the group is named develops rather quickly
from the swollen green base of each flower. It is not unusual to find a single
plant with a flattened green bud on top, several flowers in progressive stages
of development along the stem, and a puffy brown capsule or two near the
bottom. Yellow rattles are northern plants, found in all lands that touch upon
the Arctic Circle—a distribution pattern that botanists call circumboreal.

Rattlebox

Rhinanthus minor

SIZE: 8-24 in. tall; flower ½-¾ in. long.

WHAT TO LOOK FOR: flowers yellow, tubular, with
hoodlike upper lip, protruding from swollen
green base, borne along one side of upright
stems; leaves in pairs, oblong to triangular,
toothed.

HABITAT: fields, thickets, tundra, alpine meadows.

IN BLOOM: May-Sept.

Monkey Flowers *Mimulus*

Children delight in squeezing the monkey-faced flowers to make them "laugh." Those who are curious enough may discover a more subtle trait: the stigma at the end of the pistil has two spreading lobes that fold together when touched with a needle or sharp twig. If the touch leaves behind pollen from a different plant, as a bee's tongue is likely to do, the lobes remain closed and the pistil sets seed. But if there is no pollen, or if the pollen is from the same flower, the lobes soon reopen.

Dwarf Monkey Flower

Mimulus nanus

SIZE: 1-4 in. tall; flower ¼-½ in. wide.

WHAT TO LOOK FOR: flowers magenta with yellow patches in throat, profuse; leaves in pairs, lance-shaped; plant branching, downy.

HABITAT: pinelands, sandy prairies, chaparral.

IN BLOOM: May-Aug.

Allegheny Monkey Flower

Mimulus ringens

SIZE: 1-4 ft. tall; flower ½-¾ wide.

WHAT TO LOOK FOR: flowers blue to lavender, with puffy lower lip, borne on wiry stalks; leaves in pairs, oblong to lance-shaped; stems square.

HABITAT: wet woods, meadows, marshes, streambanks.

IN BLOOM: June-Sept.

Yellow Monkey Flower
Mimulus guttatus

SIZE:
2-40 in. tall; flower ½-¾ in. wide.

WHAT TO LOOK FOR:
flowers yellow with red markings, bell-shaped with flat "faces," borne in loose clusters; leaves in pairs, oval, toothed.

HABITAT:
wet meadows, ditches, streams, swamps, marshes.

IN BLOOM:
Mar.-Sept.

Scarlet Monkey Flower
Mimulus cardinalis

SIZE:
1-3 ft. tall; flower 1½-2 in. long.

WHAT TO LOOK FOR:
flowers red, velvety, tubular, with backswept upper and lower lips; leaves in pairs, oblong, toothed, sticky, hairy.

HABITAT:
streambanks, canyon seeps, wet meadows.

IN BLOOM:
Apr.-Oct.

Beardtongues *Penstemon*

Both the scientific and the common name of this group refer to the prominent fifth stamen, a projection lacking the pollen cases that crown the ends of the other four. In most beardtongue species, this infertile stamen is covered instead with a fuzzy growth of hair, which all but closes the throat of the flower. Because the shape of the opening, as well as the color of the flower, varies from species to species, different kinds of beardtongue attract and admit different kinds of pollinators. In this way, even though several species may grow in the same area, each maintains its individuality.

Scarlet Bugler

Penstemon eatonii

Size:
1-4 ft. tall; flower 1-1¼ in. long.

What to look for:
flowers scarlet, tubular, in spike at top of upright stem; leaves straplike, in pairs along stem, clustered at base.

Habitat:
deserts, scrublands, rocky slopes.

In bloom:
Mar.-July.

Foxglove Beardtongue

Penstemon digitalis

SIZE:
1-5 ft. tall; flower ¾-1¼ in. wide.

WHAT TO LOOK FOR:
flowers white (often purple-tinted), bell-shaped, open-throated, with lightly bearded "tongue"; leaves lance-shaped, in pairs and clustered at base.

HABITAT:
dry fields, open woods, prairies.

IN BLOOM:
May-July.

Pink Plains Beardtongue

Penstemon ambiguus

SIZE:
6-30 in. tall; flower ¼ in. wide.

WHAT TO LOOK FOR:
plants branching, shrubby; flowers pink, tubular, with flat faces; leaves in pairs, straplike.

HABITAT:
dry plains.

IN BLOOM:
May-Aug.

Large-flowered Beardtongue

Penstemon grandiflorus

SIZE: 1-4 ft. tall; flower 1½-2 in. long.

WHAT TO LOOK FOR: flowers blue-lavender, bell-shaped, with fuzzy "tongue," in spike at top of upright stem; leaves in pairs, rounded to oblong.

HABITAT: dry prairies, plains, meadows.

IN BLOOM: May-Aug.

Mat Beardtongue

Penstemon caespitosus

SIZE: stem to 8 in. long; flower ⅛ in. wide.

WHAT TO LOOK FOR: plants low, mat-forming; flowers lavender, with fuzzy yellow "tongue"; leaves small, grayish, fuzzy.

HABITAT: deserts, dry hillsides, scrublands.

IN BLOOM: June-Aug.

Foxgloves *Digitalis*

In 1775, the English physician-poet William Withering learned from an old woman in Shropshire how to cure dropsy with a concoction made from the Common Foxglove. He tested it on charity cases for 10 years, then published a report, *An Account of the Fox-Glove*, that is a classic of medical literature. As a result, science learned that dropsy can be symptomatic of heart disease, and that digitalis, the drug derived from foxgloves, is an effective treatment—as well as a dangerous poison. Withering later expressed his discovery in poetic form: "The fox-glove's leaves, with caution given.../ The rapid pulse it can abate,/ The hectic flush can moderate."

Common Foxglove

Digitalis purpurea

SIZE:
2-5 ft. tall; flower 1½-2 in. long.

WHAT TO LOOK FOR:
flowers purple to white, thimble-shaped, drooping from wandlike cluster; leaves lance-shaped to oval.

HABITAT:
moist clearings, fields, streambanks.

IN BLOOM:
June-Sept.

Birdbeaks *Cordylanthus*

Only some species in this western group bear flowers that suggest the open mouths of hungry young birds. In several others, the beaklike lips are rounded and nearly closed, suggesting the name clubflowers, by which these plants are often known.

Birdbeak

Cordylanthus wrightii

SIZE: 1-2 ft. tall; flower ¾-1¼ in. long.

WHAT TO LOOK FOR: flowers purple or yellow, with two beaklike lips, borne among greenish bracts at ends of wiry branches; leaves hairlike.

HABITAT: sandy plains, mesas, deserts.

IN BLOOM: July-Oct.

Turtleheads *Chelone*

The two-lipped flowers of many members of the snapdragon family call to mind various animals, such as snakes, monkeys, elephants, birds, and, of course, snapping dragons. But none are more precisely evocative than the flowers of the turtle-heads, several kinds of which are popular in garden borders.

White Turtlehead

Chelone glabra

SIZE: 1-5 ft. tall; flower 1-1½ in. long.

WHAT TO LOOK FOR: flowers white (often lavender-tinged), shaped like turtles' heads, in dense cluster atop slender stem; leaves in pairs, oval to straplike, toothed.

HABITAT: wet meadows, thickets, streambanks.

IN BLOOM: July-Oct.

Owl Clovers *Orthocarpus*

The owl clovers' flowers, like those of the Indian paintbrushes, are clustered among showy bracts. They are usually more conspicuous, however, and in some species look like little roosting owls. Those of the Escobita, or Little Broom, often blend in with the purplish bracts, but occasionally are bright yellow.

Escobita

Orthocarpus purpurascens

SIZE: 4-16 in. tall; flower ½-1 in. long.

WHAT TO LOOK FOR: flowers purple to yellow, borne in dense clusters among hairy purple-tipped bracts; leaves threadlike.

HABITAT: deserts, dry plains, pastures, open woods.

IN BLOOM: Mar.-May.

Mohaveas *Mohavea*

This group's two species grow in the Mojave Desert and a few surrounding areas. The Ghost Flower is the larger and more widespread of the two; the Lesser Mohavea (*Mohavea breviflora*), with small, bright yellow flowers, is common only from the central Mojave to Death Valley.

Ghost Flower

Mohavea confertiflora

SIZE: 4-16 in. tall; flower 1-1½ in. long.

WHAT TO LOOK FOR: flowers pale yellow with purple dots, translucent; leaves narrow, lance-shaped, hairy.

HABITAT: desert scrublands, sandy washes, dry slopes.

IN BLOOM: Mar.-Apr.

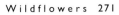

Kittentails *Synthyris*

Even though their flowers lack the distinctive lower lip that, in most members of the snapdragon family, serves as a landing platform for bees, the kittentails are generally bee-pollinated. The insects cling to the flower cluster's fuzzy surface, composed of two stamens projecting from each blossom.

Mountain Kittentails

Synthyris missurica

SIZE: 4-24 in. tall; flower ½ in. long.

WHAT TO LOOK FOR: flowers blue-purple, in dense fuzzy spike; leaves heart- to kidney-shaped, arising from base of plant and in pairs along stem.

HABITAT: open mountain slopes, pine forests.

IN BLOOM: May-June.

Besseyas *Besseya*

To the untrained eye, it is hard to tell the difference between the besseyas (named for the American botanist Charles Bessey) and the kittentails. Some botanists, in fact, have lumped both groups together, usually under the name *Synthyris*.

Alpine Besseya

Besseya alpina

SIZE: 2-6 in. tall; flower ¼ in. long.

WHAT TO LOOK FOR: flowers pale purple, in dense fuzzy spike; leaves oval to heart-shaped, arising from base of plant and scattered along stem.

HABITAT: rocky meadows at high elevations.

IN BLOOM: Aug.-Sept.

False Foxgloves *Aureolaria*

The colonists found many plants in the New World that reminded them of familiar European species. Among them were these tall semiparasites (they draw part of their sustenance from the roots of oaks), whose wandlike clusters of yellow flowers are reminiscent of the pink, purple, or white blossoms of the true foxgloves. The American Indians used some species medicinally in much the same way that true foxgloves were used in Europe.

Northern False Foxglove

Aureolaria flava

SIZE:
2-8 ft. tall; flower 1½-2¼ in. long.

WHAT TO LOOK FOR:
flowers yellow, funnel-shaped, with 5 rounded petals, borne in wandlike cluster; leaves in pairs, deeply cleft; stem often purplish.

HABITAT:
woods, thickets.

IN BLOOM:
July-Sept.

Speedwells *Veronica*

No one knows how these plants came to be called speedwells. One theory is that the English peasants, who brewed the leaves of some species into an expectorant for treating coughs and congestion, may have called them "spit-wells." Whatever the origin of the name, it has belonged exclusively to these members of the snapdragon family since the 16th century or earlier.

Water Speedwell

Veronica anagallis-aquatica

SIZE: 1-4 ft. long; flower ¼ in. wide.

WHAT TO LOOK FOR: stems creeping, with upright tips; flowers lilac-blue, in wands from bases of leaves near stem tips; leaves in pairs, oval to straplike.

HABITAT: streams, banks, marshes, ditches, ponds.

IN BLOOM: May-Sept.

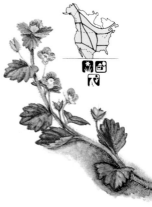

Birdseye Speedwell

Veronica persica

SIZE: 4-12 in. long; flower ¼-½ in. wide.

WHAT TO LOOK FOR: stems spreading, hairy; flowers blue with dark lines and pale centers, borne on slender stalks from leaf bases; leaves oval, toothed, scattered along stems.

HABITAT: lawns, fields, waste places.

IN BLOOM: Apr.-Aug.

Culver's Roots *Veronicastrum*

The identity of Dr. Culver is unknown, beyond the belief that a man by that name, sometime before 1716 (when Cotton Mather wrote of the plant), popularized the use of the dried root as a laxative and cathartic. Only two species exist—one in North America, the other in Siberia.

Culver's Root

Veronicastrum virginicum

SIZE:
2-7 ft. tall; flower ⅛-¼ in. wide.

WHAT TO LOOK FOR:
flowers white to purplish, in dense spikes near top of upright stem; leaves lance-shaped, in whorls around stem.

HABITAT:
open woods, thickets, moist meadows, prairies.

IN BLOOM:
June-Sept.

Mulleins *Verbascum*

Most of these Eurasian weeds are biennial—they require two years to complete their life cycle. In the first summer they form large, ground-hugging rosettes of leaves that last through the winter. (It is for the texture of its leaves that the Common Mullein is also known as Velvet Plant and Flannel Leaf.) The upright flowering stems arise from the centers of these rosettes the following spring and bear their blossoms, a few at a time, all summer long. The Common Mullein's tall, stout stem has inspired such names as Jacob's Staff and Shepherd's Club; the Moth Mullein is named for the flowers themselves, with their spreading petals and antennalike stamens.

Common Mullein

Verbascum thapsus

Size:
1-8 ft. tall; flower ¼-1 in. wide.

What to look for:
flowers yellow, in dense spike at top of stout stem; leaves oblong, velvety, gray-green, clustered at base of plant and along stem.

Habitat:
fields, old pastures, roadsides.

In bloom:
June-Sept.

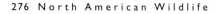

Moth Mullein

Verbascum blattaria

SIZE: 1-3 ft. tall; flower 1 in. wide.

WHAT TO LOOK FOR: flowers yellow or white with widespread petals and fuzzy purplish center, borne in open wand at top of slender stem; leaves lance-shaped to oval, toothed, clustered at base of plant and scattered along stem.

HABITAT: fields, waste places, roadsides.

IN BLOOM: June-Sept.

Toadflax *Linaria*

A patch of color marking the narrow entrance to the nectar supply suggests that these flowers are pollinated during the day; such nectar guides are useless in the dark. The nectar is in a long spur, which tells us that the pollinators are probably hummingbirds and long-tongued insects.

Butter and Eggs

Linaria vulgaris

SIZE:
6-36 in. tall; flower 1 in. long.

WHAT TO LOOK FOR:
flowers yellow with orange patch in throat, spurred, in spikes at tips of leafy stems; leaves grasslike.

HABITAT:
fields, waste places, roadsides.

IN BLOOM:
May-Sept.

WHITE FLOWER

Louseworts *Pedicularis*

To reach the nectar within a Wood Betony blossom, a bee lifts the right side of the flower's upper lip (the left side is sealed), causing the pollen-receptive stigma to dip down and touch its body. Inside, the bee receives fresh pollen on the place that will be touched by the next flower's stigma. The Elephant Heads' blossoms contain no nectar, but bumblebees seek the pollen itself. To coat itself with a cloud of pollen, a bee lands on the "trunk" and vibrates its wings; meanwhile the trunk has curled around and touched the front of the bee's abdomen with the stigma, receiving pollen from a flower visited earlier.

Towering Lousewort
Pedicularis bracteosa

SIZE:
1-4 ft. tall; flower ½-1 in. long.

WHAT TO LOOK FOR:
flowers yellow, rose, or purple, with beaklike upper lip, in dense spike; leaves divided, scattered along stem.

HABITAT:
mountain meadows, slopes, open woods.

IN BLOOM:
June-Aug.

Wood Betony

Pedicularis canadensis

SIZE:
6-16 in. tall; flower ½-1 in. long.

WHAT TO LOOK FOR:
flowers brownish red to yellow, with beaklike upper lip, in short, dense spike; leaves deeply lobed.

HABITAT:
open woods, thickets, prairies.

IN BLOOM:
Apr.-June.

Elephant Heads

Pedicularis groenlandica

SIZE:
8-24 in. tall; flower ¾-1 in. long.

WHAT TO LOOK FOR:
flowers pink to purple, shaped like elephants' heads with upraised trunks, in dense spike; leaves divided or deeply lobed, clustered at base of plant and scattered along stem.

HABITAT:
wet mountain meadows, open woods.

IN BLOOM:
June-Aug.

Broomrapes *Orobanche*

Like all members of the cancerroot family, the broomrapes contain no chlorophyll and cannot manufacture their own food. Instead, they sink parasitic roots into the roots of other plants and draw out nourishment. The broomrape group is named for a European plant that lives on the roots of broom plants.

Naked Broomrape

Orobanche uniflora

SIZE: 1-6 in. tall; flower ½-1 in. long.

WHAT TO LOOK FOR: flowers creamy white to pale lavender, with yellow throats, borne singly atop pale stalks; leaves scalelike, at base of stalks.

HABITAT: damp woods, thickets.

IN BLOOM: Apr.-June.

Louisiana Broomrape

Orobanche ludoviciana

SIZE: 4-12 in. tall; flower ¾-1¼ in. long.

WHAT TO LOOK FOR: flowers purplish with yellow throats, in dense spikes among scaly brown bracts; stems often clustered.

HABITAT: deserts, sandy prairies, scrublands.

IN BLOOM: Mar.-Aug.

Beechdrops *Epifagus*

Although Beechdrops is a parasite of beech trees, it does little or no harm to its host. Instead of penetrating the tree's roots with its own, as other members of the cancerroot family do, it gets its nutrients with the help of an intermediate fungus in the soil. The upper flowers of Beechdrops are often visited by bees, but these blossoms are usually sterile; the lower, unopened flowers produce abundant seed by self-pollination.

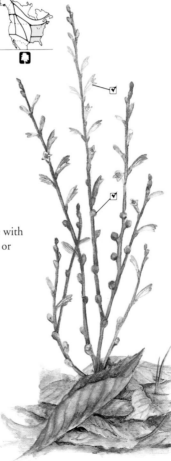

Beechdrops

Epifagus virginiana

SIZE:
5-16 in. tall; flower ¼-½ in. long.

WHAT TO LOOK FOR:
stems pale brown, branching; flowers white with brownish purple stripes, tubular (near tips) or budlike (near base).

HABITAT:
beech woods, thickets.

IN BLOOM:
Aug.-Oct.

Squawroots *Conopholis*

The scaly stems of these members of the cancerroot family look somewhat like clusters of pine cones standing on end. There is little chance of confusing them with real pine cones, however, since they are parasites on the roots of deciduous trees—chiefly oaks. The soft, yellow scales (actually modified leaves) turn hard and brown after the flowers have faded.

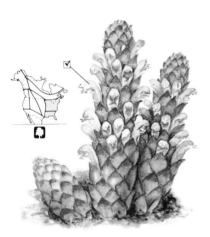

Squawroot

Conopholis americana

SIZE:
2-10 in. tall; flower ½ in. long.

WHAT TO LOOK FOR:
stems covered with overlapping, tawny yellow scales (turning brown); flowers yellow with hooded upper lip, borne between scales on upper part of stem.

HABITAT:
rich woods (often oak).

IN BLOOM:
Apr.-July.

Cross Vines *Bignonia*

If you cut through the stem of a Cross Vine you will see the pattern of a cross on the face of the cut—a key symbol in the eyes of the priests and missionaries who accompanied many of the early explorers to the Southeast. The group has only one species.

Trumpet Creepers

Campsis

One species of this group is native to North America; the only other, *Campsis grandiflora,* is Asian in origin. Both species are cultivated for the sake of their colorful flowers, but the rampant habit of our native species has made it a troublesome weed in many places.

Trumpet Creeper

Campsis radicans

SIZE: to 50 ft. high; flower 2½-3 in. long.

WHAT TO LOOK FOR: stems climbing or sprawling; flowers orange to scarlet, trumpet-shaped, in showy clusters; leaves divided into 7-11 leaflets.

HABITAT: moist woods, thickets, streambanks.

IN BLOOM: July-Sept.

◄Cross Vine

Bignonia capreolata

SIZE:
to 75 ft. high; flower 2 in. long.

WHAT TO LOOK FOR:
stems thick, climbing; flowers red and orange, bell-shaped, in showy clusters; leaves divided into two leaflets, with a climbing tendril between each pair.

HABITAT:
rich woods, swamps, bottomlands.

IN BLOOM:
Apr.-June.

Ruellias *Ruellia*

It seems odd that a group of plants as showy and distinctive as these has never acquired a common name. (Some low-growing species resemble petunias and are occasionally called wild petunias, but the name has never gained currency.) About 20 of the group's 250 species grow in temperate and subtropical North America; the rest are limited to the tropics.

Ruellia

Ruellia strepens

SIZE:
1-4 ft. tall; flower 1 in. wide.

WHAT TO LOOK FOR:
flowers blue-violet, tubular, with 5 spreading petals, on short leafy stalks along stem; leaves in pairs, oblong.

HABITAT:
open woods, thickets.

IN BLOOM:
May-July.

Water Willows *Justicia*

Although these water-loving plants are unrelated to the willows (*Salix*), their name is not inappropriate. Colonies of their supple stems arising from streams, ponds, and the edges of lakes are often mistaken for low-growing willows, because of both the shape of their leaves and their watery habitat.

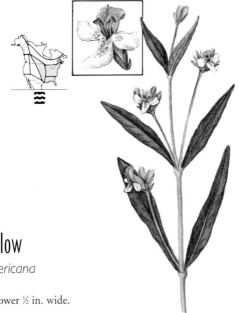

Water Willow

Justicia americana

SIZE:
1-3 ft. tall; flower ½ in. wide.

WHAT TO LOOK FOR:
stems erect, rising in colonies from water; leaves lance-shaped, in pairs; flowers white with violet markings, on long stalks arising at leaf bases.

HABITAT:
streams, ponds, lakeshores, swamps.

IN BLOOM:
June-Oct.

Butterworts *Pinguicula*

Small insects alighting on a butterwort leaf are trapped by its sticky yellowish surface. After a time, the leaf edges curl over, and the plant secretes enzymes that extract nitrogen and other vital elements from the accumulated victims. Then the leaf reopens.

Butterwort

Pinguicula vulgaris

SIZE: 2-6 in. tall; flower ¼-½ in. wide.

WHAT TO LOOK FOR: flowers violet, with spurs; leaves greenish yellow, buttery, sticky, clustered at base of stalks.

HABITAT: wet rocks, meadows, boggy areas.

IN BLOOM: June-Aug.

Unicorn Plants *Proboscidea*

Early in their development, the fruits are green and fleshy, with a single unicornlike "horn" at the end. They are edible and may be pickled like cucumbers. Dried fruits split open, forming two hooks that catch on livestock. Ranchers call them devil's claws.

Unicorn Plant

Proboscidea louisianica

SIZE: 1-3 ft. tall; flower 1½ in. wide.

WHAT TO LOOK FOR: flowers pink with yellow throats, bell-shaped, with large lower lip; leaves heart-shaped, sticky, downy; stems downy; fruits fleshy, green, with single horn on end (becoming hard, brown, with 2 claws).

HABITAT: fields, streambanks, waste places, roadsides.

IN BLOOM: June-Sept.

DRY FRUIT

Bladderworts *Utricularia*

Each little bladder among the plumelike underwater leaves of these carnivorous plants has a trapdoor triggered by sensitive hairs. When tiny water animals touch the hairs, the door opens and the creatures are sucked in, to be digested for the nutrients in their bodies. The Purple Bladderwort (*Utricularia purpurea*), with its whorled leaves, is one of the few native species in this group whose flowers are not yellow.

Swollen Bladderwort

Utricularia inflata

SIZE: to 10 ft. across; stalk 5-12 in. tall; flower ½-¾ in. wide.

WHAT TO LOOK FOR: flowers yellow, shieldlike, clustered atop leafless stalk; stems swollen, floating beneath surface; leaves feathery, bearing many small bladders.

HABITAT: ponds, ditches.

IN BLOOM: May-Aug.

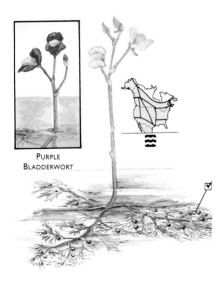

PURPLE BLADDERWORT

Greater Bladderwort

Utricularia vulgaris

SIZE:
to 7 ft. across; stalk 4-24 in. tall; flower ½-¾ in. wide.

WHAT TO LOOK FOR:
flowers yellow, snapdragon-shaped, clustered atop leafless stalk; leaves feathery, floating beneath surface, bearing many small bladders.

HABITAT:
ponds, bays, marshes.

IN BLOOM:
May-Sept.

Bellflowers *Campanula*

In some plants, cross-pollination occurs because the pollen-producing stamens and seed-producing pistil develop in different flowers; sometimes they are even borne on different plants. In others, the two organs are in separate parts of the same flower. In the bellflowers, however, each blossom has two distinct stages of development. First the stamens produce pollen, and the stigmas at the tip of the pistil remain closed. The pollen falls and collects inside the flower, to be picked up on the bodies of bees and carried to older blossoms, where the stigmas have opened. As a last resort, if the pistil remains unfertilized, its tip curls around to pick up a little loose pollen from inside its own flower.

Tall Bellflower

Campanula americana

SIZE:
2-7 ft. tall; flower 1 in. wide.

WHAT TO LOOK FOR:
flowers blue, star-shaped, borne at bases of upper leaves and clustered at top of wandlike, hairy stem; leaves lance-shaped to oval, toothed.

HABITAT:
moist woods, thickets, shady roadsides.

IN BLOOM:
June-Sept.

Southern Harebell

Campanula divaricata

SIZE: 1-3 ft. tall; flower ¼ in. wide.

WHAT TO LOOK FOR: flowers blue, bell-shaped, with 5 upturned petals, and long, protruding pistil, hanging from slender stalks; leaves lance-shaped to oval, toothed; stems slender, branching.

HABITAT: dry woods, rocky hillsides.

IN BLOOM: July-Sept.

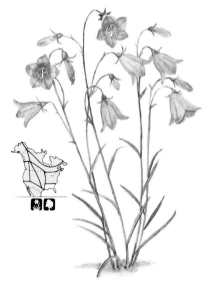

Harebell

Campanula rotundifolia

SIZE: 4-20 in. tall; flower ¾ in. wide.

WHAT TO LOOK FOR: flowers blue to lavender, bell-shaped, on hairlike stalks from tops of stems; leaves slender, scattered along stems (round, long-stalked leaves at base of stems are gone by flowering time).

HABITAT: fields, prairies, cliffs, rocky banks, dry open woods.

IN BLOOM: June-Oct.

Venus' Looking Glasses *Triodanis*

This group's name is borrowed from a European cousin, whose seeds are round, flat, and nearly mirror-bright. The seeds of the North American plants are not so precisely shaped, but they are hard and shiny enough to warrant the looking-glass name. Unlike the original Venus' Looking Glass, these plants produce self-pollinating flowers that remain closed, as well as open blossoms lower on the stem.

Venus' Looking Glass

Triodanis perfoliata

SIZE:
4-30 in. tall; flower ½-¾ in. wide.

WHAT TO LOOK FOR:
flowers blue or violet, bowl-shaped, borne at bases of leaves (those at top of stem budlike); leaves shell-like, clasping stem.

HABITAT:
open woods, fields, waste places.

IN BLOOM:
May-June.

Downingias *Downingia*

At first glance, these low-growing plants of the western states might be taken for violets, blanketing muddy wetlands with their blue to purple blossoms. A closer look, however, shows them to be members of the lobelia family. The flowers have two lobed lips, rather than the violets' five separate petals, and the stamens are fused into a central column.

Horned Downingia

Downingia bicornuta

SIZE:
3-10 in. tall; flower ¼-½ in. wide.

WHAT TO LOOK FOR:
flowers blue, with pale centers and 2 yellow horns on lower lip; leaves small, straplike.

HABITAT:
muddy places, ditches, moist open woods.

IN BLOOM:
Apr.-July.

Calico Flower

Downingia elegans

SIZE:
4-16 in. tall; flower ¼-½ in. wide.

WHAT TO LOOK FOR:
flowers blue, with white spot and 2 yellow ridges on lower lip, long stamen column protruding from center; leaves straplike.

HABITAT:
wet ditches, woods, muddy places.

IN BLOOM:
June-Sept.

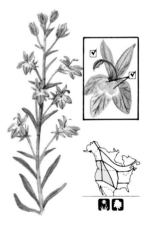

Lobelias *Lobelia*

Among this group's more than 375 species are plants contrasting sharply in size: there are treelike African giants with stems nearly 30 feet tall as well as 2- to 6-inch dwarfs, used by gardeners for edging. All bear tubular flowers that are divided into two lips, the upper one with two lobes and the lower with three, and all have five stamens united into a tube. Pollen at the end of this tube is deposited onto pollinating animals—hummingbirds in the case of the odorless red Cardinal Flower, bees or butterflies for the other two species shown on these two pages.

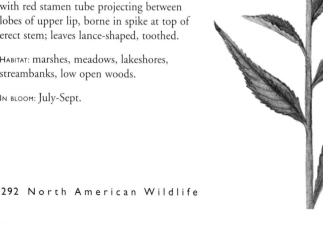

Cardinal Flower
Lobelia cardinalis

Size: 1-5 ft. tall; flower 1½-1¾ in. long.

What to look for: flowers bright red, tubular, with red stamen tube projecting between lobes of upper lip, borne in spike at top of erect stem; leaves lance-shaped, toothed.

Habitat: marshes, meadows, lakeshores, streambanks, low open woods.

In bloom: July-Sept.

Indian Tobacco
Lobelia inflata

SIZE:
4-36 in. tall; flower ¼ in. long.

WHAT TO LOOK FOR:
flowers blue to white, bell-shaped, protruding from inflated green cup, borne in open wands; leaves oblong.

HABITAT:
fields, open woods, waste places.

IN BLOOM:
June-Oct.

Great Blue Lobelia
Lobelia siphilitica

SIZE:
1-4 ft. tall; flower ¾-1¼ in. long.

WHAT TO LOOK FOR:
flowers blue, tubular, with stamen tube above upper lip; leaves lance-shaped to oval, toothed.

HABITAT:
marshes, meadows, lakeshores, stream-banks, open woods.

IN BLOOM:
Aug.-Sept.

Bluets *Houstonia*

The bluets, with their masses of dainty four-petaled blossoms covering large patches of woodland and meadow, were among the colonists' favorite springtime plants, and they still remain favorites. More than two dozen species are found in North America, but a botanist's trained eye is required to differentiate among many of them. Some bear clusters of flowers at the tips of branching stems; others, such as Quaker Ladies, bear one or two bonnetlike blossoms atop each stem.

Bluets

Houstonia purpurea

SIZE: 6-20 in. tall; flower ¼-½ in. wide.

WHAT TO LOOK FOR: flowers white to purple, 4 petaled, in clusters at stem tips; leaves in pairs, lance-shaped to oval; plant branching.

HABITAT: dry open woods, pine barrens, prairies.

IN BLOOM: May-July.

Quaker Ladies

Houstonia caerulea

SIZE:
2-8 in. tall; flower ¼-½ in. wide.

WHAT TO LOOK FOR:
flowers pale blue with yellow centers, 4-petaled, borne at stem tips; leaves oval to spoonlike, clustered at base and scattered in pairs along stems.

HABITAT:
moist meadows, open woods, fields.

IN BLOOM:
Apr.-June.

Bouvardias *Bouvardia*

Few of this group's 30 species grow naturally outside the tropics of Mexico and Central America. Those with white or yellow blossoms have a jasminelike scent attractive to insects. Such red-flowered species as the Trompetilla, however, are odorless; they attract hummingbird pollinators by their color.

Trompetilla
Bouvardia ternifolia

SIZE: 1-3 ft. tall; flower ¾-1¼ in. long.

WHAT TO LOOK FOR: flowers scarlet, trumpetlike, with 4 flaring petals, fuzzy, in clusters at stem tips; plant shrubby; leaves oval to lance-shaped, in clusters of 3-4.

HABITAT: deserts, rocky slopes, plains. IN BLOOM: May-Nov.

Twinberries *Mitchella*

North America has one of the world's two twinberry species. (The other grows in Japan.) The paired flowers at the stem tips are joined at the base like Siamese twins; as they mature, their ovaries fuse, finally forming the edible, two-part fruits for which the group is named.

Partridgeberry
Mitchella repens

SIZE: to 3 ft. long; flower ¼ in. wide.

WHAT TO LOOK FOR: stems creeping, matted; flowers white to purplish, fuzzy, 4-petaled, borne in pairs; leaves in pairs, round, evergreen with white markings; berries red, double.

HABITAT: woods. IN BLOOM: May-July.

Bedstraws *Galium*

Bedstraw foliage was once prized as mattress stuffing, but this is perhaps the least of the group's virtues. Shoots and young plants are tasty and nutritious when steamed for about five minutes (this was the dish known in old England as Lenten pottage). The acidic leaves are still used by cheesemakers to curdle milk; they can also be brewed into a tea that has served variously as a bracing tonic, a treatment for skin diseases, and a dye. The roasted fruits make a good caffeineless coffee substitute. Although the ubiquitous Cleavers—whose bristly leaves and fruits cleave to anything they touch—is best known, many other species are equally useful.

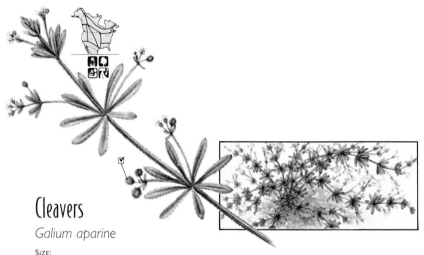

Cleavers

Galium aparine

SIZE:
1-5 ft. long; flower ⅛ in. wide.

WHAT TO LOOK FOR:
flowers white, in open clusters at tips of slender stalks; stems square, sprawling, bristly; leaves lance-shaped, bristly, in whorls along stems; fruits bristly.

HABITAT:
moist woods, fields, meadows, waste places.

IN BLOOM:
May-June.

Rough Bedstraw

Galium asprellum

Size: 2-6 ft. tall; flower ⅛ in. wide.

What to look for: flowers white, in open clusters at branch tips; stem square, erect or sprawling, branching, bristly; leaves lance-shaped, bristly, in whorls along stem.

Habitat: wet woods, thickets. In bloom: May-Aug.

Teasels *Dipsacus*

Well into this century, teasels were cultivated in Europe for their spiny flowerheads. The dried heads were mounted on rods and used by manufacturers of woolen goods to tease, or raise the nap of cloth. This ancient method was preferred over the use of metal devices because, when meeting a firm obstruction, the spines would break instead of tearing the material. Teasels, like many weeds, probably came to North America by accident, their seeds mixed in with imported hay. (It was many decades before enough land had been cleared in the New World to allow the colonists the luxury of pastures and hayfields.)

Teasel

Dipsacus fullonum

Size: 2-6 ft. tall; flower ¼ in. wide.

What to look for: flowers purple, tubular, borne in 1-2 dense bands around spiny egg-shaped heads; stems spiny, branching; leaves in pairs, lance-shaped, with spiny midribs, clasping stem.

Habitat: fields, ditches, waste places.

In bloom: July-Oct.

Honeysuckles *Lonicera*

Any child who has picked a honeysuckle blossom to taste the sweet nectar from its nipplelike base can appreciate the group's evocative name. There are many native North American species, but none is so widespread or pervasive as the imported Japanese Honeysuckle. Introduced as a fragrant ornamental for screenings and trellises and used as a ground cover for road banks and other easily eroded sites, it soon outgrew its assigned roles. With the help of birds that relish the small black fruits, the seeds have spread far and wide, producing tangled vines that have overgrown and now threaten to strangle whole forests in the East.

Trumpet Honeysuckle

Lonicera sempervirens

SIZE:
to 10 ft. high; flower 1-2¼ in. long.

WHAT TO LOOK FOR:
vine climbing or trailing; flowers trumpetlike, red with yellow throats, borne in whorled clusters; leaves oblong, in pairs, upper pairs often joined around stem.

HABITAT:
woods, thickets.

IN BLOOM:
Mar.-Sept.

Japanese Honeysuckle

Lonicera japonica

SIZE: to 60 ft. high; flower 1-1½ in. long.

WHAT TO LOOK FOR: vine climbing or trailing; flowers white (turning yellow), very fragrant, tubular, with backswept petals and showy stamens; leaves in pairs, oval to oblong.

HABITAT: fields, forests, thickets, waste places, fencerows.

IN BLOOM: Apr.-Nov.

Twinflowers *Linnaea*

It is unheard-of for a botanist to name a plant after himself, and so Carolus Linnaeus asked a friend to give his name to this smallest member of the honeysuckle family. The creator of the system of biological classification later described his favorite plant as "... a plant of Lapland, lowly, insignificant, flowering for but a brief space—from Linnaeus, who resembles it." In his best-known portrait, he holds a sprig of Twinflower in his hand. There is only one species, which is common in northern regions of Eurasia and North America.

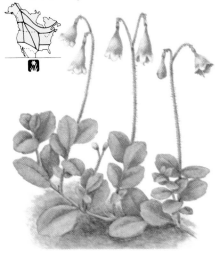

Twinflower

Linnaea borealis

SIZE: to 3 ft. long; flower ½ in. long.

WHAT TO LOOK FOR: vine slender, trailing; flowers pink, bell-shaped, nodding in pairs atop slender, downy stalks; leaves in pairs, round to oval, thick.

HABITAT: cool moist woods, peat bogs.

IN BLOOM: June-Aug.

Bonesets *Eupatorium*

Although the bonesets have no proven medicinal value, folklore credited them with many curative powers, including the setting of broken bones. Those species known as joe-pye-weeds were named for an Indian healer who used one of them to treat several ailments; he was even said to have used it to stop a typhus epidemic. The White Snakeroot is toxic.

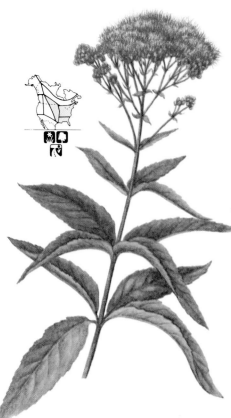

Sweet Joe-pye-weed

Eupatorium purpureum

SIZE:
2-7 ft. tall; flowerhead ⅛ in. wide.

WHAT TO LOOK FOR:
flowerheads pinkish purple, borne in domed clusters atop stout stem; leaves in pairs or whorls, toothed.

HABITAT:
woods, thickets, fields, meadows, ditches.

IN BLOOM:
July-Sept.

Western Joe-pye-weed

Eupatorium occidentale

SIZE: 1-3 ft. tall; flowerhead ⅓ in. wide.

WHAT TO LOOK FOR: flowerheads pink to purple, borne in dense clusters atop clumped stems; leaves oval to triangular, toothed, often purplish.

HABITAT: mountain streambanks, rocky clearings, evergreen forests.

IN BLOOM: July-Sept.

FLOWERHEAD

Mistflower

Eupatorium coelestinum

SIZE:
1-3 ft. tall; flowerhead ¼ in. wide.

WHAT TO LOOK FOR:
flowerheads blue to violet, in dense clusters at tops of branching stems; leaves in pairs, trowellike.

HABITAT:
moist woods, meadows, streambanks.

IN BLOOM:
July-Oct.

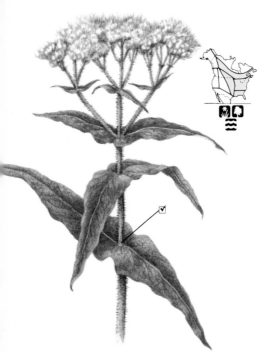

Thoroughwort

Eupatorium perfoliatum

SIZE:
2-5 ft. tall; flowerhead ¼ in. wide.

WHAT TO LOOK FOR:
flowerheads white, borne in flat-topped clusters atop hairy stem; leaves in pairs, lance-shaped, joined at base around stem.

HABITAT:
moist woods, clearings, meadows, marshes.

IN BLOOM:
July-Oct.

White Snakeroot

Eupatorium rugosum

SIZE:
1-5 ft. tall; flowerhead ¼ in. wide.

WHAT TO LOOK FOR:
flowerheads white, in flat-topped clusters atop erect stems; leaves in pairs, oval to heart-shaped, toothed.

HABITAT:
woods, pastures.

IN BLOOM:
July-Oct.

Ironweeds *Vernonia*

The huge composite family is marked by dense flowerheads, so tightly packed that each head looks like a single blossom. The individual flowers (florets) that make up the flowerheads of an ironweed or a boneset are all tubular and contain a rich nectar. Beekeepers value ironweeds for honey; farmers named them for their tough stems that stand upright through the winter.

Tall Ironweed

Vernonia altissima

Size:
2-10 ft. tall; flowerhead ⅓ in. wide.

What to look for:
flowerheads red-purple, bristly, borne in open clusters at top of tough stem; leaves lance-shaped, toothed, with downy undersides.

Habitat:
rich woods, bottomlands, moist meadows, clearings.

In bloom:
Aug.-Oct.

Golden Asters *Chrysopsis*

The flowerheads of golden asters, like those of asters, sunflowers, and many other members of the composite family, are composed of two kinds of florets. Those in the center, called disk flowers, are like the tubular florets found on the other plants on this page. Those around the outside, called ray flowers, look more like petals than blossoms, but each is a separate floret with five petals of its own, fused into a flat surface.

Golden Aster

Chrysopsis villosa

SIZE: 4-20 in. tall; flowerhead 1-1½ in. wide.

WHAT TO LOOK FOR: flowerheads yellow, with central disk surrounded by oblong ray flowers, borne in loose clusters at tops of hairy, branching stems; leaves spatula- to lance-shaped, hairy.

HABITAT: dry prairies, hillsides, chaparral, desert scrublands.

IN BLOOM: June-Oct.

Climbing Hempweeds *Mikania*

Members of this largely tropical group are among the few vines in the composite family. Three of the group's 150 species are found in North America, but only the Climbing Boneset is widespread (the others are confined to Florida). Like the bonesets, the climbing hempweeds bear flowerheads that are made up entirely of five-petaled, tubular florets.

Gumweeds *Grindelia*

The Indians boiled the roots and flowerheads of these plants to extract the gummy resin, which they used to treat such respiratory ailments as asthma, bronchitis, and whooping cough. Today, several gumweed species are commercially grown for this extract, which is used in cough drops and soothing syrups. The Common Gumweed, like most of the group, is native to the West, but its seeds were carried over much of the continent in cattle cars filled with animals that had eaten the plant. Its flowerheads usually contain both tubular disk flowers and petallike ray flowers; the heads emerge from a cuplike structure of green bracts—their pointed tips curled out and downward. Some individuals, however, like some other gumweed species, lack ray flowers altogether.

Common Gumweed

Grindelia squarrosa

SIZE: 6-30 in. tall; flowerhead 1-1½ in. wide.

WHAT TO LOOK FOR: flowerheads yellow, with disk and ray flowers emerging from gummy, cuplike base of pointed green bracts; leaves oblong, toothed, covered with translucent dots.

HABITAT: dry fields, mountain meadows, prairies, waste places, railroad sidings.

IN BLOOM: July-Sept.

◄Climbing Boneset

Mikania scandens

SIZE: to 20 ft. high; flower ¼ in. wide.

WHAT TO LOOK FOR: flowerheads white to pinkish, borne in dense clusters on short stalks along twining stem; leaves in pairs, heart-shaped, long-stalked.

HABITAT: swamps, wet thickets, hammocks.

IN BLOOM: June-Oct.

Blazing Stars *Liatris*

The pioneers who crossed the tallgrass prairies of the Midwest in late summer and fall made their way through unbroken miles of purple blazing stars intermixed with goldenrods in bloom—an awesome vista that has now all but vanished. Like the goldenrods, the blazing stars constitute a most distinctive group in which the species are variable and hybridize quite freely, so that precise identification is often difficult. The flowerheads of a blazing star are thistlelike, each composed of many tubular disk flowers emerging from a base of overlapping bracts. (The shape of these bracts is a help in identifying species.) The group is unusual in that flowering begins at the top of a stem and proceeds downward; as the flowerheads develop into fruiting heads, they put forth a growth called the pappus, made up of long, feathery bristles atop the one-seeded fruits.

Rough Blazing Star

Liatris aspera

SIZE:
1-4 ft. tall; flowerhead ¾-1¼ in. wide.

WHAT TO LOOK FOR:
flowerheads purple, with tubular disk flowers and bristly pappus emerging from cuplike base of rounded pinkish bracts, borne in leafy spike at top of wandlike stem; leaves narrow, straplike, rough-textured.

HABITAT:
dry fields, prairies, roadsides.

IN BLOOM:
Aug.-Oct.

Gayfeather

Liatris spicata

SIZE:
1-5 ft. tall; flowerhead ¼ in. wide.

WHAT TO LOOK FOR:
flowerheads rose-purple, with tubular disk flowers and feathery pappus emerging from cuplike base of wedge-shaped purplish bracts, borne in dense spike at top of wandlike stem; leaves narrow, straplike.

HABITAT:
meadows, moist prairies, edges of marshes.

IN BLOOM:
July-Sept.

Goldenrods *Solidago*

Because goldenrods are the most obvious weeds in bloom at the height of the hay fever season, they have long been unjustly blamed for the torments suffered by victims of that pollen allergy. The true culprits are ragweeds and other wind-pollinated plants with less spectacular flowers. Goldenrod pollen is too heavy to blow in the wind. It is carried by insects from one gobletlike flowerhead (composed of nectar-filled, tubular disk flowers surrounded by petallike ray flowers) to another. Goldenrods are the state flowers of Kentucky and Nebraska.

Tall Goldenrod

Solidago canadensis

SIZE:
2-8 ft. tall; flowerhead ¼ in. wide.

WHAT TO LOOK FOR:
flowerheads golden, in arching spikes that form pyramid at top of downy stem; leaves lance-shaped, rough-textured.

HABITAT:
fields, prairies, clearings.

IN BLOOM:
Aug.-Nov.

FLOWERHEAD

Silverrod

Solidago bicolor

SIZE: 1-3 ft. tall; flowerhead ¼ in. wide.

WHAT TO LOOK FOR: flowerheads cream-colored (yellow disk flowers surrounded by white ray flowers), in clusters along top of downy wandlike stem; leaves spatula-shaped.

HABITAT: dry fields, open woods, roadsides.

IN BLOOM: July-Oct.

Alpine Goldenrod

Solidago multiradiata

SIZE:
5-18 in. tall; flowerhead ⅓ in. wide.

WHAT TO LOOK FOR:
flowerheads golden, in rounded clusters; leaves mostly at base of stem, spatula-shaped.

HABITAT:
rocky plains, mountain clearings, tundra.

IN BLOOM:
June-Sept.

Gray Goldenrod

Solidago nemoralis

SIZE: 6-30 in. tall; flowerhead ⅛ in. wide.

WHAT TO LOOK FOR: flowerheads yellow, in dense, arching clusters at top of hairy gray-green stems; leaves spatula-shaped, covered with gray hairs, with 2 small leaves at base.

HABITAT: dry fields, prairies, open woods.

IN BLOOM: June-Dec.

Stemless Daisies *Townsendia*

Not truly stemless, these low-growing plants of the western mountains bear a profusion of such disproportionately large, daisylike flowerheads that the stems seem to disappear beneath a cushion of bloom.

Easter Daisy

Townsendia exscapa

SIZE: 1-4 in. tall; flowerhead 1-2¼ in. wide.

WHAT TO LOOK FOR: flowerheads with white to purplish ray flowers around yellow, often bristly, central disk, on short stems; leaves grasslike or spatula-shaped, clustered at base.

HABITAT: dry hillsides, grassy plains.   IN BLOOM: Mar.-June.

◄ Seaside Goldenrod

Solidago sempervirens

SIZE:
2-8 ft. tall; flowerhead ¼ in. wide.

WHAT TO LOOK FOR:
flowerheads yellow, in dense clusters at top of stout stem;
leaves lance-shaped, fleshy.

HABITAT:
salt marshes, ocean beaches.

IN BLOOM:
June-Dec.

Fleabanes *Erigeron*

Fleabanes are often confused with asters, but they tend to be smaller and weedier and usually bloom earlier in the year. The ray flowers that fringe their flowerheads are narrower and more numerous than those of asters, and at the base of each flowerhead is a single circle of small green bracts, rather than several overlapping circles as in most asters. It was once common practice to hang fleabane in houses in order to rid them of fleas.

Daisy Fleabane

Erigeron philadelphicus

SIZE: 8-28 in. tall; flowerhead ½-1 in. wide.

WHAT TO LOOK FOR: flowerheads with many white or pink ray flowers around yellow central disk, borne in loose clusters; leaves spatula-shaped, clustered at base and scattered along hairy stem.

HABITAT: moist meadows, woods, streambanks.

IN BLOOM: Apr.-Aug.

Yellow Fleabane

Erigeron linearis

SIZE: 2-12 in. tall; flowerhead ½-1 in. wide.

WHAT TO LOOK FOR: flowerheads yellow, borne singly atop upright, often branching stems; leaves grasslike, clustered at base of plant and scattered along stems.

HABITAT: dry mountain slopes, scrublands, open woods.

IN BLOOM: May-Aug.

Marsh Fleabanes *Pluchea*

These foul-smelling marsh plants seem to have little in common with the fleabanes, beyond the facts that both groups are members of the composite family and that both have been used to drive away fleas. The flowerheads of the marsh fleabanes are composed entirely of tubular disk flowers, quite unlike the fringed fleabane blossoms. The leaves of most species emit a fetid odor when bruised, strongest and most repulsive in the Stinking Fleabane.

Stinking Fleabane

Pluchea foetida

SIZE:
20-36 in. tall; flowerhead ⅓ in. wide.

WHAT TO LOOK FOR:
flowerheads creamy white, borne in rounded clusters at branch tips; leaves oval, toothed, clasping downy stem.

HABITAT:
swamps, marshes, ditches, coastal savannas.

IN BLOOM:
July-Oct.

Asters *Aster*

The starburst flowerheads of wild asters are among the familiar pleasures of late summer and autumn. (The name aster is from the Greek for "star," and the plants were once commonly known in England as starworts.) Some of the group's nearly 600 species are popular garden flowers. Others, such as the coarse White Heath Aster, are troublesome weeds; because masses of its tough stems have been known to break mowing blades, it has also been called Steelweed.

New England Aster

Aster novae-angliae

SIZE:
2-7 ft. tall; flowerhead 1-2 in. wide.

WHAT TO LOOK FOR:
flowerheads with pink to purple ray flowers around yellow central disk, clustered at top of hairy, sticky stems; leaves lance-shaped, clasping stem.

HABITAT:
moist fields, meadows, roadsides.

IN BLOOM:
July-Oct.

Stiff Aster

Aster linariifolius

SIZE:
4-24 in. tall; flowerhead ¾-1¼ in. wide.

WHAT TO LOOK FOR:
flowerheads with blue to pink ray flowers around yellow central disk, borne at tips of wiry stems; leaves needlelike.

HABITAT:
dry prairies, meadows, open woods.

IN BLOOM:
July-Oct.

White Heath Aster

Aster ericoides

SIZE:
1-3 ft. tall; flowerhead ½ in. wide.

WHAT TO LOOK FOR:
plant bushy; flowerheads profuse, with white ray flowers around small yellow central disk; leaves narrow, straplike.

HABITAT:
dry prairies, fields, roadsides.

IN BLOOM:
July-Dec.

Blue Wood Aster

Aster cordifolius

SIZE:
1-4 ft. tall; flowerhead ½-1 in. wide.

WHAT TO LOOK FOR:
flowerheads with short blue or violet ray flowers around yellow central disk, in dense clusters on branching stems; leaves heart-shaped, toothed, hairy.

HABITAT:
open woods, thickets, clearings.

IN BLOOM:
Aug.-Oct.

Leafy Aster

Aster foliaceus

SIZE:
4-36 in. tall; flowerhead 1-2 in. wide.

WHAT TO LOOK FOR:
flowerheads with narrow blue to rose-purple ray flowers around yellow central disk, borne at top of leafy stem; leaves oval to lance-shaped, upper leaves clasping stem.

HABITAT:
mountain ridges, meadows, open slopes, moist woods.

IN BLOOM:
July-Sept.

Inulas *Inula*

About 2,400 years ago Hippocrates prescribed the root of Elecampane for lung disorders. It continued to be used medicinally through the centuries, known sometimes as Elfwort (when the ailment was called "elf sickness") and sometimes as Horseheal (when the patients were draft animals). It is the only member of this Eurasian group found in the New World, to which it was brought by the colonists.

Elecampane
Inula helenium

SIZE:
2-6 ft. tall; flowerhead 2-4 in. wide.

WHAT TO LOOK FOR:
flowerheads yellow, with long scraggly ray flowers around darker central disk; leaves clasping stem, large, toothed, rough-textured above, woolly below.

HABITAT:
fields, waste places, roadsides.

IN BLOOM:
May-Sept.

Cockleburs *Xanthium*

The two seeds in a cocklebur's spiny fruit are covered by airtight coats. Because the seeds need oxygen to germinate, they remain dormant until these coats begin to wear away. One seed invariably requires much more oxygen than the other, and so remains dormant a year longer. Thus each bur produces two generations of offspring—one reason these weeds are notoriously difficult to eradicate.

Cocklebur

Xanthium strumarium

SIZE:
1-6 ft. tall; flowerhead minute.

WHAT TO LOOK FOR:
plant bushy; leaves oval to wedge-shaped, toothed; flowerheads greenish, borne in short-lived spikes (male) and clusters at leaf bases (female); fruits egg-shaped, prickly.

HABITAT:
fields, waste places.

IN BLOOM:
Aug.-Oct.

Everlastings _Anaphalis_

Several other members of the composite family are also known as everlastings, including the cudweeds and the pussytoes. All bear long-lasting flowerheads that are popular in dried arrangements. Of this group's nearly three dozen species, only the Pearly Everlasting is native to North America. The flowerheads are composed entirely of disk flowers; the pearly white fringe around the outside is made up of bracts rather than the more familiar ray flowers.

Pearly Everlasting
Anaphalis margaritacea

SIZE:
1-3 ft. tall; flowerhead ¼-½ in. wide.

WHAT TO LOOK FOR:
flowerheads of yellowish disk flowers surrounded by pearly white bracts, borne in flat-topped clusters atop woolly stem; leaves straplike to lance-shaped, woolly below.

HABITAT:
dry plains, fields, mountain slopes, roadsides.

IN BLOOM:
July-Sept.

Ragweeds *Ambrosia*

The Common Ragweed and Giant Ragweed are best known for the widespread suffering they cause among North America's hay fever victims. The drab male flowerheads release vast quantities of pollen into the air. Each grain is covered with minute hooks and barbs so that it clings to whatever it touches—whether the stigma of a seed-producing female flower or the bronchial tissue of an allergic human being.

GIANT
RAGWEED
(Ambrosia trifida)

COMMON
RAGWEED

Common Ragweed

Ambrosia artemisiifolia

SIZE:
1-5 ft. tall;
flowerhead ⅛ in. wide.

WHAT TO LOOK FOR:
flowerheads greenish, borne in slender spikes (male) and in clusters at leaf bases (female); leaves deeply lobed, ragged; stems hairy, branching.

HABITAT:
fields, meadows, roadsides, waste places.

IN BLOOM:
July-Oct.

Cudweeds *Gnaphalium*

When a cow loses its cud, the cause is usually a stomach inflammation. Though old-time dairy farmers did not know that the cudweeds, like the closely related everlastings and pussytoes, contain a soothing antibiotic, they were well aware that feeding cudweed to afflicted cattle helped to restore digestion.

Fragrant Cudweed
Gnaphalium obtusifolium

SIZE: 4-30 in. tall; flowerhead ⅛-¼ in. wide.

WHAT TO LOOK FOR: flowerheads white, with yellow tuft, fragrant, clustered near top of cottony stem; leaves narrow, straplike, woolly below.

HABITAT: dry prairies, fields, clearings.

IN BLOOM: July-Nov.

Pussytoes *Antennaria*

The tubular disk flowers that make up the pussy-toes' fluffy flowerheads can produce seed with or without fertilization (the latter case is called apomixis). Thus, individual variations that arise from cross-pollination are later preserved in clonelike off-spring. The result is a confusing array of species and varieties.

Field Pussytoes
Antennaria neglecta

SIZE: 2-10 in. tall; flowerhead ¼-½ in. wide.

WHAT TO LOOK FOR: flowerheads fluffy, clustered atop woolly stalks; leaves spoon-shaped, woolly, clustered at base.

HABITAT: dry prairies, hayfields. IN BLOOM: Apr.-July.

Rosinweeds *Silphium*

The tall, rough-textured rosinweeds are often mistaken for sunflowers in bloom. When they go to seed, however, the difference is clear: a sunflower's abundant crop of one-seeded fruits is produced by the flowers of the flat central disk, while in a rosinweed only the petallike yellow ray flowers produce fruits. Another difference is the resinous sap for which the rosinweeds are named; if a stem is broken, a blob of this sap collects and gels into a pleasant-tasting gum. The Compass Plant, on the next page, was useful to travelers across the plains because its deeply lobed basal leaves nearly always align north-and-south.

Prairie Dock

Silphium terebinthinaceum

SIZE:
2-10 ft. tall; flowerhead 1½-3½ in. wide.

WHAT TO LOOK FOR:
flowerheads yellow, with flat disk surrounded by petallike ray flowers, in loose clusters at top of branching stem; leaves heart-shaped, rough, toothed, clustered at base of stem.

HABITAT: moist prairies.

IN BLOOM:
July-Sept.

Compass Plant

Silphium laciniatum

SIZE:
5-10 ft. tall; flowerhead 2-5 in. wide.

WHAT TO LOOK FOR:
flowerheads yellow, with flat central disk surrounded by large petallike ray flowers, scattered along upper part of stout, hairy stem; leaves very large, deeply lobed, rough, hairy, mostly clustered at base of plant.

HABITAT: prairies. IN BLOOM: July-Sept.

Cup Plant

Silphiurn perfoliatum

SIZE: 3-9 ft. tall; flowerhead 2-4 in. wide.

WHAT TO LOOK FOR: flowerheads yellow, with flat disk surrounded by petallike ray flowers, in loose clusters at top of square stem; leaves in pairs, oval, toothed (upper ones join at base to form cup around stem).

HABITAT: moist prairies, open woods, fields, streambanks.

IN BLOOM: July-Sept.

Purple Coneflowers *Echinacea*

Botanists once classified all the coneflowers in one group. The purple coneflowers were reclassified, not because of their distinctive color but because of such structural differences as the spiny bristles among their disk flowers.

Pale Purple Coneflower

Echinacea pallida

SIZE:
4-40 in. tall; flowerhead 1-4 in. wide.

WHAT TO LOOK FOR:
flowerheads with bristly conical center of brown-purple disk flowers surrounded by drooping magenta to pale purple ray flowers; leaves lance-shaped, clustered at base and scattered along hairy reddish stem.

HABITAT:
dry prairies, fields.

IN BLOOM:
May-Aug.

Prairie Coneflowers *Ratibida*

Subtle differences in fruit structure are the botanist's key in distinguishing this group's five species from the other coneflowers. A more obvious characteristic is the aniselike odor of the floral cone when it is crushed or bruised. Indians extracted a yellow-orange dye from the blossoms of prairie coneflowers; they also brewed a tea from the blossoms and leaves.

Coneflowers *Rudbeckia*

Maryland's state flower, the Black-eyed Susan, is native to the East but has spread across the continent as a garden flower. Many cultivated forms (sold under the name Gloriosa Daisy) have large, multicolored flowerheads, and in some the number of ray flowers has been doubled and redoubled by genetic manipulation. These often escape to the wild; later generations tend to revert to the original form.

◄ Prairie Coneflower
Ratibida pinnata

SIZE: 2-5 ft. tall; flowerhead 1½-3 in. wide.

WHAT TO LOOK FOR: flowerheads with high, rounded button of dark brown disk flowers surrounded by drooping yellow ray flowers; leaves deeply divided, clustered at base and scattered along hairy stem.

HABITAT: prairies, fields, dry open woods.

IN BLOOM: June-Sept.

Black-eyed Susan
Rudbeckia hirta

SIZE: 1-3 ft. tall; flowerhead 2-3 in. wide.

WHAT TO LOOK FOR: flowerheads with conical center of purplish-brown disk flowers surrounded by deep yellow ray flowers; leaves oval to straplike, hairy, scattered along coarse, hairy stems.

HABITAT: fields, prairies, open woods, waste places.

IN BLOOM: June-Oct.

Zinnias *Zinnia*

The showy garden zinnias are a far cry from their ancestors. Like many other New World wildflowers, the zinnias were transformed in Old World gardens, especially those of England. The 18th-century German botanist Johann Zinn collected seeds of the Common Zinnia (*Zinnia elegans*) in Mexico; from the progeny, plant breeders created the first of the myriad colors and forms found in today's catalogs.

Rocky Mountain Zinnia
Zinnia grandiflora

SIZE: 4-8 in. tall; flowerhead 1-1¾ in. wide.

WHAT TO LOOK FOR: plants low, clumped; flower-heads with 4-5 yellow ray flowers around tufted brick-red central disk; leaves small, hairy, straplike.

HABITAT: dry slopes, prairies, deserts.

IN BLOOM: May-Oct.

Mule Ears *Wyethia*

These are long-lived plants of mountain slopes and mesas, with heavy taproots that put forth aromatic leaves each spring. They are named for these large, hairy leaves, although a few species growing in exceptionally dry places produce narrow, water-conserving foliage instead.

Mule Ears
Wyethia arizonica

SIZE: 1-2 ft. tall; flowerhead 1½-2½ in. wide.

WHAT TO LOOK FOR: flowerheads yellow, with long ray flowers around flat central disk; leaves large, hairy, mostly clustered at base of plant.

HABITAT: mountain pinelands, clearings, streambanks, thickets.

IN BLOOM: May-Aug.

Greenthreads *Thelesperma*

The finely divided leaves for which this group is named were brewed into tea by various Indian peoples of the Southwest.

Navajo Tea

Thelesperma subnudum

SIZE: 4-15 in. tall; flowerhead 1½-2½ in. wide.

WHAT TO LOOK FOR: flowerheads with yellow ray flowers around brownish central disk; leaves divided into threadlike leaflets, mostly clustered at base of plant.

HABITAT: dry plains, open hillsides, deserts. IN BLOOM: May-July.

Sticktights *Bidens*

Beggar's ticks, stickseeds, devil's pitchforks, harvest lice, cow lice, Spanish needles—most of the names by which these widespread weeds are none-too-fondly known refer to their small, one-seeded fruits. These cling to fur, feathers, and clothing by means of barbed prongs. The flowerheads of most species have only tubular disk flowers; those with yellow ray flowers are often called bur marigolds.

FRUIT

Bur Marigold

Bidens cernua

SIZE: 6-36 in. tall; flowerhead ¾-2 in. wide.

WHAT TO LOOK FOR: flowerheads yellow, with broad ray flowers around slightly darker, buttonlike central disk, profuse, nodding; leaves in pairs, lance-shaped to oblong, toothed.

HABITAT: wet meadows, marshes, lakeshores, streambanks. IN BLOOM: Aug.-Oct.

Sunflowers *Helianthus*

The reason sunflowers face the sun is, paradoxically, that light inhibits growth in the stem; hence the shaded side of the stem grows faster, tipping the flowerhead toward the sun. The Common Sunflower, grown worldwide for its oil-rich seeds, is both the state flower of Kansas and the floral emblem of the Soviet Union. The Jerusalem Artichoke, whose name is a corruption of the Italian *girasole* ("turns to the sun"), is widely cultivated for its edible tubers— the so-called artichokes.

Jerusalem Artichoke

Helianthus tuberosus

SIZE:
3-10 ft. tall;
flowerhead 2-4 in. wide.

WHAT TO LOOK FOR:
flowerheads yellow, with long ray flowers around flat central disk, loosely clustered at top of hairy, branching stem; leaves in pairs, oval to lance-shaped, toothed.

HABITAT:
moist fields, open woods, thickets, waste places, bottomlands.

IN BLOOM:
Aug.-Oct.

Common Sunflower

Helianthus annuus

SIZE: 2-12 ft. tall; flowerhead 3-10 in. wide.

WHAT TO LOOK FOR: flowerheads with petallike yellow ray flowers around flat brownish central disk, nodding sunward atop stout, hairy stem; leaves oval to heart-shaped, toothed, rough.

HABITAT: fields, prairies, waste places.

IN BLOOM: June-Oct.

Wingstems *Verbesina*

This group's single species is also known as the Golden Ironweed because of its tough stem. The edges of the leaves seem to run down into narrow ridges, or wings, along the stem.

Wingstem

Verbesina alterniflora

SIZE: 2-6 ft. tall; flowerhead 1-2 in. wide.

WHAT TO LOOK FOR: flowerheads yellow, with rounded central disk surrounded by a few drooping ray flowers; leaves lance-shaped, the edges joining ridges along stem.

HABITAT: moist woods, thickets, clearings.

IN BLOOM: Aug.-Oct.

Tickseeds *Coreopsis*

One must look carefully at the petallike ray flowers of most members of the composite family in order to realize that each is actually a separate blossom with five fused petals. The notched and grooved ray flowers of a tickseed, however, illustrate this at a glance. The group is named for the appearance of its hard, flat, one-seeded fruits.

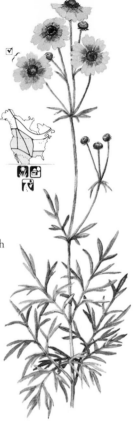

Golden Tickseed

Coreopsis tinctoria

SIZE: 1-4 ft. tall; flowerhead 1-1¾ in. wide.

WHAT TO LOOK FOR: flowerheads with notched, two-tone ray flowers around reddish central disk, clustered at top of branching stem; leaves deeply divided.

HABITAT: dry fields, prairies, scrublands.

IN BLOOM: June-Aug.

Tickseed

Coreopsis lanceolata

SIZE: 8-30 in. tall; flowerhead 1½-3 in. wide.

WHAT TO LOOK FOR: flowerheads yellow, with notched ray flowers around buttonlike central disk, borne singly atop long stalks; leaves lance-shaped, mostly clustered at base of plant.

HABITAT: dry fields, prairies.

IN BLOOM: May-Aug.

Hulseas *Hulsea*

Like many other western mountain plants, the hulseas bear most of their succulent, aromatic leaves clustered close to the ground. This huddled posture, along with the woolly gray fuzz that often covers the foliage, helps the plants survive the drying winds that sweep their rigorous habitat.

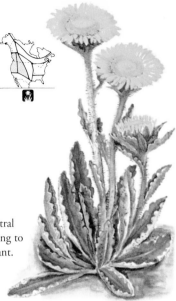

Alpine Gold
Hulsea algida

SIZE: 5-18 in. tall; flowerhead 1½-2 in. wide.

WHAT TO LOOK FOR: flowerheads yellow, with bristly central disk fringed by many narrow ray flowers; leaves oblong to spatula-shaped, densely hairy, clustered at base of plant.

HABITAT: high mountain slopes. IN BLOOM: July-Aug.

Layias *Layia*

"Tidy tips" is a name shared by many of this group's 15 species that have yellow ray flowers neatly tipped with white. Several species have solid yellow flowerheads, and a few, such as the White Daisy (*Layia glandulosa*) of the Pacific Coast, have pure white ray flowers.

Tidy Tips
Layia chrysanthemoides

SIZE: 4-20 in. tall; flowerhead 1-1¾ in. wide.

WHAT TO LOOK FOR: flowerheads mostly yellow, with notched, white-tipped ray flowers around brown-specked central disk; leaves deeply lobed.

HABITAT: oak woods, meadows (California's Coast Ranges).

IN BLOOM: Mar.-June.

Desert Marigolds *Baileya*

When water is available, the stems and leaves of these desert dwellers grow firm and juicy; as the water disappears during dry spells, the plants become thin and spindly. The dense woolly coat that shades their leaves helps retain moisture, and each soft hair collects a drop of morning dew. The ray flowers become dry and papery as they age, so that water loss from them is kept to a minimum.

Desert Marigold

Baileya pleniradiata

SIZE: 6-25 in. tall; flowerhead 1-1½ in. wide.

WHAT TO LOOK FOR: flowerheads golden to pale yellow, with many ray flowers that dry and droop with age; leaves narrow, deeply lobed, covered with woolly hair.

HABITAT: deserts, dry scrublands.

IN BLOOM: Mar.-June; Sept.-Nov.

Sneezeweeds *Helenium*

Indians used the powdered flowerheads of sneezeweeds as snuff to provoke violent sneezing and rid the body of evil spirits. Several species are toxic to sheep; cattle that eat Bitterweed give bitter milk.

Bitterweed
Helenium amarum

SIZE: 6-30 in. tall; flowerhead 1 in. wide.

WHAT TO LOOK FOR: stem branching, shrubby, covered with narrow leaves; flowerheads yellow, with domelike central disk surrounded by ragged ray flowers.

HABITAT: dry fields, prairies.

IN BLOOM: July-Oct.

GROWTH FORM

Mountain Sunflowers *Hymenoxys*

Western stockmen watch for these toxic plants on their range-land, for they are a clear sign of overgrazing. Sheepherders dread their appearance on another count as well: at least two species are especially poisonous to their woolly charges.

◄Mountain Sunflower
Hymenoxys acaulis

SIZE: 4-12 in. tall; flowerhead 1-2 in. wide.

WHAT TO LOOK FOR: flowerheads yellow, with domelike central disk surrounded by notched ray flowers; leaves straplike, silky, clustered at base of plant.

HABITAT: dry hillsides, plains, open pine woods. IN BLOOM: Apr.-July.

Lasthenias *Lasthenia*

At the height of its blooming period, Goldfields blankets thousands of acres—from Oregon's mountain woodlands to the dry islands of Baja California—with golden yellow.

Goldfields

Lasthenia chrysostoma

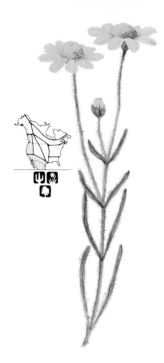

SIZE: 1-16 in. tall; flowerhead ¾-1½ in. wide.

WHAT TO LOOK FOR: flowerheads yellow, with dome-like central disk surrounded by ray flowers; leaves narrow, in pairs along hairy stems.

HABITAT: meadows, open woods, plain, deserts.

IN BLOOM: Mar.-May.

Pincushions *Chaenactis*

The pincushions are also called false yarrows. Unlike true yarrows, they have only tubular disk flowers in their "cushions," although the outer flowers are often large enough to look somewhat like the yarrows' ray flowers.

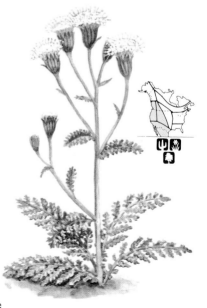

Blanketflowers *Gaillardia*

One reason for the blanketflowers' popularity among gardeners is that their spectacular flowerheads—like those of most members of the composite family—last for a long while. The tubular disk flowers open one at a time, beginning at the outer edge of the disk and proceeding in a spiral, and the petallike ray flowers remain showy throughout the process.

Firewheel

Gaillardia pulchella

SIZE:
4-25 in. tall; flowerhead 1-3 in. wide.

WHAT TO LOOK FOR:
flowerheads showy, with reddish disk surrounded by ray flowers of red, orange, and yellow; leaves usually toothed or lobed, hairy.

HABITAT:
dry plains, sandy fields, prairies.

IN BLOOM:
May-Aug.

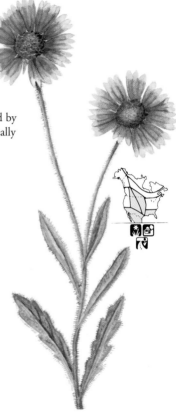

◄Dusty Maiden

Chaenactis douglasii

SIZE: 4-18 in. tall; flowerhead ¾-1 in. wide.

WHAT TO LOOK FOR: flowerheads white, pinkish, or lavender, tufted, with many tubular disk flowers, numerous at tips of branching stem; leaves lacily divided.

HABITAT: dry mountain slopes, deserts, open woods, chaparral.

IN BLOOM: June-Aug.

Chrysanthemums *Leucanthemum*

Garden mums are hybrids of several Oriental species belonging to this group. The Oxeye Daisy, which is actually a chrysanthemum, is one of many similar-looking plants called daisies. Chaucer's "dayeseye, or . . . eye of day" and Shakespeare's "daisies pied" refer to the English Daisy (*Bellis perennis*).

Oxeye Daisy

Leucanthemum vulgare

SIZE: 8-30 in. tall; flowerhead 1¼-2½ in. wide.

WHAT TO LOOK FOR: flowerheads with "dented" yellow disk surrounded by white petallike ray flowers; leaves lobed, toothed.

HABITAT: prairies, fields.

IN BLOOM: May-Oct.

Brass Buttons *Cotula*

The little yellow flowerheads for which these plants are named seem to contain only tubular disk flowers, but a close look at the edges reveals a fringe of tiny ray flowers.

Tansies *Tanacetum*

Tansy leaves and flowerheads have been used medicinally since ancient times, but always with great care, for an overdose can be fatal. The leaves contain an effective insect repellent; it was once common practice to rub raw meat with them in order to ward off flies. They were also used in burial rites.

Common Tansy

Tanacetum vulgare

SIZE:
1-5 ft. tall; flowerhead ¼-½ in. wide.

WHAT TO LOOK FOR:
flowerheads yellow, buttonlike, borne in dense, flat-topped clusters at top of upright stem; leaves divided, toothed.

HABITAT:
fields, waste places, roadsides.

IN BLOOM:
July-Oct.

◄ Brass Buttons

Cotula coronopifolia

SIZE: 6-16 in. long; flowerhead ¼-½ in. wide.

WHAT TO LOOK FOR: stems sprawling; flowerheads yellow, buttonlike, borne singly on upright stalks; leaves straplike to lance-shaped, lobed.

HABITAT: tidal flats, wet meadows, ditches.   IN BLOOM: Mar.-Dec.

Wild Chamomiles *Matricaria*

The fernlike leaves of several species in this group give off the odor of fresh pineapple when bruised. Most members of the group bear daisylike flowerheads, with the yellow center disk surrounded by white ray flowers. The Pineapple Weed's spherical flowerheads, however, have only tubular disk flowers.

Pineapple Weed

Matricaria matricarioides

Size: 4-16 in. tall; flowerhead ¼ in. wide.

What to look for: flowerheads yellow, spherical, borne at tips of leafy branches; leaves finely divided, pineapple-scented.

Habitat: fields, waste places, roadsides, railroad embankments. In bloom: May-Sept.

Coltsfoots *Tussilago*

The distinctive leaves for which the Coltsfoot is named appear in summer after the flowers have died back. The single species has been so highly regarded as a medicinal plant that the outline of its leaf was used as a symbol for apothecary shops in Europe.

Coltsfoot

Tussilago farfara

Size: 4-20 in. tall; flowerhead ¾-1 in. wide.

What to look for: flowerheads yellow, with central disk fringed by narrow ray flowers, borne on scaly stalks; leaves broad, toothed, borne after flowering.

Habitat: fields, streambanks, waste places. In bloom: Mar.-June.

Fireweeds *Erechtites*

These tall, weedy plants, their light seeds carried far in parachutelike fruits, are often among the first plants to become established in the open, nutrient-rich soil left by a fire. Other plants known as fireweeds for the same reason include species of willow herbs, plantains, ragworts, and thornapples.

Fireweed

Erechtites hieracifolia

SIZE:
1-10 ft. tall; flowerhead ½-¾ in. long.

WHAT TO LOOK FOR:
flowerheads green, swollen at base, with brushlike tip of white to yellow disk flowers, borne in loose clusters at ends of branches; seedheads white, fluffy; leaves lance-shaped, toothed, scattered along stem.

HABITAT:
fields, burns, waste places, open woods.

IN BLOOM:
July-Nov.

Groundsels *Senecio*

Groundsels have a long history of medicinal use. Golden Ragwort, for example, is also known as Squaw Weed because it was used to ease the pain of childbirth. Among the group's nearly 3,000 species is the popular Florist's Cineraria (*Senecio hybridus*).

Spotted Knapweed

Golden Ragwort

Senecio aureus

SIZE: 1-3 ft. tall; flowerhead ½-¾ in. wide.

WHAT TO LOOK FOR: flowerheads golden yellow, loosely clustered atop upright stem; leaves lance-shaped and lobed (along stem) or heart-shaped and long-stalked (at base of plant), often reddish below.

HABITAT: moist woods, meadows, swamps.

IN BLOOM: Apr.-July.

Knapweeds *Centaurea*

The knapweeds are named for their thistlelike flowerheads, in which tubular disk flowers emerge from a knobby cup of bracts. (*Knap* is from the Old English for "knob.") Germany's national flower, the Cornflower, or Bachelor's Button (*Centaurea cyanus*), is the group's most popular garden plant.

◄Spotted Knapweed
Centaurea maculosa

SIZE: 1-4 ft. tall; flowerhead ¾-1 in. wide.

WHAT TO LOOK FOR: flowerheads rose-pink, with long, tubular disk flowers spreading from urn-shaped base; leaves divided into narrow sections, scattered along wiry, branching stem.

HABITAT: fields, dry pastures, roadsides. IN BLOOM: June-Oct.

Yarrows *Achillea*

Yarrows contain a chemical that speeds the formation of blood clots, an attribute said to have been discovered by the Greek hero Achilles outside the walls of Troy. This medicinal use gave rise to such names as nosebleed, bloodwort, and soldier's woundwort. The Common Yarrow, widespread in Eurasia, came to North America with the colonists and soon spread across the continent.

Common Yarrow
Achillea millefolium

SIZE: 8-40 in. tall; flowerhead ¼-½ in. wide.

WHAT TO LOOK FOR: flowerheads with white to pink ray flowers around creamy central disk, borne in dense, flat-topped clusters; leaves fernlike, aromatic.

HABITAT: fields, prairies, waste places.

IN BLOOM: June-Nov.

Plumeless Thistles *Carduus*

In the flowerheads of this group, each flower is surrounded by long pappus hairs that are simple and unbranched. The plants are therefore called plumeless, setting them apart from other thistles, whose ornate blossoms have finely divided pappus hairs.

Nodding Thistle

Carduus nutans

SIZE:
2-7 ft. tall; flowerhead 1½-2½ in. wide.

WHAT TO LOOK FOR:
flowerheads rose-purple, with disk flowers and soft hairs emerging from a purplish base of spiny bracts, nodding at ends of branches; leaves divided into spine-tipped lobes, scattered along spiny, branching stem.

HABITAT:
fields, pastures, waste places.

IN BLOOM:
June-Oct.

Burdocks *Arctium*

Nearly every part of a burdock is edible. The Great Burdock (*Arctium lappa*) is cultivated in parts of Europe and Asia for its large taproot. Although the Common Burdock's root is smaller, it is no less tasty when peeled and boiled. The young leaves make a good potherb. The pithy cores of the flowering stem and of the large basal leafstalks may be eaten raw or cooked like asparagus after the bitter green rind has been stripped away.

Common Burdock

Arctium minus

SIZE:
1-5 ft. tall; flowerhead ½-1 in. wide.

WHAT TO LOOK FOR:
flowerheads purple to whitish, with disk flowers emerging from end of spiny ball of bracts, borne in clusters along upper part of stem; leaves heart-shaped, large, mostly clustered at base of plant.

HABITAT:
fields, pastures, waste places.

IN BLOOM:
July-Oct.

GROWTH FORM

Thistles *Cirsium*

It is against the law in 37 states to allow the Canada Thistle to grow on one's land. Despite its outlaw status, the spiny fugitive flourishes, spreading by means of tufted airborne fruits and fast-creeping roots. A related thistle was the emblem of the Scottish Stuart clan, and when the Stuarts became the royal house of Scotland, their thistle became the national flower.

Bull Thistle

Cirsium vulgare

SIZE: 2-6 ft. tall; flowerhead 1½-3 in. wide.

WHAT TO LOOK FOR: flowerheads rose-purple, with slender disk flowers and feathery pappus hairs emerging from cuplike base of spiny green bracts; leaves spiny, divided into spine-tipped lobes, scattered along stout, spiny stem.

HABITAT: fields, pastures, waste places, meadows.

IN BLOOM: June-Oct.

Canada Thistle

Cirsium arvense

SIZE:
1-4 ft. tall; flowerhead ½-1 in. wide.

WHAT TO LOOK FOR:
flowerheads pink to purple, with slender disk flowers and feathery pappus hairs emerging from cuplike base of prickly green bracts; leaves spiny, divided into spine-tipped lobes, scattered along slender, branching stem.

HABITAT:
fields, pastures, waste places.

IN BLOOM:
June-Aug.

Hawkweeds *Hieracium*

Hawkweeds, like the other members of the composite family shown on pages 346 to 354, bear flowerheads with no tubular disk flowers, but only flat ray flowers like the "petals" of a daisy. Although insects are drawn to their nectar, some of these plants—including hawkweeds and dandelions—produce seed without pollination. Hence, their genes are unmixed, and each offspring is a clonelike duplicate of the parent.

Orange Hawkweed

Hieracium aurantiacum

SIZE: 4-24 in. tall; flowerhead ¾ in. wide.

WHAT TO LOOK FOR: flowerheads orange, loosely clustered atop leafless, hairy stalk; leaves clustered at base, spatula-shaped to oblong, hairy.

HABITAT: fields, lawns, pastures, clearings.

IN BLOOM: June-Sept.

Rattlesnake Weed

Hieracium venosum

SIZE: 8-30 in. tall; flowerhead ½-1 in. wide.

WHAT TO LOOK FOR: flowerheads yellow, loosely clustered at top of slender stalk; leaves clustered at base, spatula-shaped, with purple veins.

HABITAT: dry open woods, clearings.

IN BLOOM: May-Oct.

Lettuces *Lactuca*

Wild lettuces are sometimes called wild opium because the milky sap of older leaves resembles that of the Opium Poppy. It is not a narcotic, but it does contain a bitter toxin that taints the milk of cows. Tender young leaves, like those of Garden Lettuce (*Lactuca sativa*), are edible.

Wild Lettuce

Lactuca canadensis

SIZE:
1-10 ft. tall;
flowerhead ½-¾ in. wide.

WHAT TO LOOK FOR:
flowerheads of yellow ray flowers emerging from cuplike base of bracts; leaves lance-shaped, toothed, often deeply divided.

HABITAT:
open woods, meadows, fields, waste places.

IN BLOOM:
July-Sept.

Skeleton Plants *Lygodesmia*

In the West, these plants of arid plains and rocky outcrops are known as skeleton plants for their narrow leaves and spindly, zigzag stems. In the Southeast, where a few species grow, they are more often called rush pinks or flowering straws.

Skeleton Plant

Lygodesmia grandiflora

SIZE: 4-12 in. tall; flowerhead 1½-2 in. wide.

WHAT TO LOOK FOR: flowerheads pink, with single row of petallike, notched ray flowers; leaves grasslike, mostly clustered at base of slender, branching stem.

HABITAT: sandy plains, gravelly slopes.

IN BLOOM: May-July.

Dandelions *Taraxacum*

No weed is more successful than the dandelion. Its leaves exude an ethylene gas that discourages competition. A small fragment of its gluttonous taproot will grow into a new plant. Its parachute-borne fruits can stay aloft almost indefinitely as long as the relative humidity is less than 70 percent—which means that when the humidity rises (often just before a life-giving rain), dandelion seeds come to earth.

SEEDHEAD

Dandelion

Taraxacum officinale

SIZE: 1-20 in. tall; flowerhead ¾-2 in. wide.

WHAT TO LOOK FOR: flowerheads yellow, atop hollow stalks; seedheads white, fluffy; leaves clustered at base, deeply toothed.

HABITAT: fields, lawns, woods, swamps, prairies. IN BLOOM: all year.

Mountain Dandelions *Agoseris*

The flower stalks of mountain dandelions (also known as false dandelions) are not hollow like those of true dandelions, and their milky sap contains more latex (dried, it has been chewed as gum). The young leaves of both groups are tasty and nutritious, cooked or uncooked, and the flowers can be used to make delicately flavored tea, beer, or the ever-popular dandelion wine.

Pale Mountain Dandelion

Agoseris glauca

SIZE: 4-24 in. tall; flowerhead 1-1½ in. wide.

WHAT TO LOOK FOR: flowerheads yellow, flat-topped, with ray flowers only; leaves slender, toothed, clustered at bases of stalks.

HABITAT: mountain meadows, wooded slopes, scrublands.

IN BLOOM: July-Aug.

Orange Mountain Dandelion

Agoseris aurantiaca

SIZE: 4-20 in. tall; flowerhead 1-2 in. wide.

WHAT TO LOOK FOR: flowerheads burnt orange, flat-topped, with ray flowers only; leaves slender, often toothed, clustered at base.

HABITAT: coniferous mountain woods.

IN BLOOM: July-Aug.

Rattlesnake Roots *Prenanthes*

Snakebite victims were once treated by applying poultices soaked in the bitter, milky juice of these plants—said to taste like rattlesnake venom.

Rattlesnake Root

Prenanthes racemosa

SIZE:
1-5 ft. tall; flowerhead ½ in. wide.

WHAT TO LOOK FOR:
flowerheads pinkish or purplish white, with ray flowers only, borne in clusters at leaf bases along stout stem; leaves spatula-shaped and toothed (base of stem) or oval (clasping stem).

HABITAT:
moist plains, meadows, streambanks.

IN BLOOM:
Aug.-Sept.

Prairie Dandelions *Nothocalais*

Most dandelions bloom quickly and often. Unlike daisy-type flowerheads, whose disk flowers open one at a time over a long period, each head of this type is filled with ray flowers that open all at once. It soon becomes a puff-ball of parachute-topped, one-seeded fruits.

Prairie Dandelion

Nothocalais cuspidata

SIZE: 2-13 in. tall; flowerhead ¾-1¼ in. wide.

WHAT TO LOOK FOR: flowerheads of yellow ray flowers only, borne singly atop leafless stalks; leaves strap-like, often with wavy edges, clustered at base.

HABITAT: dry prairies. IN BLOOM: Apr.-June.

Dwarf Dandelions *Krigia*

These spring bloomers are dwarfs in the sense that their flowerheads are much smaller than those of dandelions and their leaves and stems are generally slenderer, though not necessarily shorter. Unlike true dandelions, some dwarf dandelion species bear more than one flowerhead on a stalk, and several develop leafy branching stems later in the season.

Virginia Dwarf Dandelion

Krigia virginica

SIZE: 1-16 in. tall; flowerhead ½-¾ in. wide.

WHAT TO LOOK FOR: flowerheads of yellow ray flowers, borne singly atop slender stalks; leaves spatula-shaped, toothed, clustered at base.

HABITAT: dry fields, meadows, open woods.

IN BLOOM: Mar.-Aug.

Chicories *Cichorium*

Common Chicory is native to the Mediterranean region, but it long ago spread throughout much of the world as a result of the popularity of its roots. Roasted and ground, chicory root is commonly mixed with—and often substituted for—coffee. The plant is also cultivated for its young leaves, which are sold, along with those of its cousin *Cichorium endivia*, as endive or escarole.

Common Chicory

Cichorium intybus

SIZE: 1-5 ft. tall; flowerhead ¾-1½ in. wide.

WHAT TO LOOK FOR: flowerheads of spreading blue ray flowers, profuse, scattered along stems; leaves lance-shaped to oblong, toothed.

HABITAT: fields, waste places, roadsides.

IN BLOOM: July-Nov.

Common Chicory

Desert Chicory

Glyptopleuras *Glyptopleura*

Mankind has yet to find a use for either of this group's two species, and neither has ever been given a common name. Both are exquisite spring flowers of the Mojave Desert. The species shown below is also found in Utah and Arizona, while the tiny-flowered *Glyptopleura marginata* ranges northward into Nevada and Oregon.

Glyptopleura
Glyptopleura setulosa

SIZE:
½-2 in. tall; flowerhead 1-2 in. wide.

WHAT TO LOOK FOR:
flowerheads of creamy or yellow rays, borne singly on short stalks; leaves lobed, toothed, clustered at base.

HABITAT: deserts, dry plains. IN BLOOM: Apr.-June.

Plumeseeds *Rafinesquia*

In the wake of spring rains that drench the dry lands of the Southwest, soil that had seemed barren brings forth an abundance of plant life. One of the commonest flowers is the Desert Chicory, usually found growing beneath and around small desert shrubs, themselves returning to life. The only other species, the smaller-flowered California Plumeseed (*Rafinesquia californica*), is limited to the Pacific Coast.

◀ Desert Chicory
Rafinesquia neomexicana

SIZE:
8-21 in. tall; flowerhead 1-1¼ in. wide.

WHAT TO LOOK FOR:
flowerheads of notched white ray flowers with pink to purple veins; leaves toothed or lobed, clustered at base and scattered along slender, branching stem.

HABITAT: deserts, dry mesas. IN BLOOM: Feb.-May.

Goatsbeards *Tragopogon*

The plants of this group have several names. They are called goatsbeards for their huge, white-plumed seedheads; some are known as oyster plants for the distinctive flavor of their boiled roots—strongest in the purple-flowered Salsify (*Tragopogon porrifolius*). Three species of this Old World group have long been established in North America, and in recent years it has been found that two new species have arisen in the Northwest as a result of hybridization.

SEEDHEAD

Goatsbeard

Tragopogon dubius

SIZE:
1-3 ft. tall; flowerhead 1-2 in. wide.

WHAT TO LOOK FOR:
flowerheads of spreading yellow ray flowers and long pointed green bracts open in morning only; leaves grasslike, mostly clustered at base of stalks; seedheads large, white, fluffy.

HABITAT:
fields, prairies, rocky banks, roadsides.

IN BLOOM:
May-Aug.

Desert Dandelions *Malacothrix*

This group's 20 or so species are all native to arid regions of the Southwest. Most are dandelionlike annuals that carpet the desert landscape with flowerheads of pale yellow or white after a rain. A few bear pink-tinted blossoms; and one—the pink-flowered *Malacothrix blairii,* found only on San Clemente Island—is a shrub that grows up to 7 feet tall.

Desert Dandelion

Malacothrix glabrata

SIZE:
5-15 in. tall; flowerhead 1½-2½ in. wide.

WHAT TO LOOK FOR:
flowerheads of white or yellow ray flowers (often reddish near center), fragrant; leaves divided into many narrow sections, often woolly, clustered at base and sparsely scattered along hairy stems.

HABITAT:
deserts, dry plains, scrublands.

IN BLOOM:
Mar.-June.

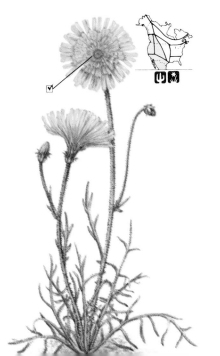

Arrowheads *Sagittaria*

The starchy, new–potato–like tubers of arrowheads were a dietary staple of many Indian peoples; Lewis and Clark learned the name Wapato from the Chinooks of the Pacific Northwest. The tubers form along the roots within 5 feet of the parent plant. Because they float when broken loose from the root, barefoot waders could easily gather them from the muddy bottoms of rivers and lakes.

Water Plantains *Alisma*

Throughout the Northern Hemisphere, members of this group can be found growing in shallow water and wet ground. They are unrelated to plantains, but owe their name to the similar shape of their long-stalked leaves. In deep enough water they often bear ribbonlike underwater leaves as well.

Wapato

Wapato

Sagittaria latifolia

SIZE: 1-5 ft. tall; flower ¾-1½ in. wide.

WHAT TO LOOK FOR: leaves arrowhead-shaped, on long stalks; flowers white, 3-petaled, with fuzzy yellow centers (male) or green mounds (female), in whorls of 3; fruits in dense round heads.

HABITAT: rivers, lakes, ponds, marshes.

IN BLOOM: July-Sept.

Water Plantain

Burheads _Echinodorus_

Despite their spiny fruits, these members of the water plantain family are often mistaken for arrowheads (not all arrowhead species bear arrowhead-shaped leaves). Burhead flowers are bisexual, while arrowheads bear separate male and female flowers in two tiers on the same stalk.

Texas Mudbaby

Echinodorus cordifolius

SIZE:
5-16 in. tall; flower ½-1 in. wide.

WHAT TO LOOK FOR:
leaves heart-shaped to oval, on long stalks; flowers white, 3-petaled, borne in whorls on upright stalks and along arched rooting stems; fruits in bristly round heads.

HABITAT:
muddy banks, shallow water.

IN BLOOM:
July-Oct.

◄ Water Plantain

Alisma subcordatum

SIZE:
4-36 in. tall; flower ¼ in. wide.

WHAT TO LOOK FOR:
leaves oval to heart-shaped, on long stalks; flowers white, 3-petaled, profusely borne at tips of branching stalk.

HABITAT: rivers, lakes, ditches, muddy shores.

IN BLOOM: June-Sept.

Tapegrasses *Vallisneria*

This group's female flowers are borne at the ends of spiraling stalks that maintain just enough tension to form dimples on the water surface. The tiny male flowers are released to float free. They are drawn into the dimples and pollination occurs, after which the stalks coil tighter and the developing fruits are pulled underwater.

Elodeas *Elodea*

When you buy a handful of greenery for your aquarium, it is probably a member of this group. Although elodea flowers are pollinated on the surface of the water, the plants are propagated chiefly by means of broken fragments of the weak, buoyant stems.

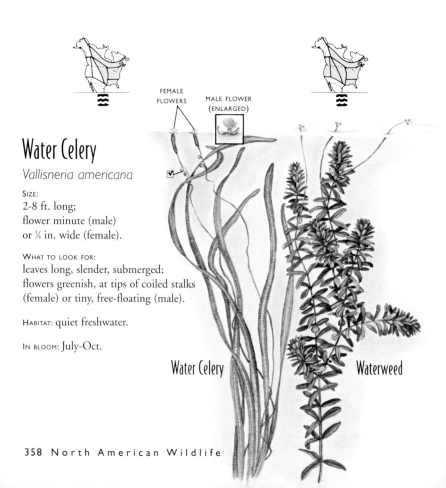

FEMALE FLOWERS

MALE FLOWER (ENLARGED)

Water Celery

Vallisneria americana

SIZE:
2-8 ft. long;
flower minute (male)
or ¼ in. wide (female).

WHAT TO LOOK FOR:
leaves long, slender, submerged;
flowers greenish, at tips of coiled stalks
(female) or tiny, free-floating (male).

HABITAT: quiet freshwater.

IN BLOOM: July-Oct.

Water Celery

Waterweed

Eelgrasses *Zostera*

These plants use ocean tides for pollination in the same way grasses use the wind. Their tiny male flowers, hidden in sheaths along with the females, release clouds of pollen into the water. When a threadlike grain touches the stigma of a female flower, it anchors itself by curling and twisting around it.

Eelgrass

Zostera marina

SIZE: 1-4 ft. long; flower minute.

WHAT TO LOOK FOR: leaves grasslike, forming dense mats from creeping stems, submerged at high tide; flowers green, borne in long sheaths at leaf bases.

HABITAT: bays, shoals, seashores. IN BLOOM: June-Sept.

◀ Waterweed

Elodea canadensis

SIZE:
1-10 ft. long; flower ⅛-½ in. wide.

WHAT TO LOOK FOR:
stems submerged or floating; leaves oval, densely borne in whorls of 3; flowers white, 3-petaled, with yellow centers (male) or 3 purple pistils (female), borne atop slender stalks above water surface.

HABITAT: lakes, ponds, springs, quiet streams.
IN BLOOM: July-Sept.

Pondweeds *Potamogeton*

No flowering plant plays a more crucial role in the ecology of freshwater lakes than the pondweeds. They are a vital food source for waterfowl, as well as for many forms of aquatic life. Fish, frogs, snakes, and snails are among the creatures that feed and breed among their leaves.

Pondweed

Potamogeton illinoensis

SIZE:
1-8 ft. long; flower ⅛ in. wide.

WHAT TO LOOK FOR:
plants submerged, forming dense colonies; leaves elliptical (floating) or lance-shaped (submerged); flowers green, in dense spikes above water.

HABITAT:
ponds, lakes, streams.

IN BLOOM:
June-Sept.

Spiderworts *Tradescantia*

Spiderworts are among the world's most sensitive—and certainly the most attractive—devices for detecting nuclear radiation. The stamen hairs on a plant that has been exposed to low-level radiation change from blue to pink in proportion to the dose received. By counting, under a microscope, the number of cells in a hair that have so changed, a scientist can index the severity of radiation.

Spiderwort

Tradescantia ohiensis

SIZE:
8-36 in. tall; flower 1-1½ in. wide.

WHAT TO LOOK FOR:
flowers blue to purple (occasionally white), 3-petaled, borne in loose clusters at base of a pair of leaves at stem tip; leaves long, narrow, with large sheaths at base.

HABITAT:
prairies, open woods, thickets, meadows.

IN BLOOM:
Apr.-July.

WHITE
FLOWER

Yellow-eyed Grasses *Xyris*

Despite their grasslike leaves, the yellow-eyed grasses are more closely related to the pineapple family than they are to the grass family—a kinship that is revealed by a close look at the knobby head from which the small yellow flowers emerge, one or two at a time. Most North American species are confined to the coastal bogs and marshes of the Southeast; Twisted Yellow-eyed Grass spreads much farther north and west.

Twisted Yellow-eyed Grass

Xyris torta

SIZE: 6-36 in. tall; flower ⅛-¼ in. wide.

WHAT TO LOOK FOR: flowers yellow, 3-petaled, borne from conelike head atop leafless, wiry stalk; leaves clustered at base, stiff, grasslike, often twisted.

HABITAT: bogs, meadows, shores.

IN BLOOM: July-Sept.

Dayflowers *Commelina*

Each of a dayflower's many short-lived blossoms (they last but a single morning) has two large, showy blue petals and one insignificant white petal. This characteristic prompted Linnaeus to name the group after the three Commelin brothers: two were notable Dutch botanists of the 17th century, and the third died young "... before accomplishing anything in botany."

Asiatic Dayflower

Commelina communis

SIZE: 6-30 in. long; flower ¾-1 in. wide.

WHAT TO LOOK FOR: stems fleshy, sprawling; flowers blue, with 2 large round petals above a single inconspicuous white petal, borne one at a time from small green cups; leaves lance-shaped.

HABITAT: yards, fields, open woods, waste places.

IN BLOOM: June-Oct.

Pipeworts *Eriocaulon*

Most of this group's nearly 400 species are tropical and subtropical. However, several are abundant along lakeshores and riverbanks throughout the Southeast and the Middle Atlantic States. The Northern Pipewort (*Eriocaulon aquaticum*) is found as far north as Newfoundland. The species all look much alike; several are called Hatpins.

◄Hatpins

Eriocaulon compressum

SIZE: 8-30 in. tall; flowerhead ¼-½ in. wide.

WHAT TO LOOK FOR: flowers white, minute, borne in dense buttonlike head atop wiry, leafless stalk; leaves clustered at base, grasslike, soft.

HABITAT: bogs, pond edges.

IN BLOOM: May-July.

Rushes *Juncus*

Prehistoric peoples used rush stems for binding and basketmaking. The resilient stems still serve these purposes and are woven into mats, hats, chair seats, boats, and other items as well. Although the papery leaves and small flower clusters resemble those of sedges and grasses, the group is more closely related to the lily family. Its three-petaled flowers—though wind-pollinated and much less showy than those of most lilies—have the same basic structure; its fruits are lilylike seed-filled capsules rather than the grains of grasses and sedges.

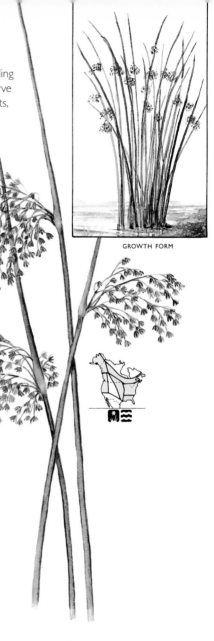

GROWTH FORM

Soft Rush

Juncus effusus

SIZE:
1-6 ft. tall; flower ⅛ in. wide.

WHAT TO LOOK FOR:
stems erect, grasslike, each ending in a tubular, sharp-pointed leaf; leaves at base of stems small, spearlike; flowers straw-colored to brown, borne in dense clusters near tops of stems.

HABITAT:
marshes, bogs, riverbanks, lakeshores, ditches, wet thickets.

IN BLOOM:
June-Sept.

Bulrushes *Scirpus*

This is not the bulrush of the Bible; it is a sedge. Many kinds of birds and animals depend on the bulrush for food and cover. Songbirds and waterfowl nest in dense stands of bulrushes and eat the seeds and stems. The rootstocks nourish muskrats; otters and raccoons are among the animals that hide and hunt under the cover of the plants.

Great Bulrush

Scirpus tabernaemontani

SIZE: 2-10 ft. tall; flowerhead ¼-½ in. long.

WHAT TO LOOK FOR: stems erect, tubular, leafless; flowers minute, petalless, borne in scaly, spearlike reddish-brown heads that form drooping clusters near top of stems.

HABITAT: bogs, marshes, shallow water. IN BLOOM: June-Sept.

Spikerushes *Eleocharis*

The 40 to 45 spikerush species that grow in North America range from a few inches tall to shoulder-high. In most species, the leafless stems are round. Some have square or triangular stems, and a few, such as the Water Spikerush (*Eleocharis elongata*) of southern ponds and marshes, have long, thread-like underwater stems.

GROWTH FORM

Spikerush

Eleocharis engelmanii

SIZE: 4-18 in. tall; flowerhead ¼-½ in. long.

WHAT TO LOOK FOR: stems erect, wiry, leafless; flowers minute, petalless, in scaly, spearlike brown heads atop stems.

HABITAT: marshes, swamps, wet meadows, shores.

IN BLOOM: May-Oct.

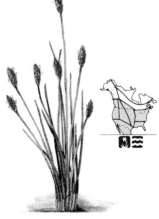

Chufa

Umbrella Sedges *Cyperus*

The umbrella sedges are typical of the sedge family—
wetland plants whose triangular stems are topped by
clusters of compact flowerheads. In this group, the clusters
splay from an umbrellalike whorl of leaves. Chufa is also
known as Yellow Nutgrass for its edible tubers.

Chufa

Cyperus esculentus

SIZE: 6-30 in. tall;
flowerhead ¼-1 in. long.

WHAT TO LOOK FOR: flowers minute,
borne in scaly heads that form
loose clusters atop triangular stem;
leaves grasslike, stiff, clustered at
base and in umbrellalike whorl at
top of stem.

HABITAT: wet fields, meadows,
pastures.

IN BLOOM: Aug.-Oct.

Cottongrass

Cottongrasses *Eriophorum*

Like a snowfall out of season, compact stands of
cottongrass clothe northern bogs and meadows with
a soft blanket of white in summer and fall. North
America's 10 species are largely circumboreal—that
is, they are found growing in all lands that touch upon
the Arctic Circle.

Sedges *Carex*

Most of the world's nearly 2,000 species of sedge grow in wet ground, but at least a few are common in nearly every habitat, from arid plains to high mountain slopes. Such northern species as the Bear Sedge (*Carex ursina*) and the Russet Sedge (*Carex saxatilis*) dominate large stretches of the Arctic tundra.

Porcupine Sedge

Carex hystericina

SIZE: 1-3 ft. tall; flowerhead 1-2½ in. long.

WHAT TO LOOK FOR: leaves long, rough textured, clustered at base and scattered along triangular stems; flowers greenish, in narrow spike atop stem (male) and drooping, bristly spikes near top of stem (female).

HABITAT: marshes, swamps, ditches, shores.

IN BLOOM: June-Oct.

Porcupine Sedge

◄ Cottongrass

Eriophorum angustifolium

SIZE:
1-2 ft. tall; flowerhead 1-2 in. wide.

WHAT TO LOOK FOR:
flowers with silky white hairs, forming cottony tufts atop triangular stems; leaves grasslike, sparsely scattered along stem.

HABITAT:
tundra, bogs, moist prairies, meadows.

IN BLOOM:
May-Aug.

Bluegrasses *Poa*

No grass is more highly prized for pasturage than the bluegrasses, and among the group of about 250 species, none ranks higher than Kentucky Bluegrass. Like the similar Canada Bluegrass (*Poa compressa*), it originated in the Old World but has spread across North America.

Kentucky Bluegrass

Poa pratensis

SIZE:

2-36 in. tall; spikelet ⅛-¼ in. long.

WHAT TO LOOK FOR:

leaves ribbonlike, in tufts and scattered on stem; spikelets in open branching clusters atop wiry stems; plants sod-forming.

HABITAT:

lawns, fields, prairies, meadows, open woods.

IN BLOOM:

May-Aug.

Bamboos *Arundinaria*

Among the grass family's bamboo tribe (comprising about 60 groups with more than 700 species), only the Giant Cane is native to North America. Like many other bamboos, it flowers only once every 40 to 50 years, spreading in the meantime by underground stems, or rhizomes. All the plants in a given area blossom at once; then the stems die back, no matter how young each may actually be. Within a period of four to five years, all the individuals of a species anywhere in the world flower, set seed, and die.

Giant Cane

Arundinaria gigantea

SIZE:
5-30 ft. tall; spikelet 1½-2½ in. long.

WHAT TO LOOK FOR:
stems tough, woody, forming dense thickets, or canebrakes; leaves elliptical to lance-shaped; spikelets scaly, in branching clusters.

HABITAT:
swamps, wet woods, streambanks, bottomlands.

IN BLOOM:
Apr.-May (infrequently).

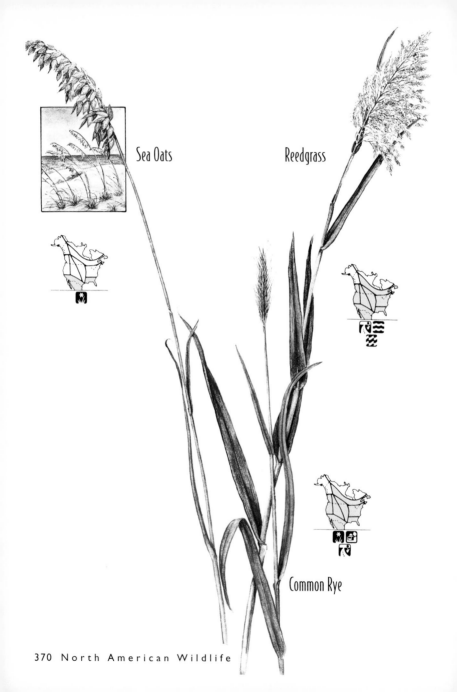

Sea Oats

Reedgrass

Common Rye

Spikegrasses *Uniola*

To appreciate the diverse beauty of the huge grass family—shown on pages 368 through 381—it helps to view its members as a field mouse might. Note the form and texture of the narrow leaf blades. Then study how the intricately structured flowerheads (called spikelets) are clustered high atop the hollow stems. In Sea Oats (an endangered species), they form many elegantly drooping spikes that sway in the coastal breezes.

Reedgrasses *Phragmites*

Second in height only to the Giant Cane among native grasses, reedgrasses form dense and enormous stands in ponds, marshes, and streams throughout much of the world. The plumelike clusters of silky-haired spikelets are attractive but unproductive; the plants seldom produce seed but spread by means of rootstocks that may be 30 feet long.

Ryes *Secale*

Like many cereal grasses, the ryes bear compact spikelets that usually contain only two seed-producing flowers and are tightly clustered in a single spike. Common Rye originated in Eurasia and is cultivated in many parts of the world. In North America, it is often planted along roadsides to control erosion.

Sea Oats

Uniola paniculata

SIZE: 3-6 ft. tall; spikelet ½-1 in. long.

WHAT TO LOOK FOR: spikelets straw-colored to violet, in flat spikes that form flaglike clusters at top of stout stem; leaves ribbonlike, curling.

HABITAT: coastal dunes. IN BLOOM: June-Nov.

Reedgrass

Phragmites australis

SIZE: 4-15 ft. tall; spikelet ½ in. long.

WHAT TO LOOK FOR: spikelets tawny to purplish, with many soft hairs, borne in long spikes that form plumelike cluster atop stout stem; leaves straplike to lance-shaped, stiff, scattered along stem.

HABITAT: marshes, shores, streambanks, ditches. IN BLOOM: July-Sept.

Common Rye

Secale cereale

SIZE: 18-36 in. tall; spikelet ½ in. long.

WHAT TO LOOK FOR: spikelets with bristly awns atop erect stem; leaves soft, ribbonlike, scattered along stem.

HABITAT: fields, waste places, roadsides.

IN BLOOM: June-Aug.

June Grasses *Koeleria*

At the base of each floral spikelet of a grass plant are a pair of small green bracts called glumes. Above these glumes the petalless flowers are borne, each cupped in another bract, known as the lemma, and covered by yet another, called a palea. There may be one or many such flowers in a herringbone pattern. In the June grasses, the spikelets are themselves similarly arranged in dense spikes atop the slender stems.

LONG-
AWNED
SPIKE

June Grass

Koeleria cristata

SIZE: 1-2 ft. tall; spikelet ¼ in. long.

WHAT TO LOOK FOR: plants in clumps; leaves slender, stiffly upright; spikelets pale green, in dense spikes atop slender stems.

HABITAT: prairies, open woods.

IN BLOOM: Apr.-Aug.

June Grass

Porcupine Grass

Prairie Three-awn

Wheat

Wheats *Triticum*

It has been at least 10,000 years since mankind first cultivated wheat, using wild species in which each grain fell away as it ripened. When these early farmers reaped, they chose spikes that still held grain, and so domestic strains were bred in which the grains held tightly to the spike, to be threshed free after all had ripened. Our modern species developed from these ancient strains.

Needlegrasses *Stipa*

In most grasses, the tiny green lemma that cups each flower tapers into a bristlelike awn. In needlegrasses, this awn may be 10 inches long. Porcupine Grass is one of several species (sometimes called augerseeds) whose awns coil as they dry and uncoil as they absorb moisture. When the one-seeded grains fall, they are literally drilled into the ground by the corkscrew action of the awns in response to nightly changes in humidity.

Three-awns *Aristida*

Many of North America's 40 species of three-awn are known as wiregrasses or needlegrasses because of the three sharp-pointed awns that project from the tip of each lemma. Another name often applied to various members of the group is poverty grass because they flourish in arid and impoverished soil.

Wheat

Triticum aestivum

SIZE: 2-3 ft. tall; spikelet ½ in. long.

WHAT TO LOOK FOR: spikelets plump, forming dense spike at top of upright stem, often with long, bristly awns; leaves ribbonlike, scattered along stem.

HABITAT: fields, waste places, roadsides.

IN BLOOM: May-Aug.

Porcupine Grass

Stipa spartea

SIZE: 2-5 ft. tall; spikelet 1-1½ in. long.

WHAT TO LOOK FOR: spikelets straw-colored to greenish, with long spirally twisted awns, in loose spike atop tall stem; leaves ribbonlike, rough-textured, scattered along stem.

HABITAT: dry prairies, barrens.

IN BLOOM: May-July.

Prairie Three-awn

Aristida oligantha

SIZE: 6-20 in. tall; spikelet ¾-1 in. long.

WHAT TO LOOK FOR: plants in low, bushy clumps; spikelets with 3 long awns, loosely clustered along upright stem; leaves threadlike to ribbonlike.

HABITAT: dry prairies, fields, open slopes.

IN BLOOM: July-Oct.

Gramas *Bouteloua*

In the days when vast herds of Bison roamed the western prairies, the gramas made up a large part of their diet. Today, these grasses serve as forage for many other wild and domesticated grazers. They are especially well adapted to the northern High Plains and to the arid Southwest, where they grow rapidly during the short rainy season and are cured by the dry winds that follow into a high-protein standing hay.

Sideoats Grama

Bouteloua curtipendula

SIZE: 18-32 in. tall;
spikelet ¼ in. long.

WHAT TO LOOK FOR: plants in clumps; leaves ribbonlike, rough-textured, clustered at base and scattered on stem; spikelets forming short spikes that hang like pennants from one side of slender stem.

HABITAT: dry plains, desert grasslands.

IN BLOOM: June-Sept.

Indian Rice

Sideoats Grama

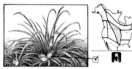

BUFFALO GRASS
FEMALE PLANT

Buffalo Grass

Blue Grama

Bouteloua gracilis

SIZE: 6-20 in. tall; spikelet ¼ in. long.

WHAT TO LOOK FOR: plants in tufts; leaves slender, ribbonlike; spikelets borne in one-sided, arching spikes at and near top of upright stem.

HABITAT: dry plains, prairies, desert grasslands.

IN BLOOM: July-Sept.

Blue Grama

Wild Rices *Zizania*

Every autumn Indians of the northern lake regions traveled to "ricing camps" where they collected the grain from stands of Indian Rice by threshing the tops of living plants across their canoe gunwales. This inefficient technique left behind enough seed to guarantee a crop the following year. Like the closely related domestic rice (*Oryza*), wild rices bear one-flowered spikelets; in this group, however, the male spikelets are separate from grain-producing female spikelets.

Indian Rice

Zizania aquatica

SIZE: 2-10 ft. tall; spikelet ¼-1 in. long.

WHAT TO LOOK FOR: spikelets on broomlike, tufted branches (male) and dangling from spreading branches immediately below (female), at top of slender stem; leaves ribbonlike, scattered along stem.

HABITAT: shallow water of lakes, ponds, backwaters, swamps. IN BLOOM: June-Sept.

Buffalo Grasses *Buchloe*

This group's only species is the most important short forage grass of the central Great Plains. Because of its creeping underground runners, or stolons, it is one of the few western grasses capable of forming soil-binding sod; most others grow in bunches. Early settlers on the Great Plains stacked slabs of this sod to make their houses, which they called soddies.

Buffalo Grass

Buchloe dactyloides

SIZE: 2-6 in. tall; spikelet ¼ in. long.

WHAT TO LOOK FOR: plants spreading, sod-forming; leaves gray-green, narrow; spikelets in flaglike clusters on wiry stems (male plants) or in small heads among leaves (female plants).

HABITAT: plains, prairies. IN BLOOM: May-Aug.

Bluestems *Andropogon*

Also known as beardgrasses for their feathery clusters of spikelets, the bluestems are found throughout much of the earth. Big Bluestem, whose splayed clusters have earned it the name Turkeyfoot, was the dominant plant of the tallgrass prairies that once stretched across the upper Midwest. Little Bluestem is commonest on the Great Plains and dry prairies farther west, although it grows in dry uplands of the East as well.

Broomsedge

Andropogon virginicus

SIZE: 2-4 ft. tall; spikelet ⅛ in. long.

WHAT TO LOOK FOR: plant stiff, bushy; leaves ribbonlike, dense at base; spikelets in loose spikes with many long silky hairs, arising from bases of long straw-colored bracts.

HABITAT: old fields, meadows, waste places.

IN BLOOM: Aug.-Nov.

Little Bluestem

Andropogon scoparius

SIZE: 1-4 ft. tall; spikelet ¼ in. long.

WHAT TO LOOK FOR: leaves ribbonlike, clustered at base and scattered along slender stems; spikelets with hairy prongs, borne in zigzag spikes among small yellowish bracts.

HABITAT: dry uplands, prairies, fields.

IN BLOOM: July-Oct.

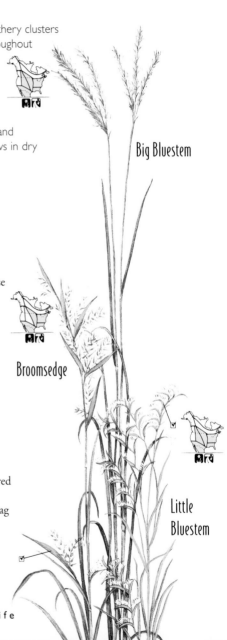

Big Bluestem

Broomsedge

Little Bluestem

◄ Big Bluestem

Andropogon gerardii

SIZE:
2-8 ft. tall; spikelet ¼-½ in. long.

WHAT TO LOOK FOR:
leaves ribbonlike, often drooping at tips, clustered at base and
abundant along slender stem; spikelets green to purple-bronze,
with hairlike awns, in slender spikes that form forked clusters.

HABITAT: prairies, fields, shores, cliffs, wetlands. IN BLOOM: June-Sept.

Sandburs *Cenchrus*

Each spiny bur borne by these spreading grasses is a complete flowering
spike, containing one or more single-flowered spikelets. The spines, covered
with minute backward-pointing barbs, are actually modified branchlets—
termed sterile because they bear no spikelets of their own.

Mat Sandbur

Cenchrus carolinianus

SIZE:
2-36 in. long; spike ¼ in. wide.

WHAT TO LOOK FOR:
leaves ribbonlike, scattered along sprawling
stems; spikelets minute, enclosed in spiny,
purple to straw-colored burs.

HABITAT:
beaches, sandy fields, desert grasslands.

IN BLOOM:
June-Oct.

Indian Grasses *Sorghastrum*

The deep, black topsoil that nourished
vast sweeps of such plants as Yellow Indian
Grass and Big Bluestem proved ideal for
growing another kind of tall American
grass. And so, behind the plows of settlers,
the tallgrass prairies were transformed in
the course of a few decades into today's
productive corn belt.

Yellow Indian Grass

Sorghastrum nutans

SIZE:
3-10 ft. tall; spikelet ¼-½ in. long.

WHAT TO LOOK FOR:
leaves ribbonlike, rough-textured, clustered at
base and scattered along slender stem; spikelets
golden brown, hairy, with long awns, borne in
2's or 3's, forming plumelike cluster.

HABITAT:
moist prairies, fields, barrens.

IN BLOOM:
Aug.-Sept.

Sorghums *Sorghum*

These grasses were prized in ancient Africa and Asia as a source of grain, forage, and syrup. Many kinds are now grown in North America for the same purposes. Johnson Grass is said to have been imported from Turkey in the 1830s, by William Johnson of Alabama, for testing as a hay crop. It soon escaped cultivation and has become a troublesome weed.

Johnson Grass

Sorghum halepense

SIZE:
3-5 ft. tall; spikelet ¼ in. long.

WHAT TO LOOK FOR:
leaves straplike, scattered on stem; spikelets purplish, with long awns, in loose spikes forming branched, pyramidal cluster.

HABITAT:
fields, waste places, bottomlands.

IN BLOOM:
June-Sept.

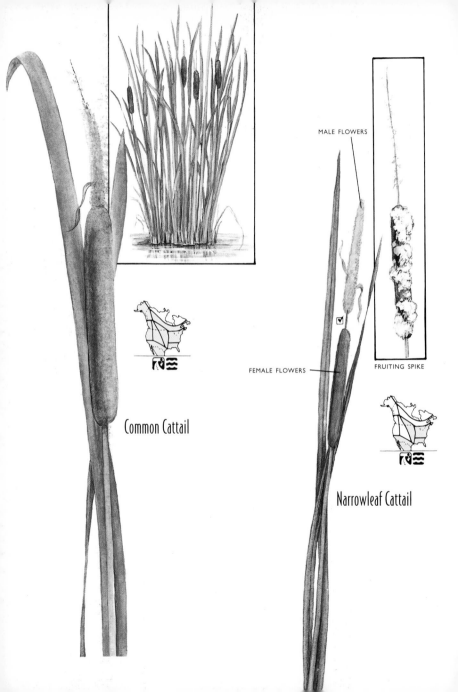

MALE FLOWERS

FEMALE FLOWERS

FRUITING SPIKE

Common Cattail

Narrowleaf Cattail

Cattails *Typha*

One need never starve where cattails grow. In fall and winter, the starchy rhizomes can be peeled and cooked like potatoes or dried and pounded into flour. The dormant sprouts that grow from them are tastiest steamed, a dish known as Russian asparagus. In spring and early summer, the young shoots can be eaten raw or cooked, and the immature flower spikes can be boiled and eaten like miniature ears of corn. Later on, the abundant pollen produced by the male flowers that make up the top half of the flowering spike can be used without grinding as a fine-textured flour. The leaves are not edible, but they have been woven into mats, chair seats, baskets, and even roofs. The fluffy white fruits have been used to stuff pillows, and campers have found them a good emergency replacement for down in sleeping bags and jackets.

Common Cattail

Typha latifolia

Size: 2-10 ft. tall; flower minute.

What to look for: flowers brown (female) and greenish or yellow (male), in dense 2-part spike atop stout stalk; leaves long, swordlike, arising from base of stalk; fruits fluffy, white, on lower part of spike.

Habitat: lakes, ponds, marshes, ditches, rivers.

In bloom: May-July.

Narrowleaf Cattail

Typha angustifolia

Size: 2-8 ft. tall; flower minute.

What to look for: flowers brown (female) and greenish or yellow (male), in dense 2-part spike (the parts separated) atop slender stalk; leaves long, narrow, arising from base of stalk; fruits fluffy, white, on lower part of spike.

Habitat: marshes, ponds, ditches.

In bloom: May-July.

Tree Mosses *Tillandsia*

Despite their evil reputation, neither Spanish Moss nor Bunchmoss is parasitic. Like most members of the pineapple (or bromeliad) family, they are epiphytes; they attach themselves to trees for support but take no direct nourishment from their hosts. (The worst damage they are likely to cause is the loss of a weak branch, weighed down during a tropical storm by the additional wet foliage.) They live on nutrients leached from leaves and dead bark by the rain. They even make use of dust particles trapped by the silvery scales covering their branches and leaves, and so can flourish on fence posts and phone wires.

TREE WITH SPANISH MOSS

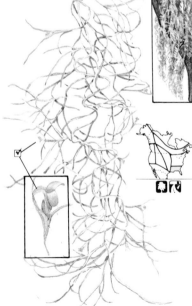

Spanish Moss

Tillandsia usneoides

SIZE: to 25 ft. long; flower ¼ in. wide.

WHAT TO LOOK FOR: stems gray, covered with scale-like gray-green leaves, hanging in mosslike swags; flowers green, small, rarely seen.

HABITAT: tree limbs, wires, poles.

IN BLOOM: Apr.-July.

◄ Bunchmoss

Tillandsia recurvata

SIZE: 2-6 in. tall; flower ½ in. long.

WHAT TO LOOK FOR: leaves gray, fuzzy, hairlike, forming rounded clump; flowers blue to violet, borne in slender spikes at tips of wiry stems.

HABITAT: trees, wires, poles, gutters, fences.

IN BLOOM: all year.

Air Plants *Guzmania*

This group is one of several in the pineapple family whose epiphytic members are known as air plants. Like many others in the family, they collect water in the cups formed by the bases of their leaves and, through the leaves, absorb nutrients dissolved in the water. Only one of the group's 126 species is native to North America; most come from the forests of tropical America.

Strap-leaved Air Plant

Guzmania monostachia

SIZE:
1-2 ft. tall; flower ¼-½ in. long.

WHAT TO LOOK FOR:
leaves straplike, in rosette with cuplike base; flowers white, borne among green to vermilion bracts at top of erect stalk.

HABITAT:
hammocks, subtropical forests.

IN BLOOM:
all year.

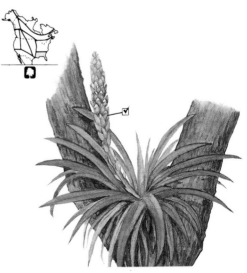

Sweet Flags *Acorus*

The spadix of a sweet flag seems to jut from halfway up one of the plant's upright leaves. A closer look shows that it grows atop a flattened stalk, with a leaflike spathe rising above it. The underground stems, or rhizomes, were once used to make a popular gingery candy, and the leaves have been used since ancient times as a sweet-smelling floor covering.

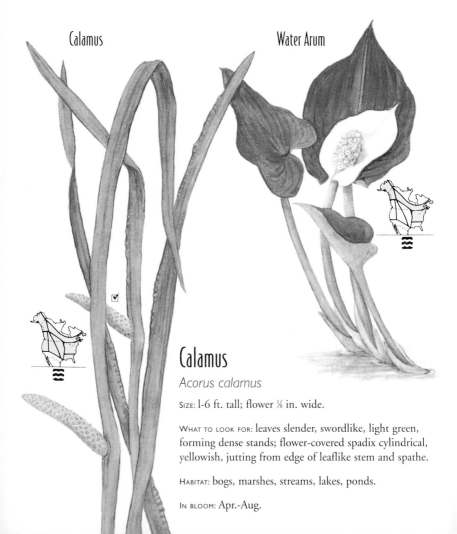

Calamus

Water Arum

Calamus
Acorus calamus

SIZE: 1-6 ft. tall; flower ⅛ in. wide.

WHAT TO LOOK FOR: leaves slender, swordlike, light green, forming dense stands; flower-covered spadix cylindrical, yellowish, jutting from edge of leaflike stem and spathe.

HABITAT: bogs, marshes, streams, lakes, ponds.

IN BLOOM: Apr.-Aug.

Water Arums *Calla*

Water Dragon, Wild Calla, Swamp Robin—all are names for this group's single species, which grows in shady bogs and swamps all around the Northern Hemisphere. The plant's white floral spathe resembles that of the popular calla lilies (*Zantedeschia*) of southern Africa—distant relatives within the arum family. Insects are major pollinators, but water snails also play a role.

Water Arum

Calla palustris

SIZE: 4-10 in. tall; flower ⅛-¼ in. wide.

WHAT TO LOOK FOR: flower-covered spadix knobby, yellow, at base of open white spathe; leaves heart-shaped, leathery.

HABITAT: bogs, swamps, ponds.

IN BLOOM: Apr.-Aug.

Golden Clubs *Orontium*

Unlike most of the arum family, the Golden Club appears to have no spathe, but only a yellow spadix at the tip of a clublike stalk. The spathe exists, however, in the form of a leaflike collar at the base of the stalk. The single species is also called Neverwet because its waxy leaves repel water.

Golden Club

Orontium aquaticum

SIZE: 1-2 ft. tall; flower ⅛-¼ in. wide.

WHAT TO LOOK FOR: flower-covered spadix golden yellow, at tip of long white and red stalk with small spathe at base; leaves long-stalked, oblong, pointed.

HABITAT: swamps, ponds, streams.

IN BLOOM: Apr.-June.

BERRIES

Dragon Arums *Arisaema*

Members of the largely tropical arum family bear their small flowers on the surface of a fleshy spike, called a spadix ("Jack" in Jack-in-the-pulpit), which is usually surrounded by a large bract, called a spathe. In the dragon arums the flowers occur near the base of the spathe and are pollinated by insects.

Jack-in-the-pulpit

Arisaema triphyllum

Size: 1-3 ft. tall; flower ⅛ in. wide.

What to look for: spathe with purple and green stripes, hooded, enclosing clublike spadix (flowers clustered at base); leaves divided into 3 oval leaflets; berries red, clustered.

Habitat: moist woods. In bloom: Apr.-July.

Green Dragon

Arisaema dracontium

Size: 1-4 ft. tall; flower ⅛ in. wide.

What to look for: spadix long, slender (flowers clustered at base), emerging from green spathe; single leaf divided into many leaflets.

Habitat: moist woods, streambanks. In bloom: Apr.-June.

Swamp Pinks *Helonias*

This group's only species is in real danger of disappearing forever because of the steady destruction of the swamps and bogs where it lives. The peril is compounded by its bright flowers, easily the most eye-catching springtime bloom in its habitat. It may be only a matter of time until some hiker unknowingly picks the world's last Swamp Pink.

Fly Poisons *Amianthium*

It is a rule of survival among hikers and campers to eat no wild plant that looks like an onion but does not smell like one. This group's only species is one good reason why. It was named by the colonists, who mashed the bulb and mixed the pulp with sugar to kill flies. The entire plant contains alkaloids strong enough to kill livestock as well. People have died from handling the foliage and then failing to wash their hands before eating.

Stargrasses *Aletris*

Several stargrass species are known as agueroot or colicroot because their roots were used to ease chills, fevers, and the pains of colic. The effectiveness of these folk remedies, however, probably owed more to the strong whiskey or brandy with which the powdered root was mixed than it did to the root itself.

Swamp Pink

Helonias bullata

SIZE: 1-3 ft. tall; flower ¼ in. wide.

WHAT TO LOOK FOR: flowers bright pink with 6 purple stamens, in dense cluster atop hollow stalk; leaves spatula-shaped to straplike, clustered at base of stalk.

HABITAT: swamps, bogs. IN BLOOM: Apr.-May.

Fly Poison

Amianthium muscaetoxicum

SIZE: 1-4 ft. tall; flower ¼ in. wide.

WHAT TO LOOK FOR: flowers white to greenish, in oval to cylindrical cluster atop upright stalk; leaves slender, straplike, clustered at base of stalk.

HABITAT: open sandy woods, meadows, bogs.

IN BLOOM: May-July.

Colicroot

Aletris farinosa

SIZE: 1-3 ft. tall; flower ¼ in. wide.

WHAT TO LOOK FOR: flowers white, urnlike, with 6-pointed star at tip, mealy-looking, in wandlike cluster at top of upright stalk; leaves lance-shaped, at base of stalk.

HABITAT: meadows, bogs, open woods.

IN BLOOM: May-Aug.

Stars-of-Bethlehem *Ornithogalum*

Flowers of the lily family have three petals and three sepals. In the stars-of-Bethlehem, as in most members of the family, the petals and sepals are so much alike that botanists coined the term "tepals" to describe them. These poisonous plants originated in Africa and Eurasia, but a few species, imported as early-flowering garden plants, have spread to the wild in North America.

Star-of-Bethlehem
Ornithogalum umbellatum

SIZE:
4-15 in. tall; flower ¾-1 in. wide.

WHAT TO LOOK FOR:
flowers white with green stripe or tint, starlike, with 6 spreading tepals, loosely clustered atop leafless stalk; leaves grasslike, dark green with light center stripe, clustered at base of stalk.

HABITAT:
meadows, fields, lawns, roadsides, waste places.

IN BLOOM:
Apr.-June.

Alp Lilies *Lloydia*

Most members of the lily family grow either from fleshy bulbs, which help them survive arid conditions, or from rhizomes or tubers, which help them survive long winters. The alp lilies are unusual in that they have both bulbs and rhizomes. About a dozen species of these delicate-looking but stalwart little plants grow high in the mountains of Europe and Asia; only one is also found in North America's Rocky Mountains and Arctic tundra.

Alp Lily
Lloydia serotina

SIZE:
2-6 in. tall; flower ¼-½ in. wide.

WHAT TO LOOK FOR:
flowers white with purple veins, borne singly on slender stalks; leaves in clumps, grasslike to hairlike.

HABITAT:
tundra, high mountain peaks.

IN BLOOM:
July-Aug.

Ithuriel's Spear

Harvest Lily

Brodiaea Lilies *Brodiaea / Triteleia / Dichelostemma*

Surely no plant bears a common name so impressively literary as Ithuriel's Spear (Ithuriel was the angel in *Paradise Lost* who, with a touch of his spear, transformed Satan from a toad to his true image). The species is also known as Grassnut for its flavorsome bulblike corms, and is sometimes listed in catalogs as Triplet Lily. Others of the group familiar to gardeners include the Harvest Lily, Blue-dicks, and Pretty Face. The Snake Lily is unique in the lily family because of its twining, vinelike stalk, which will continue to climb and flower even after it has been severed from the ground.

Ithuriel's Spear
Triteleia laxa

SIZE:
5-30 in. tall; flower ¾-1¾ in. long.

WHAT TO LOOK FOR:
flowers purple to blue or white, funnel-shaped, loosely clustered atop leafless stalk; leaves long, slender, arising from base of stalk.

HABITAT:
fields, grassy hillsides, coastal sagebrush areas, open woods.

IN BLOOM:
Apr.-Aug.

Harvest Lily
Brodiaea elegans

SIZE:
4-18 in. tall; flower 1-1½ in. wide.

WHAT TO LOOK FOR:
flowers violet to deep purple, funnel-shaped, with 6 spreading tepals, loosely clustered atop leafless stalk; leaves long, grasslike, arising from base of stalk (often withered by flowering time).

HABITAT:
dry plains, grassy hillsides, pine forests.

IN BLOOM:
Apr.-July.

Snake Lily

Brodiaea volubilis

SIZE: 1-8 ft. long; flower ½ in. wide.

WHAT TO LOOK FOR: flowers pink, starlike, in rounded cluster with purplish urn-shaped buds, at tip of vinelike stalk (sprawling or twining up other plants); leaves straplike, sparse, at base of stalk.

HABITAT: brushy slopes of foothills.

IN BLOOM: May-June.

Blue-dicks

Brodiaea pulchella

SIZE: 1-3 ft. tall; flower ½-¾ in. long.

WHAT TO LOOK FOR: flowers blue to violet, tubular to bowl-shaped, tightly clustered atop reddish stalk (4-5 bronze-purple bracts at base of cluster); leaves long, slender, arising from base of stalk.

HABITAT: plains, hillsides, open pine forests.

IN BLOOM: Mar.-May.

Pretty Face

Brodiaea lutea

6-30 in. tall; flower ¾-1 in. wide.

flowers yellow, starlike, with 6 spreading tepals (each with a dark line down the back), loosely clustered atop slender stalk; leaves long, slender, arising from base.

pine forests, wooded foothills.

May-Aug.

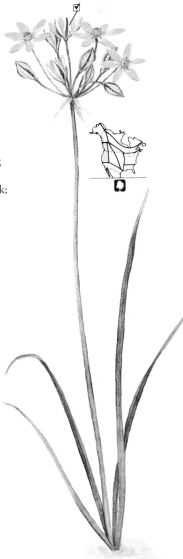

Firecracker Flower

Dichelostemma ida-maia

SIZE:
1-3 ft. tall; flower 1-1½ in. long.

WHAT TO LOOK FOR:
flowers bright red, tubular, with greenish-yellow starlike tips, in rounded cluster atop reddish stalk; leaves long, slender, arising from base of stalk.

HABITAT:
grassy slopes, open redwood forests.

IN BLOOM:
May-July.

Lilies *Lilium*

According to Korean legend, a hermit once befriended a tiger by removing an arrow from its leg. Years later, when the tiger died, its body was transformed into a lily; and after the hermit himself died, the Tiger Lily spread across the land in search of its friend. Thanks to gardeners, its search is now worldwide. Among the many other lilies whose dramatic blossoms have been the focus of myth and legend through the ages, the white Madonna Lily (*Lilium candidum*) of the Mideast is supreme. It was once emblematic of the Greek goddess Hera, and was later dedicated to the Virgin Mary.

Chaparral Lily

Lilium rubescens

SIZE:
2-7 ft. tall; flower 1½-3 in. wide.

WHAT TO LOOK FOR:
flowers white with purple dots (aging to solid wine-purple), trumpetlike, fragrant, on short stalks near top of leafy stem; leaves oval to lance-shaped, with wavy edges, borne in whorls along stem.

HABITAT:
wooded slopes, chaparral.

IN BLOOM:
June-July.

Washington Lily
Lilium washingtonianum

SIZE: 3-7 ft. tall; flower 2½-4 in. wide.

WHAT TO LOOK FOR: flowers white (aging to pink) with purple dots, trumpetlike, fragrant, on spreading stalks near top of leafy stem; leaves lance-shaped, in whorls along stem.

HABITAT: mountain forests, scrubland.

IN BLOOM: July-Aug.

Daylilies *Hemerocallis*

North America's two daylily species— the lemon-scented Yellow Daylily (*Hemerocallis flava*) is not shown here— are hybrids from Eurasian species, and neither produces viable seeds. Instead, they spread by fibrous rootstocks, quite unlike the bulbs or corms of most true lilies. Another difference is that a daylily's short-lived flowers are borne in irregular bunches on a leafless stalk.

Canada Lily

Lilium canadense

SIZE:
2-5 ft. tall; flower 2-3½ in. wide.

WHAT TO LOOK FOR:
flowers yellow to orange, bell-shaped, nodding on slender stalks at top of leafy stem; leaves lance-shaped, in whorls along stem.

HABITAT:
moist meadows, thickets, woods.

IN BLOOM:
June-Aug.

 ◀ # Orange Daylily

Hemerocallis fulva

SIZE:
2-6 ft. tall; flower 3-5 in. wide.

WHAT TO LOOK FOR:
flowers tawny orange, trumpet-shaped, borne one or two at a time at top of leafless stalk; leaves long, swordlike, arising from base of stalk.

HABITAT:
fields, meadows, waste places.

IN BLOOM:
May-July.

GROWTH FORM

Leopard Lily
Lilium pardalinum

SIZE: 2-8 ft. tall; flower 2-3 in. wide.

WHAT TO LOOK FOR: flowers red-orange with maroon spots, bell-shaped with 6 curling, outspread tepals, nodding on slender stalks at top of stout stem; leaves lance-shaped, in whorls along stem.

HABITAT: wet mountain meadows, open woods, streambanks. IN BLOOM: May-July.

Turk's-cap Lily
Lilium superbum

SIZE: 2-8 ft. tall; flower 3-5 in. wide.

WHAT TO LOOK FOR: flowers orange to reddish with purple spots, turban-like, with 6 upswept tepals, nodding on slender stalks at and near top of stout stem; leaves lance-shaped, in whorls along stem.

HABITAT: wet woods, meadows.

IN BLOOM: July-Sept.

Wood Lily

Lilium philadelphicum

SIZE: 1-3 ft. tall; flower 2-3½ in. wide.

WHAT TO LOOK FOR: flowers orange to scarlet, funnel-shaped, with 6 tepals on slender stalks, clustered atop leafy stem; leaves lance-shaped, in whorls or scattered along stem.

HABITAT: prairies, meadows, open woods.

IN BLOOM: June-Aug.

Tiger Lily

Lilium lancifolium

SIZE: 2-5 ft. tall; flower 3-5 in. wide.

WHAT TO LOOK FOR: flowers orange with purple spots, turbanlike, with 6 upswept tepals; leaves lance-shaped, scattered along hairy stem; blue-black bulbils clustered at leaf bases.

HABITAT: fields, thickets.

IN BLOOM: July-Sept.

Mariposa Lilies *Calochortus*

Before the Mormon pioneers succeeded in making the desert around the Great Salt Lake productive, they lived in part on the bulbs of mariposa lilies, as the Utes and Paiutes and other Indians of the area had been doing for centuries. And when the Mormons' first crops were destroyed by insect swarms, mariposa bulbs were all that kept them from starving. To commemorate the ordeal, Utah chose the Sego Lily as its state flower (sego is the Shoshone word for any edible bulb). The bulbs have a nutty flavor when eaten raw; cooked, they resemble potatoes. The tuliplike flowers of most species are extremely variable in color.

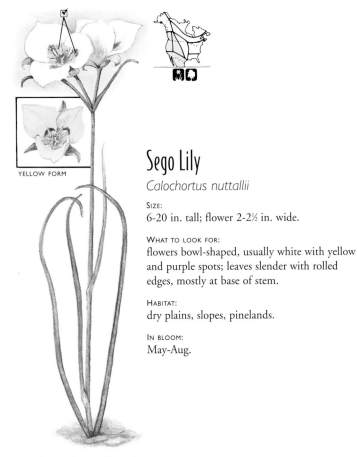

YELLOW FORM

Sego Lily

Calochortus nuttallii

SIZE:
6-20 in. tall; flower 2-2½ in. wide.

WHAT TO LOOK FOR:
flowers bowl-shaped, usually white with yellow and purple spots; leaves slender with rolled edges, mostly at base of stem.

HABITAT:
dry plains, slopes, pinelands.

IN BLOOM:
May-Aug.

Cat's Ear

Calochortus coeruleus

SIZE:
1-6 in. tall; flower ½-¾ in. wide.

WHAT TO LOOK FOR:
flowers pale blue to white, fringed, fuzzy;
leaves straplike, mostly at base of stem.

HABITAT:
open woods, rocky slopes.

IN BLOOM:
May-July.

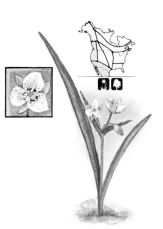

Desert Mariposa

Calochortus kennedyi

SIZE:
4-15 in. tall; flower 2-3½ in. wide.

WHAT TO LOOK FOR:
flowers bowl-shaped, yellow to vermilion, with
brown-purple spots at petal bases; leaves straplike,
mostly at base of stem.

HABITAT:
deserts, dry slopes, pinyon forests.

IN BLOOM:
Apr.-June.

White Mariposa

Calochortus venustus

SIZE:
8-24 in. tall; flower 2-3 in. wide.

WHAT TO LOOK FOR:
flowers bowl-shaped, white, yellow, red, or purple (usually with 2-3 dark blotches on each petal); leaves grasslike, mostly at base of stem.

HABITAT: dry meadows, slopes, open woods.

IN BLOOM: May-July.

PURPLE FORM

Fairybells *Disporum*

These woodland members of the lily family have two names, both descriptive of their delicate hanging flowers. In the western states they are usually called fairybells. Easterners are more likely to know their local species as mandarins or mandarin lanterns.

Yellow Mandarin

Disporum lanuginosum

SIZE: 15-30 in. tall; flower ¾-1 in. wide.

WHAT TO LOOK FOR:
flowers greenish yellow, bell-shaped, dangling at tips of leafy branches; leaves oval with pointed tips, downy.

HABITAT: rich woods, thickets.

IN BLOOM: May-June.

Indian Cucumberroots *Medeola*

This group's only species is easily recognized by the two whorls of leaves. The upper whorl usually has three leaves, and from its center droop the distinctive flowers or the dark purple berries. The cucumber-like "root" is actually an underground stem, or rhizome.

Indian Cucumberroot

Medeola virginiana

SIZE: 1-3 ft. tall; flower ½-¾ in. wide.

WHAT TO LOOK FOR: flowers greenish yellow, with 6 tepals upswept from reddish stamens and 3 fuzzy brown stigmas; leaves borne in 2 whorls along stem.

HABITAT: rich woods, bottomlands.

IN BLOOM: May-June.

Merrybells *Uvularia*

Hikers along the Appalachian Trail are charmed in spring and early summer by dainty merrybell blossoms. The asparaguslike shoots, arising from spreading rootstocks, were once eaten, but such exploitation today threatens the group's survival.

Big Merrybells

Uvularia grandiflora

SIZE: 6-32 in. tall; flower 1-2 in. long.

WHAT TO LOOK FOR: flowers yellow to orange, bell-shaped, hanging from tips of leafy branches; leaves oval with pointed tips, their bases clasping stem.

HABITAT: rich woods.

IN BLOOM: Apr.-June.

Dogtooth Violets *Erythronium*

Despite their name, the dogtooth violets belong to the lily family. The sharp-pointed "dogtooth" is the hard, bulblike corm, from which a pair of leaves arises in spring. The leaves last all summer, producing food to be stored in the corm. It may be six or seven years before a flower stalk appears, bearing one nodding blossom or—in a few species of the northwestern mountains—a cluster of flowers.

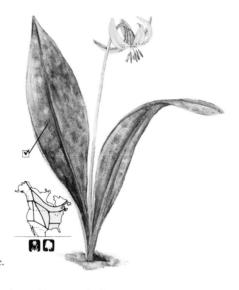

Trout Lily

Erythronium americanum

SIZE:
4-12 in. tall; flower ¾-1¼ in. wide.

WHAT TO LOOK FOR:
flowers yellow, with 6 upswept tepals, nodding atop leafless stalk; leaves leathery, with troutlike brownish-purple mottling, arising from base of stalk.

HABITAT:
moist woods, meadows, bottomlands.

IN BLOOM:
Mar.-June.

Glacier Lily

Erythronium grandiflorum

SIZE: 6-16 in. tall; flower 1½-2½ in. wide.

WHAT TO LOOK FOR: flowers yellow, with 6 upswept tepals, nodding atop leafless stalk; leaves leathery, arising from base of stalk.

HABITAT: mountain meadows, streambanks, woods (near melting snow).

IN BLOOM: Apr.-July.

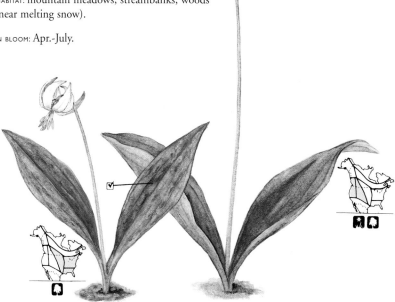

White Dogtooth Violet

Erythronium albidum

SIZE: 4-12 in. tall; flower ¾-1 in. wide.

WHAT TO LOOK FOR: flowers white, with 6 upswept tepals, nodding atop leafless stalk; leaves leathery, often mottled, arising from base of stalk.

HABITAT: moist woods, thickets.

IN BLOOM: Apr.-June.

Trilliums *Trillium*

Three leaves, three green sepals, three colored petals, and (surrounded by six stamens) a three-chambered pistil topped by three spreading stigmas—these are the unmistakable marks of the trilliums, whose name comes from the Latin for "three." (Trilliums are also among the several spring-flowering plants known as wake robins.) Although the flowers of most species are self-pollinating, a certain amount of cross-pollination takes place, generally with the help of flies.

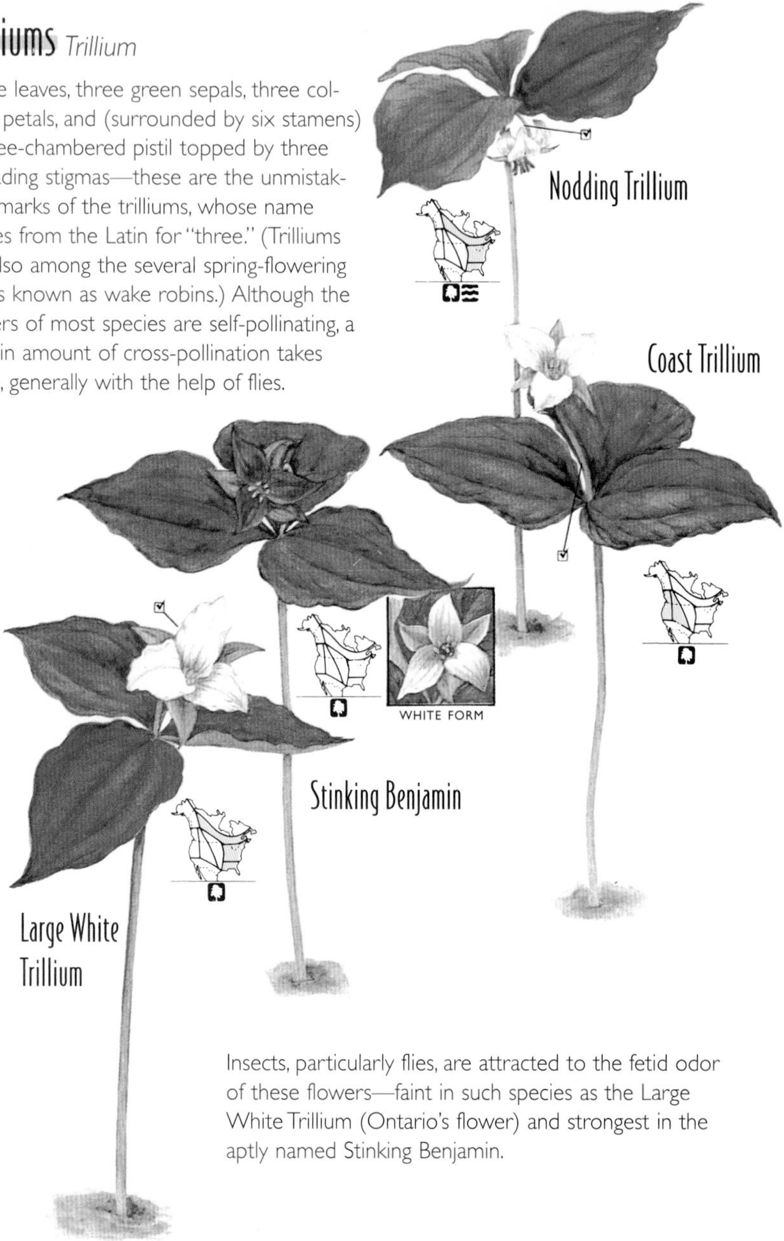

Nodding Trillium

Coast Trillium

WHITE FORM

Stinking Benjamin

Large White Trillium

Insects, particularly flies, are attracted to the fetid odor of these flowers—faint in such species as the Large White Trillium (Ontario's flower) and strongest in the aptly named Stinking Benjamin.

Nodding Trillium

Trillium cernuum

SIZE: 6-20 in. tall; flower ¾-1½ in. wide.

WHAT TO LOOK FOR: flowers white, with 3 backswept petals, hanging on slender stalk from center of whorl of 3 leaves atop erect stem; leaves diamond-shaped.

HABITAT: moist woods, bogs, swamps.

IN BLOOM: Apr.-June.

Stinking Benjamin

Trillium erectum

SIZE: 8-16 in. tall; flower 1½-2½ in. wide.

WHAT TO LOOK FOR: flowers dark red to maroon (or pale yellow to white), foul-smelling, with 3 spreading petals, on slender stalk arising from center of whorl of 3 leaves atop erect stem; leaves oval to diamond-shaped.

HABITAT: rich woods.

IN BLOOM: Apr.-May.

Toadshade

Trillium sessile

SIZE: 4-12 in. tall; flower ¾-1½ in. long.

WHAT TO LOOK FOR: flowers maroon to brownish, with 3 upright petals, borne in center of whorl of 3 leaves atop erect stem; leaves oval, mottled.

HABITAT: rich woods.

IN BLOOM: Apr.-May.

Coast Trillium

Trillium ovatum

SIZE: 4-20 in. tall; flower 2-3 in. wide.

WHAT TO LOOK FOR: flowers white to pink, with 3 broad petals on long stalk arising from center of whorl of 3 leaves atop erect stem; leaves round to oval.

HABITAT: moist woods, streambanks.

IN BLOOM: Feb.-June.

Large White Trillium

Trillium grandiflorum

SIZE: 8-20 in. tall; flower 2-3½ in. wide.

WHAT TO LOOK FOR: flowers white, with 3 ruffled petals, on short stalk arising from center of whorl of 3 leaves atop erect stem; leaves oval to diamond-shaped.

HABITAT: rich woods, thickets.

IN BLOOM: Apr.-May.

Toadshade

Asparagus *Asparagus*

Each spring, tender asparagus spears sprout from long, cordlike roots and, if not harvested, grow into tall stalks with fernlike "foliage." (To locate a productive bed, look in winter for a stand of dry stalks.) The apparent leaves are actually clusters of slender branchlets; the true leaf is a brownish scale at the base of a cluster. The popular Asparagus Fern (*Asparagus setaceus*) is among the group's tropical species often sold as houseplants.

EDIBLE SPEARS

FLOWER

Asparagus

Asparagus officinalis

SIZE:
1-7 ft. tall; flower ⅛-¼ in. wide.

WHAT TO LOOK FOR:
plants erect, branching, with clusters of needlelike green branchlets; flowers greenish white, bell-shaped, hanging on slender stalks; berries red.

HABITAT:
fields, meadows, roadsides, railway embankments.

IN BLOOM:
May-June.

Goldenstars *Bloomeria*

To tell a member of this group from a brodiaea lily, look closely at a single flower. In goldenstars, the six tepals (identical petals and sepals) are separated and the six stamens arise on slender filaments from small nectar cups. The tepals of a brodiaea lily spread from a tubelike base, and the stamens form a crownlike central cluster.

Goldenstars

Bloomeria crocea

SIZE:
5-25 in. tall; flower ¾-l in. wide.

WHAT TO LOOK FOR:
flowers golden yellow, starlike, with 6 spreading tepals (often with dark lines down the middles), loosely clustered atop slender stem; leaf solitary, slender, arising from base.

HABITAT:
dry grasslands, brushlands, oak woods.

IN BLOOM:
Apr.-June.

STRIPED FORM

Onions *Allium*

The Ojibwa Indians knew the prairies at the southern end of Lake Michigan as *she-kag-ong,* or "place of the wild onion." Today, we call the place Chicago. Onions grow throughout the Northern Hemisphere and have been used for food and seasoning everywhere. They are a problem for dairy farmers because a cow that eats the leaves—or even breathes much of the vapor from trampled plants—gives bad-tasting milk.

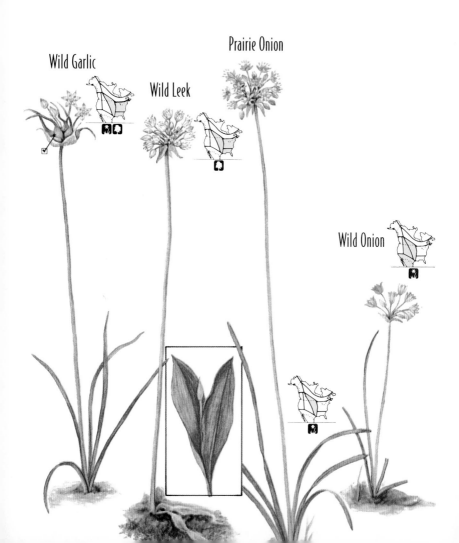

Wild Garlic

Wild Leek

Prairie Onion

Wild Onion

Wild Garlic

Allium canadense

SIZE:
8-24 in. tall; flower ¼-½ in. wide.

WHAT TO LOOK FOR:
flowers pink to white, starlike, in loose cluster with many green-brown bulblets atop leafless stem; leaves grasslike, arising from base of stem.

HABITAT:
moist meadows, prairies, open woods.

IN BLOOM:
May-June.

Wild Leek

Allium tricoccum

SIZE:
6-18 in. tall; flower ¼-½ in. wide.

WHAT TO LOOK FOR:
flowers white, starlike, in rounded cluster atop leafless stem; leaves elliptical, clustered at base of stem (withered by flowering time).

HABITAT:
rich woods.

IN BLOOM:
June-July.

Prairie Onion

Allium stellatum

SIZE:
8-30 in. tall; flower ¼-½ in. wide.

WHAT TO LOOK FOR:
flowers pink to lavender, starlike, in rounded cluster atop leafless stem; leaves grasslike, fleshy, arising from base of stem.

HABITAT:
prairies, rocky slopes.

IN BLOOM:
July-Sept.

Wild Onion

Allium drummondii

SIZE:
4-12 in. tall;
flower ¼-½ in. wide.

WHAT TO LOOK FOR:
flowers rose-purple to white, in loose cluster atop leafless stem; leaves grasslike, arising from base of stem.

HABITAT:
dry prairies, plains.

IN BLOOM:
Mar.-June.

Stargrasses *Hypoxis*

Like the stargrass described on page 391, plants in this group are not grasses at all, but members of the lily family. These stargrasses seem more deserving of the name, with their small clusters of bright white or yellow six-pointed blossoms twinkling among the tufts of slender green leaves.

Yellow Stargrass

Hypoxis hirsuta

SIZE:
2-12 in. tall; flower ½-¾ in. wide.

WHAT TO LOOK FOR:
flowers yellow, starlike, in open cluster atop leafless stem; leaves long, grasslike, in tufts.

HABITAT:
meadows, prairies, fields, open woods, thickets.

IN BLOOM:
Apr.-Sept.

California
Bog Asphodel

Yellow Stargrass

Bog Asphodels *Narthecium*

These are cousins of the Mediterranean asphodels (*Asphodeline lutea*) of classical mythology, with which the Elysian meadows were said to be strewed. The rare New Jersey Bog Asphodel (*Narthecium americanum*) of eastern pine barrens and coastal plains is smaller than its California counterpart.

◀ California Bog Asphodel
Narthecium californicum

SIZE: 1-2 ft. tall; flower ½-¾ in. wide.

WHAT TO LOOK FOR: flowers greenish yellow, starlike, with red-tipped stamens, in slender cluster near top of stem; leaves grasslike, in dense tuft at base.

HABITAT: wet meadows, marshy woods, bogs.

IN BLOOM: July-Aug.

LEAVES (AT BASE)

Soap Plants *Chlorogalum*

Western Indians made mats and brushes from the coarse fibers covering soap plant bulbs. The bulbs themselves were used for soap or thrown into ponds to suffocate fish. They were also roasted and eaten, and the juice was salvaged to make glue for feathering arrows and a paste for treating poison oak rashes.

Soap Plant
Chlorogalum pomeridianum

SIZE: 2-10 ft. tall; flower 1-2 in. wide.

WHAT TO LOOK FOR: flowers white with purple or green midveins, in branching clusters at top of stout stem; leaves straplike with wavy edges, clustered at base of stem.

HABITAT: dry plains, scrublands, open woods.

IN BLOOM: May-Aug. (evening).

Crinum Lilies *Crinum*

Greenhouse enthusiasts and southern gardeners probably know several of this group's many tropical species and even more hybrids. A few kinds, such as the Milk-and-wine Lily (*Crinum latifolium zeylanicum*), are hardy in gardens as far north as New York. The Swamp Lily is the only species native to the continental United States.

Goldencrests *Lophiola*

The Goldencrest in bloom is not likely to be mistaken for any other plant. A close look at one of the small woolly flowers underlines the plant's singularity; the six tepals are maroon inside, but their color is obscured by the bright tufts of yellow hair that cover them.

Goldencrest

Swamp Lily

Goldencrest

Lophiola aurea

SIZE:
1-3 ft. tall; flower ¼ in. wide.

WHAT TO LOOK FOR:
flowers woolly outside with tufts of bright yellow hair inside, in dense clusters at top of white woolly stem; leaves long, grasslike, arising from base of stem.

HABITAT:
bogs, wet pinelands, moist savannas.

IN BLOOM:
May-Sept.

Swamp Lily

Crinum americanum

SIZE:
1-3 ft. tall; flower 3½-5½ in. wide.

WHAT TO LOOK FOR:
flowers white with pink markings, starlike, clustered atop stout stalk; leaves straplike, slightly toothed.

HABITAT:
marshes, cypress swamps, wet forests, streambanks.

IN BLOOM:
May-Nov.

Zephyr Lilies *Zephyranthes*

The soft west wind that often follows spring rains brings with it, in the Southeast and along the Gulf Coast, the fragrant blossoms of several species of zephyr lilies, also known as rain lilies. The red-tinged Atamasco Lily (from an Algonquian word for "it is red") is one of two species sometimes used as substitutes for Easter Lilies.

Atamasco Lily

Zephyranthes atamasco

SIZE: 4-12 in. tall; flower 2-3½ in. wide.

WHAT TO LOOK FOR: flowers white with reddish tints, funnel-shaped, atop leafless stalk; leaves grasslike, arising from base of stalk.

HABITAT: wet woods, clearings, bottomlands.

IN BLOOM: Mar.-May.

Fritillaries *Fritillaria*

The bulblike corm from which a fritillary sprouts is surrounded by a peculiar mass of bulblets that look like grains of rice. Bears and rodents seek out the corms, and various browsing animals feed on the green parts. The starchy corms and green pods are tasty and nutritious raw or cooked, and were often eaten by Indians and Eskimos.

Yellow Bell

Fritillaria pudica

SIZE: 3-12 in. tall; flower ½-¾ in. wide.

WHAT TO LOOK FOR: flowers yellow, 1-3 borne nodding atop leafless stalks; leaves sparse, straplike, mostly at base of stem.

HABITAT: desert grasslands, hillsides, open woods, scrublands. IN BLOOM: Mar.-June.

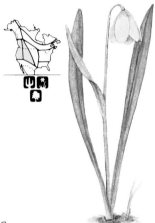

Clintonias *Clintonia*

BERRIES

The dark, beadlike berries of these woodland plants are as distinctive as their blossoms. The Speckled Wood Lily (*Clintonia umbellulata*), commoner than Bluebead in the mountains of the Southeast, has dark-spotted white flowers that produce shiny black berries. The Queen's Cup (*Clintonia uniflora*), of western mountains from Alaska to northern California, bears a single white flower and a blue berry.

Bluebead

Clintonia borealis

SIZE: 6-16 in. tall; flower ½-¾ in. long.

WHAT TO LOOK FOR: flowers yellow, bell-shaped, loosely clustered atop leafless stem; leaves (usually 3) at base, oval, shiny; berries blue.

HABITAT: rich woods, mountain slopes.

IN BLOOM: May-June.

BERRIES

Solomon's Seals *Polygonatum*

In his *Herball* (1597), John Gerard questioned whether these plants were named for the shape of the scars on their root-stocks or for their medicinal use in closing wounds. The point is still moot. "The root," he continued, ". . . taketh away in one night, or two at the most, any bruise, blacke or blew spots gotten by falls or women's wilfulnesse, in stumbling upon their hasty husbands' fists, or the like."

Solomon's Seal

Polygonatum biflorum

SIZE:
1-6 ft. tall; flower ½-1 in. long.

WHAT TO LOOK FOR:
flowers greenish white, bell-shaped, hanging in clusters from arching stem; leaves oval; berries dark blue.

HABITAT:
woods, thickets, riverbanks.

IN BLOOM:
May-July.

Mandarins *Streptopus*

The little flowers dangling like ornate Chinese lanterns inspired the name that these plants share with several fairybell species. These mandarins are also known as twisted-stalks (a translation of the scientific name) because of the peculiar way the flower stalks grow. Each arises opposite a leaf, rather than from the leaf base as in many plants; then it twists around the stem so the flower hangs beneath the leaf. In the White Mandarin, a kink halfway along the stalk gives the name added meaning.

Rose Mandarin

Streptopus roseus

SIZE: 6-30 in. tall; flower ¼-½ in. long.

WHAT TO LOOK FOR: flowers pink to purple, bell-shaped, hanging singly beneath leaves on threadlike twisted stalks; leaves oval, scattered along zigzag stem.

HABITAT: rich woods, thickets.

IN BLOOM: May-July.

White Mandarin

Streptopus amplexifolius

SIZE: 1-4 ft. tall; flower ½ in. long.

WHAT TO LOOK FOR:
flowers creamy white, bell-shaped, with 6 up-curled tepals, hanging singly beneath leaves on sharply twisted threadlike stalks; leaves oval, their bases embracing zigzag stem.

HABITAT: rich woods, thickets.

IN BLOOM: May-July.

Beargrasses *Xerophyllum*

The rootstocks and tender young leaves of beargrasses are sought by bears in spring. The flowers, stems, and seedpods are eaten by rodents and many browsing animals. Only the Mountain Goat, however, seems able to relish the dry, stiff basal leaves. The group has only two species—the Beargrass of western mountain ranges and the very similar Turkeybeard (*Xerophyllum asphodeloides*) of eastern pine barrens and mountain woods.

Beargrass

Xerophyllum tenax

SIZE:
1-6 ft. tall; flower ½ in. wide.

WHAT TO LOOK FOR:
flowers creamy, starlike, in dense, rounded cluster atop stout stalk; leaves grasslike, stiff, rough-edged, densely clustered at base and scattered along stem.

HABITAT:
dry slopes, mountain meadows, open forests.

IN BLOOM:
May-Aug.

False Hellebores *Veratrum*

These members of the lily family have little in common with true hellebores (*Helleborus*)—Eurasian members of the buttercup family—beyond the fact that the plants of both groups are poisonous. This group's toxic alkaloids work through the nervous system to depress the heartbeat and reduce blood pressure. They were used medicinally by many Indian peoples, as well as by ancient herbalists in Europe and Asia, and are part of modern medicine's arsenal for treating hypertension.

Corn Lily
Veratrum californicum

SIZE:
2-6 ft. tall; flower ½-1 in. wide.

WHAT TO LOOK FOR:
flowers white, starlike, clustered in several dense spikes at top of stout stem; leaves large, clasping stem at base, with pleatlike veins.

HABITAT:
wet woods, swamps, mountain meadows, streambanks.

IN BLOOM:
June-Aug.

Indian Poke

Veratrum viride

SIZE:
2-7 ft. tall; flower ½-¾ in. wide.

WHAT TO LOOK FOR:
flowers yellow-green, starlike, clustered in
several dense spikes (lower spikes drooping)
at top of stout stem; leaves large, clasping
stem at base, with pleatlike veins.

HABITAT:
wet woods, swamps, mountain meadows,
streambanks.

IN BLOOM:
May-Aug.

Fairy Wands

Chamaelirium

SINGLE MALE
FLOWER

This group's single
species is also called
Devil's Bit and Blazing Star. Its male and
female flowers are borne on separate plants.
The long flower cluster on a male plant
(shown here) tapers to a graceful, drooping
tip. On a female plant, the flower cluster is
shorter, and it stands upright.

Fairy Wand

Chamaelirium luteum

SIZE:
1-4 ft. tall; flower ¼ in. wide.

WHAT TO LOOK FOR:
flowers white, in dense wand atop stem;
leaves spatula-shaped, densely clustered at
base and scattered along stem.

HABITAT:
wet woods, meadows, bogs.

IN BLOOM:
May-July.

Camases *Camassia*

Baked in an oven of hot
stones, the quamash bulb was
the most important plant food
of the Indian peoples of the
Northwest. When the govern-
ment forced those peaceful
tribes to abandon lands where
the Quamash grew, the bloody
Plateau Wars began, ending
with the bitter defeat of Chief
Joseph's Nez Percé in 1877.
The bulbs of all five camas
species are nutritious, but the
plants can all too easily be confused with poisonous relatives.

Wild Hyacinth
Camassia scilloides

SIZE:
8-24 in. tall; flower ½-1 in. wide.

WHAT TO LOOK FOR:
flowers pale blue, starlike, in dense wandlike cluster atop leafless stem; leaves grasslike, clustered at base of stem.

HABITAT:
moist meadows, prairies, open woods.

IN BLOOM:
Apr.-June.

 # Quamash
Camassia quamash

SIZE:
8-30 in. tall; flower 1-2½ in. wide.

WHAT TO LOOK FOR:
flowers blue, starlike, in dense wandlike cluster atop leafless stem; leaves grasslike, clustered at base of stem.

HABITAT:
moist meadows.

IN BLOOM:
Apr.-July.

Bunchflowers *Melanthium*

As a bunchflower ages, the blossom turns from greenish white to purple, finally becoming almost black (the scientific name means "black flower"). This characteristic, along with the narrower leaves borne mostly at the base of the stem, is the easiest way to differentiate members of this North American group from the similar-looking false hellebores.

Bunchflower

Melanthium virginicum

Size: 2-5 ft. tall; flower ½-1 in. wide.

What to look for: flowers greenish white (turning purple), starlike, in dense spikes at top of erect stem; leaves grasslike, mostly clustered at base of stem.

Habitat: moist meadows, woods, prairies. In bloom: June-Aug.

Bunchflower

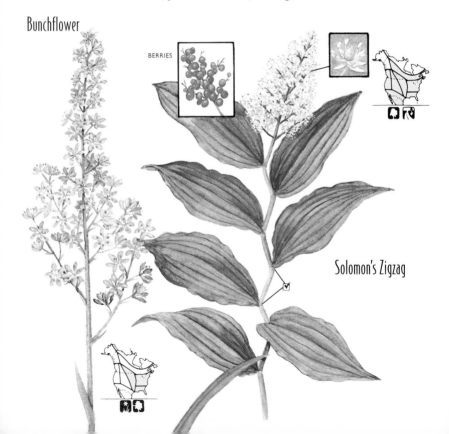

BERRIES

Solomon's Zigzag

Death Camases *Zigadenus*

The most notable difference between a camas and a death camas is that, if you eat the bulb of a death camas, you will probably die. Because camas bulbs are not at their best during flowering season, when their blue blossoms set them apart, it was important for Indian food gatherers to recognize subtle differences between the bulbs.

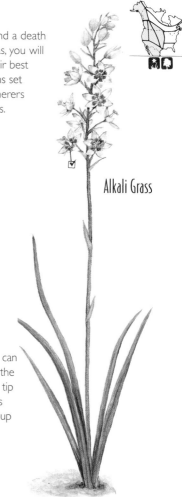

Alkali Grass

Alkali Grass

Zigadenus elegans

SIZE: 1-3 ft. tall; flower ½-1 in. wide.

WHAT TO LOOK FOR: flowers white with green centers, starlike, in wandlike cluster at top of erect stem; leaves grasslike, mostly clustered at base of stem.

HABITAT: mountain meadows, prairies, open woods.

IN BLOOM: June-Aug.

False Solomon's Seals *Smilacina*

When not in flower or fruit, a false Solomon's seal can be hard to tell from the genuine article, but when the flowers or berries are seen clustered at the stem's tip rather than dangling along its length, identification is simple. Because of this cluster, members of the group are also known as Solomon's plumes.

◄ Solomon's Zigzag

Smilacina racemosa

SIZE:
1-3 ft. tall; flower ⅛-¼ in. wide.

WHAT TO LOOK FOR:
flowers white, starlike, in dense, branching cluster at top of zigzag stem; leaves oval, alternating along stem; berries red.

HABITAT: rich woods. IN BLOOM: Mar.-July.

Sand Lilies *Leucocrinum*

The fragrant flowers of the Sand Lily nestle at ground level, amid a rosette of grasslike leaves. The stalks are underground, springing directly from the fleshy rootstock. The group's only species is also called the Mountain Lily, Star Lily, and Star-of-Bethlehem.

Sand Lily

Leucocrinum montanum

SIZE:
2-6 in. tall; flower 1-1½ in. wide.

WHAT TO LOOK FOR:
flowers white, tubular, with star-shaped flare, clustered among a clump of grasslike leaves.

HABITAT:
mountain meadows, scrublands.

IN BLOOM: Apr.-June.

False Lilies of the Valley *Maianthemum*

These woodland plants have flower parts in twos and fours rather than threes and sixes like all other lilies. In addition to the leaves borne on each flowering stem, many leaves arise singly from the rootstock, but these usually wither before flowering time.

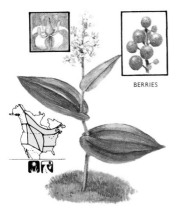

BERRIES

Canada Mayflower

Maianthemum canadense

SIZE:
2-6 in. tall; flower ⅛-¼ in. wide.

WHAT TO LOOK FOR:
flowers white, with 4 tepals, in dense spike atop stem with 2-3 leaves; leaves oval or heart-shaped; berries red, speckled.

HABITAT: moist woods, thickets, clearings.

IN BLOOM: May-July.

Desert Lilies *Hesperocallis*

The Desert Lily's deeply buried bulb was dug up and eaten by Indians of the Southwest. The Spanish found its tangy taste to their liking and called the plant *ajo* ("garlic"). The plant lent its Spanish name to the town of Ajo, Arizona, as well as to a nearby mountain range and valley.

Desert Lily

Hesperocallis undulata

SIZE:
1-6 ft. tall; flower 1½-2½ in. wide.

WHAT TO LOOK FOR:
flowers white with silvery green stripes, funnel-shaped, clustered along top of stem; leaves blue-green, straplike, with crisped edges, mostly at base.

HABITAT:
sand flats, dunes.

IN BLOOM:
Feb.-May.

Spider Plants *Anthericum*

The "spiders" for which this group is named are new plantlets produced on ground-level offshoots, or stolons. Most of the 50-odd species come from Africa; the gardeners' St. Bernard's Lily (*Anthericum liliago*) is European. The spider plant grown indoors in hanging baskets is a close relative, *Chlorophytum comosum*, once considered part of this group.

Crag Lily
Anthericum torreyi

SIZE:
2-3 ft. tall; flower ¾-1 in. wide.

WHAT TO LOOK FOR:
flowers amber with greenish lines, starlike, clustered at top of leafless stem; leaves grasslike, arising at base of stem.

HABITAT:
canyons, desert scrublands, pine forests.

IN BLOOM:
June-Nov.

Blue-eyed Grasses *Sisyrinchium*

The blue-eyed grasses are identifiable as part of the iris family by the way in which their leaves overlap at the base and by the three stamens in the center of each flower. In this group the stamens are joined to form a central column around the pistil.

White Blue-eyed Grass

Sisyrinchium albidum

SIZE:
4-16 in. tall; flower ½ in. wide.

WHAT TO LOOK FOR:
flowers white to pale blue, starlike, borne on wiry stalks atop flat stem; leaves grasslike, stiff, mostly at base.

HABITAT:
dry fields, meadows.

IN BLOOM:
Apr.-June.

Blue-eyed Grass

Sisyrinchium angustifolium

SIZE:
6-24 in. tall; flower ¾-1 in. wide.

WHAT TO LOOK FOR:
flowers blue to violet, starlike, borne on wiry stalks atop flat stems; leaves grasslike, stiff, mostly at base.

HABITAT:
wet meadows, fields, woods.

IN BLOOM:
May-July.

Irises *Iris*

Iris was the Greek goddess of the rainbow, whose role was often to bring peace after one of the gods' stormy confrontations. The plants of this bright, colorful group well deserve her name. An iris blossom seems to have nine petals; the outer three (called falls) are really sepals, the next three (the standards) are true petals, and the center three are crestlike branches of the pistil. The base of each fall combines with one of the crests to form a tube, its entrance marked by lines, a splotch of color, or a fuzzy beard. When a pollinating insect or bird seeks the nectar at the base of the tube, the stigma at the top of the crest dips down to receive pollen from its body. Inside the tube, the stamen waits to dust the creature with more pollen. The iris is Tennessee's state flower.

Red Flag

Iris fulva

SIZE:
2-5 ft. tall; flower 3-4 in. wide.

WHAT TO LOOK FOR:
flowers reddish brown to bronze, with dark veins on spreading falls and standards; leaves swordlike, densely clustered at base and scattered along branching stalk.

HABITAT:
wet meadows, marshes, streambanks.

IN BLOOM:
Apr.-June.

Southern Blue Flag

Iris virginica

SIZE:
18-30 in. tall;
flower 2½-3½ in. wide.

WHAT TO LOOK FOR:
flowers pale lavender to violet (downy yellow blotches on falls), with spreading standards; leaves swordlike, arching, mostly clustered at base of lax, arching stalk.

HABITAT: marshes, swamps, lakeshores.

IN BLOOM: Apr.-July.

Yellow Flag

Iris pseudacorus

SIZE: 2-3 ft. tall; flower 3-4 in. wide.

WHAT TO LOOK FOR: flowers yellow (dark lines on broad falls), with small upright standards; leaves stiff, swordlike, mostly at base of stalk.

HABITAT: wet meadows, marshes, swamps, streambanks, lakeshores. IN BLOOM: Apr.-Aug.

Dwarf Blue Flag

Iris verna

SIZE:
5-12 in. tall; flower 1½-2 in. wide.

WHAT TO LOOK FOR:
flowers violet (yellow blotches on falls), with upright standards; leaves stiff, mostly clustered at base of stalk.

HABITAT:
pine barrens, sandy woods, peaty soil.

IN BLOOM:
Mar.-May.

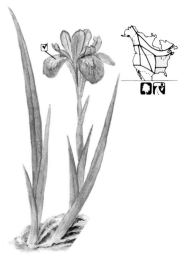

Rocky Mountain Iris

Iris missouriensis

SIZE:
1-3 ft. tall; flower 2½-3 in. wide.

WHAT TO LOOK FOR:
flowers blue to lilac (yellow, white, and purple markings on falls), with upright standards; leaves swordlike, pale green, densely clustered at base of stout stalk.

HABITAT:
moist meadows, flatlands.

IN BLOOM:
May-July.

Celestial Lilies *Nemastylis*

Each year, these members of the iris family produce new bulbs. They differ from most plants that reproduce in this fashion, however, in that the new bulb grows directly beneath the old one. As many as six bulbs may accumulate, one atop another. The stem and leaves of the bulbs on the bottom push up past the bulbs on top. These flowers also reproduce by seed.

Prairie Iris

Nemastylis geminiflora

SIZE:
5-24 in. tall; flower 1¾-2½ in. wide.

WHAT TO LOOK FOR:
flowers blue with white centers, borne singly or in pairs atop stem; leaves swordlike, with crease down center, mostly at base of stem.

HABITAT: prairies.

IN BLOOM: Mar.-June.

Century Plants *Agave*

This group's name is an exaggeration at best: no century plant has been known to reach the age of 100 years, although many species live several decades before putting forth their treelike flower stalks. The tubular flowers are pollinated by long-tongued bats, which crawl down the spikes or hover in midair while lapping the sweet nectar. (Some bats migrate northward from Mexico every year, following the flowering season.) Although many agave species, including the Utah Century Plant, die after flowering, the False Aloe and some other bulbous species produce a new cluster of spine-tipped leaves and a new flowering stalk each summer.

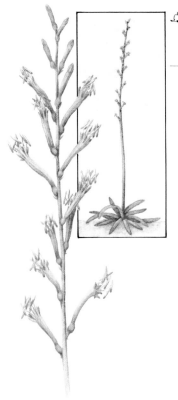

False Aloe

Agave virginica

SIZE:
3-6 ft. tall; flower 1½-2 in. long.

WHAT TO LOOK FOR:
flowers tubular, greenish yellow with long reddish stamens, in loose spike along top of upright stalk; leaves leathery, often purple-blotched, spreading from cluster at base of stalk.

HABITAT:
dry woods, thickets, slopes, clearings.

IN BLOOM:
June-Aug.

Utah Century Plant

Agave utahensis

SIZE:
1-20 ft. tall; flower 1-1½ in. long.

WHAT TO LOOK FOR:
leaves hard, thick, with hooked white teeth along edges, tipped with long spines, forming a compact rosette; flowers yellow, with long stamens, in dense clusters along upper part of stout stalk.

HABITAT:
deserts, dry plains, slopes.

IN BLOOM:
May-June.

Yuccas *Yucca*

The pollination of a yucca is a task that can be performed by only one group of moths. Conversely, the continued existence of yucca moths depends on their ability to pollinate yuccas. An adult yucca moth never eats. Its mouthparts have but one function: to gather grains of yucca pollen and knead them into a ball. After mating, a female moth makes such a ball and flies with it to a different flower. There she injects her eggs into the embryonic seedpod at the base of the pistil, then climbs to the top of the pistil and stuffs the ball of pollen down inside. Caterpillars hatching from the eggs live on some of the developing seeds until they pupate. New Mexico's state flower is a yucca, and so is the Joshua-tree.

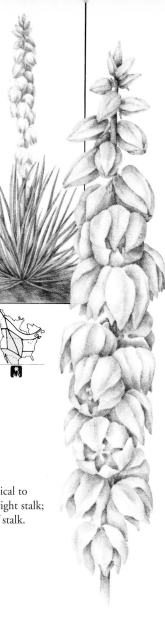

Soapweed

Yucca glauca

SIZE:
2-6 ft. tall; flower 1½-2¼ in. long.

WHAT TO LOOK FOR:
flowers greenish white to pinkish, spherical to bell-shaped, densely clustered along upright stalk; leaves slender, wiry, in cluster at base of stalk.

HABITAT: dry plains, dunes, hillsides.

IN BLOOM: May-July.

Adam's Needle

Yucca filamentosa

<small>SIZE:</small>
2-10 ft. tall; flower ¾-1½ in long.

<small>WHAT TO LOOK FOR:</small>
flowers greenish white, spherical to bell-shaped, densely clustered along branches at top of stout stalk; leaves swordlike, with threadlike fibers along the edges, in cluster at base of stalk.

<small>HABITAT:</small>
beaches, dunes, sandy fields, pine woods.

<small>IN BLOOM:</small>
May-Sept.

Greenbriers *Smilax*

Most greenbrier species are woody vines whose thorny stems can form nearly impen-etrable tangles in eastern forests. The rootstocks of several tropical kinds yield the drug sarsaparilla, used as a tonic and an aphrodisiac (not to be confused with the beverage that was once flavored with birch oil and sassafras bark). The Carrion Flower, named for the fly-attracting odor of its greenish-white flowers, is among the few herbaceous greenbriers, whose thornless stems die back to the ground each winter.

Catbrier

Smilax rotundifolia

Size:
5-40 ft. high; flower ¼ in. wide.

What to look for:
stems climbing or sprawling, thorny; flowers greenish white, in round clusters along stems; leaves round to heart-shaped, leathery, with long tendrils at base; berries black.

Habitat:
open woods, thickets.

In bloom:
Apr.-June.

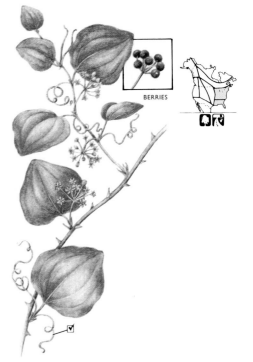

BERRIES

Carrion Flower

Smilax herbacea

SIZE:
2-9 ft. high; flower ⅛-¼ in. wide.

WHAT TO LOOK FOR:
flowers greenish white, in round clusters along climbing stems; leaves oval to heart-shaped, with long tendrils at base; berries blue to purple.

HABITAT:
woods, thickets, fencerows.

IN BLOOM:
May-June.

BERRIES

Calypsos *Calypso*

At first glance, this group's only species might be taken for one of the lady's slippers (it is often called Fairy Slipper). The only resemblance, however, is the shape of the lip petal. Odorless and nectarless, the Calypso attracts insects with the tuft of yellow hairs on its lip, which look like the stamens of some nectar-rich flowers.

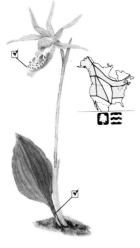

Calypso

Calypso bulbosa

SIZE: 2-8 in. tall; flower 1-2 in. wide.

WHAT TO LOOK FOR: flowers rose-pink, with yellow and purplish markings on pouchlike lip; leaf oval, solitary, at base of stem.

HABITAT: cool mossy woods, bogs.

IN BLOOM: Apr.-July.

Showy Lady's Slipper

Cypripedium reginae

SIZE:
1-3 ft. tall; flower 2-4 in. wide.

WHAT TO LOOK FOR:
flowers with rose-pink slipperlike lip
and white tepals, borne singly or in
pairs; leaves clasping stem.

HABITAT:
woods, bogs.

IN BLOOM:
May-Aug.

Showy Lady's Slipper

Yellow Lady's Slipper

Mountain
Lady's
Slipper

Lady's Slippers *Cypripedium*

The Showy Lady's Slipper is the provincial emblem of Prince Edward Island and the state flower of Minnesota. Like the rest of this group, it depends for pollination on the gullibility of insects. Although no nectar is contained in the slipperlike pouch formed by the lower petal, or lip, bees are attracted by a nectar-like scent from within. Once inside, the unsatisfied insect can escape only by squeezing through one of two small channels at the rear of the pouch, where its back is coated with pollen. Undaunted, it proceeds to another blossom and repeats the process, still getting no nectar but leaving some pollen on the female stigma as it pushes toward an exit channel.

Mountain Lady's Slipper
Cypripedium montanum

SIZE:
10-28 in. tall; flower 2-4 in. wide.

WHAT TO LOOK FOR:
flowers with white slipperlike lip and purplish spiral side petals, 1-3 borne near top of stem; leaves clasping stem.

HABITAT:
open woods, slopes.

IN BLOOM:
May-July.

Yellow Lady's Slipper
Cypripedium calceolus

SIZE:
4-24 in. tall; flower 2-6 in. wide.

WHAT TO LOOK FOR:
flowers yellow, with slipperlike lip and brown to green spiral side petals, borne singly or in pairs; leaves oval, clasping stem.

HABITAT:
rich woods, swamps, bogs.

IN BLOOM:
Apr.-Aug.

Moccasin Flower
Cypripedium acaule

SIZE:
6-16 in. tall; flower 2-5 in. wide.

WHAT TO LOOK FOR:
flowers magenta to white, with veined slipperlike lip and purplish-brown twisted side petals; leaves oval, paired, at base of stem.

HABITAT:
woods, thickets, pine barrens, bogs.

IN BLOOM:
Apr.-July.

White Lady's Slipper
Cypripedium candidum

SIZE:
6-14 in. tall; flower 1-2 in. wide.

WHAT TO LOOK FOR:
flowers with white slipperlike lip and greenish spiral side petals; leaves oblong, sheathing stem.

HABITAT:
moist meadows, prairies, bogs.

IN BLOOM:
Apr.-June.

Pogonias *Pogonia*

At the tip of the column overhanging the fringed lip of a pogonia blossom are paired bags of pollen (pollinia), and beyond them is the pollen-receptive stigma. As an insect enters the fragrant flower, a flap covers the pollinia, so that the insect's back touches only the stigma. Withdrawing, the insect uncovers the pollinia, and bits of pollen adhere to its back, to be carried to the stigma of another pogonia flower.

Rose Pogonia

Pogonia ophioglossoides

SIZE:
3-24 in. tall; flower ½-1 in. wide.

WHAT TO LOOK FOR:
flowers rose-pink to white, with yellow bristles in center of fringed lip; leaf oval to elliptical, solitary, partway up slender stem.

HABITAT:
wet meadows, bogs, swamps, ditches.

IN BLOOM:
May-Aug.

Nodding Pogonias *Triphora*

Flowers of the orchid family have three sepals and three petals arranged around a central column, or gynostemium, which contains both the pollen-producing stamens and the pollen-receptive stigma of the pistil. The lowermost petal is enlarged to form a lip, which in this group serves as a landing strip for insects.

Three Birds

Triphora trianthophora

SIZE: 3-12 in. tall; flower ½-¾ in. wide.

WHAT TO LOOK FOR: flowers pale pink to white, with greenish markings on ruffled lip, usually borne in 3's, nodding, at top of leafy stem; leaves oval, fleshy, clasping stem.

HABITAT: rich woods. IN BLOOM: July-Oct.

Dragon's Mouths *Arethusa*

This is a rare bog orchid, which blooms briefly before producing its grasslike leaf. Pollinating insects (usually bumblebees), attracted by the flower's sweet scent, land on the lip and are guided by three yellow-crested ridges to the nectar in the throat.

Dragon's Mouth

Arethusa bulbosa

SIZE: 2-10 in. tall; flower 1-1½ in. wide.

WHAT TO LOOK FOR: flowers magenta-pink, with purplish markings and yellow bristles on broad lip; leaf solitary, grasslike, borne after flower fades.

HABITAT: bogs. IN BLOOM: May-Aug.

Spreading Pogonias *Cleistes*

In these orchids, the three spreading sepals are clearly different from the petals, which form a tube around the central column. (In the Calypso and many other orchids, only the lip petal is markedly different; the other five nearly identical parts are often called tepals, as are the petals and sepals found in much of the lily family.) The Rosebud Orchid is North America's only representative of this largely tropical group.

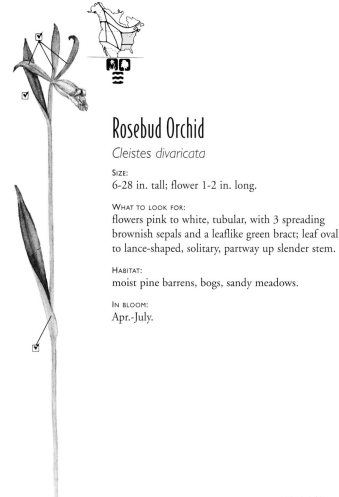

Rosebud Orchid

Cleistes divaricata

SIZE:
6-28 in. tall; flower 1-2 in. long.

WHAT TO LOOK FOR:
flowers pink to white, tubular, with 3 spreading brownish sepals and a leaflike green bract; leaf oval to lance-shaped, solitary, partway up slender stem.

HABITAT:
moist pine barrens, bogs, sandy meadows.

IN BLOOM:
Apr.-July.

Twayblades *Listera*

When an insect, following a trail of nectar up the split lip of a twayblade blossom, touches a sensitive trigger at the tip of the column, a squirt of quick-drying glue shoots out, and with it two pollinia. The startled insect flies away, carrying the pollinia on its back. The trigger mechanism then rises, exposing the stigma to receive pollen from the back of the next insect.

GREEN
FLOWER

Heartleaf Twayblade

Listera cordata

SIZE:
3-11 in. tall; flower ⅛-¼ in. wide.

WHAT TO LOOK FOR:
flowers green to purplish, with 2 small prongs at base of cleft lip, in wandlike clusters; leaves heart-shaped, paired on stem.

HABITAT: rich woods.

IN BLOOM: May-Aug.

Twayblades *Liparis*

These twayblades have little in common with the twayblades shown opposite, beyond the fact that the plants of both groups are wild orchids with only two leaves. (*Tway* is from the Old English for "two.") The large leaves of this group spring from the base of the plant, whereas the *Listera* twayblades bear a pair of small leaves midway up the stem.

Large Twayblade

Liparis lilifolia

SIZE:
4-12 in. tall; flower ½-¾ in. wide.

WHAT TO LOOK FOR:
flowers with purplish lip, threadlike side petals, and greenish rolled sepals, borne on long stalks along stem; leaves shiny, paired at base of stem.

HABITAT:
rich woods.

IN BLOOM:
May-July.

Coralroots *Corallorhiza*

An orchid seed contains no stored nutrients. Before it can develop, it must be "infected" by a specialized fungus that establishes a symbiotic relationship, sharing food and enzymes until the young plant can survive on its own. Coralroots, however, never become self-sufficient. Despite the name, they have no roots but only hard, branching rhizomes, which continue to derive nourishment from fungi in the soil. After several years, the leafless flower stalk sprouts, containing little or no food-producing chlorophyll. Its only function is to develop seeds.

Striped Coralroot

Corallorhiza striata

Size:
9-20 in. tall; flower ¾-1 in. wide.

What to look for:
flowers yellowish with pink to purple stripes, in wandlike cluster at top of magenta to yellowish leafless stalk.

Habitat:
rich woods.

In bloom:
May-Aug.

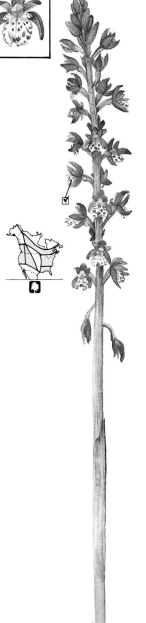

Spotted Coralroot

Corallorhiza maculata

SIZE:
8-30 in. tall; flower ½ in. wide.

WHAT TO LOOK FOR:
flowers purplish, with purple spots on ruffled white lip, in wandlike cluster at top of purple to yellowish leafless stalk.

HABITAT:
rich woods.

IN BLOOM:
Apr.-Sept.

Rein Orchids *Platanthera*

"If insects had not been developed on the face of the Earth," wrote Charles Darwin, "our plants would not have been decked with beautiful flowers, but only such poor flowers as we see... on grasses, spinach, docks, and nettles, which are all pollinated by the agency of the wind." The flowers of the orchid family, more clearly than any others, illustrate the great naturalist's thesis. Many seem to have been designed by a humorous and infinitely clever mind to attract and exploit specific insects. When a long-tongued moth or butterfly sips nectar from the deep spur of a rein orchid blossom, a stalked pollinium or two becomes glued to its head in such a way that the pollen must touch the stigma of the next blossom visited. Some tiny orchids of the Far North use nectar-drinking mosquitoes in the same way.

Round-leaved Rein Orchid

Platanthera orbiculata

SIZE:
6-24 in. tall; flower ¾-1½ in. wide.

WHAT TO LOOK FOR:
flowers greenish white, with slender lip and long spur, in wandlike cluster; leaves round, shiny, paired at base of stem.

HABITAT:
rich, moist woods.

IN BLOOM:
June-Sept.

Purple Fringed Orchid

Platanthera psycodes

SIZE:
1-3 ft. tall; flower ½-¾ in. wide.

WHAT TO LOOK FOR:
flowers lavender to purple, with 3-part fringed lip and long spur, in dense spike at top of leafy stem.

HABITAT:
wet woods, meadows, ditches, swamps, bogs.

IN BLOOM:
June-Aug.

Orange Fringed Orchid

Orange Fringed Orchid

Platanthera ciliaris

SIZE:
1-3 ft. tall; flower ½-¾ in. wide.

WHAT TO LOOK FOR:
flowers bright orange, with feathery lip and long spur, in dense spike at top of leafy stem.

HABITAT:
moist woods, meadows, bogs.

IN BLOOM:
June-Sept.

Purple Fringed Orchid

Prairie Fringed Orchid
Platanthera leucophaea

SIZE:
1-4 ft. tall; flower ¾-1½ in. wide.

WHAT TO LOOK FOR:
flowers white, with 3-part fringed lip and long spur, in open spike at top of stout leafy stem; leaves lance-shaped, their bases sheathing stem.

HABITAT: wet prairies, meadows, bogs.

IN BLOOM: May-Aug.

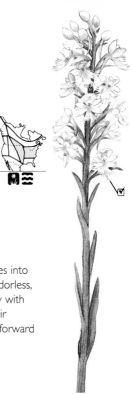

Orchises *Galearis*

No one knows why bees or dragonflies thrust their tongues into the spur at the rear of an orchis blossom—the flower is odorless, the spur nectarless—but they do so regularly, coming away with one or two stalked clumps of pollen (pollinia) glued to their heads like horns. The stalks dry within 30 seconds, arching forward so the pollen will touch the stigma of the next blossom.

Showy Orchis
Galearis spectabilis

SIZE:
5-12 in. tall; flower ½-¾ in. wide.

WHAT TO LOOK FOR:
flowers purple to pink, helmetlike, with white lip and spur, clustered among leaflike bracts; leaves shiny, paired at base of stem.

HABITAT:
rich woods.

IN BLOOM:
Apr.-June.

Puttyroots *Aplectrum*

This group's single species is often called Adam-and-Eve because of the way one bulblike corm develops from another. The corm from which the leaf arises in summer also produces a second corm, at the end of a short underground branch. The leaf lasts through the winter, fading before the flower stalk sprouts from the offshoot corm. The original corm withers as the cycle is repeated. Settlers made glue from crushed puttyroot corms.

Puttyroot

Aplectrum hyemale

SIZE:
1-2 ft. tall; flower ½-¾ in. wide.

WHAT TO LOOK FOR:
flowers yellowish to purple with purple-spotted white lip, in loose spike at top of leafless stalk; leaf solitary, withered before flower stalk arises.

HABITAT:
moist, rich woods.

IN BLOOM:
May-June.

Cranefly Orchids *Tipularia*

Like a swarm of crippled craneflies clinging to a straw, the delicate flower stalk of a Cranefly Orchid presents a bizarre image to sharp-eyed observers. Each year a new corm forms at the tip of a row of old corms. In most years, the lead corm produces only a single overwintering leaf. Occasionally, a flower stalk arises instead.

Cranefly Orchid

Tipularia discolor

SIZE:
4-24 in. tall;
flower ¼-½ in. wide.

WHAT TO LOOK FOR:
flowers pale greenish purple, with slender lip and long spur, lopsided (3 tepals on one side); leaf solitary, withering before stalk arises.

HABITAT: rich woods. IN BLOOM: June-Sept.

Downy Rattlesnake Plantain

Goodyera repens

SIZE:
7-18 in. tall; flower ¼-½ in. wide.

WHAT TO LOOK FOR:
flowers greenish white, in dense spike at top of downy stalk; leaves clustered at base, hairy, with white markings.

HABITAT: woods, thickets.

IN BLOOM: July-Aug.

Downy
Rattlesnake
Plantain

Cranefly
Orchid

Rattlesnake Plantains *Goodyera*

It is easy to see why these orchids are called plantains, with their slender flower stalks arising from plantainlike rosettes of broad leaves. The other part of their name refers to the evergreen leaves, usually marked with a white pattern reminiscent of snakeskin. The flowers, like those of the related ladies' tresses, are mostly pollinated by bumblebees seeking nectar from the pouchy lip.

Menzies' Rattlesnake Plantain

Goodyera oblongifolia

SIZE:
12-18 in. tall; flower ¼-½ in. wide.

WHAT TO LOOK FOR:
flowers greenish white, in spiral or one-sided spike at top of hairy stalk; leaves clustered at base, usually with faint white mottling.

HABITAT: woods.

IN BLOOM: June-Sept.

Menzies'
Rattlesnake
Plantain

Ladies' Tresses *Spiranthes*

A bumblebee sipping nectar invariably starts at the bottom of a floral spike and works its way up. The ladies' tresses, like the rattlesnake plantains, take advantage of this habit to ensure cross-pollination. When a flower first opens, the lip and the overhanging column are so close together that a bee cannot reach the nectar inside. As it tries, however, a pair of pollinia from the tip of the column become glued to its head or back. Later, the lip drops a little, and a bee can then crawl inside, brushing against the sticky stigma on the underside of the column. Because the flowers at the bottom of the braidlike spike open first, a bumblebee carries pollen from the young flowers at the top of one spike to the older flowers at the bottom of another.

Leafless Beaked Orchid

Spiranthes lanceolata

SIZE:
12-30 in. tall; flower ¼-½ in. wide.

WHAT TO LOOK FOR:
flowers red, in dense spike at top of stout, reddish stalk; leaves large, elliptical, clustered at base, usually withered by flowering time.

HABITAT:
meadows, fields, open woods.

IN BLOOM:
Apr.-July.

Nodding Ladies' Tresses

Spiranthes cernua

SIZE: 3-20 in. tall; flower ⅛-½ in. wide.

WHAT TO LOOK FOR: flowers white, nodding, in dense spirals at top of leafless stalk; leaves grasslike, arising from base of stalk.

HABITAT: moist meadows, bogs; fields, prairies.

IN BLOOM: Aug.-Nov.

Nodding Ladies' Tresses

Slender Ladies' Tresses

Slender Ladies' Tresses

Spiranthes lacera

SIZE: 8-30 in. tall; flower ⅛-¼ in. wide.

WHAT TO LOOK FOR: flowers greenish white, in long spiral at top of slender stalk; leaves oval, clustered at base, often withered by flowering time.

HABITAT: dry meadows, fields, prairies, open woods.

IN BLOOM: June-Oct.

Grass Pinks *Calopogon*

These are among the few orchids whose flowers are right-side-up. (Most orchid blossoms rotate as they develop, so the lip is on the bottom.) The flowers have no nectar, but the stamenlike fringe on the lip makes them resemble flowers that do, and they often grow among such plants. When an insect in search of nectar lands on these false stamens, the lip dips forward and drops the creature indecorously on the column beneath. Scrambling to right itself, the insect either picks up or leaves behind a load of pollen.

Grass Pink

Calopogon tuberosus

SIZE:
1-3 ft. tall; flower ¾-1½ in. wide.

WHAT TO LOOK FOR:
flowers purplish pink with yellow tuft near top of upright lip, in loose cluster at top of slender stalk; leaf solitary, long, grasslike, arising from base of stalk.

HABITAT:
bogs, swamps, wet meadows, streambanks.

IN BLOOM:
May-Aug.

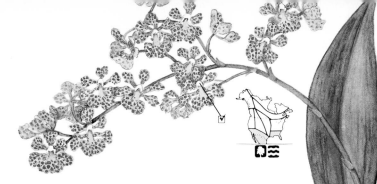

Dancing Ladies *Oncidium*

The nectarless flowers of this group's more than 500 species deceive potential pollinators in various ways. Some look like the males of a kind of territorial bee and buzz threateningly at the breath of a breeze—provoking an attack from a real male bee, during which pollen is transferred. The Dingy Dancing Lady seems to mimic other flowers that offer nectar.

Dingy Dancing Lady

Oncidium undulatum

SIZE:
1-6 ft. long; flower 1-1½ in. wide.

WHAT TO LOOK FOR:
flowers yellow with reddish mottling and white center, in large spray on arching leafless stalk; leaf solitary, elliptical, often tinged with red; plants forming clumps on tree branches.

HABITAT:
swamps, hammocks, forests.

IN BLOOM:
Dec.-June.

Epidendrums *Epidendrum*

There are no parasitic orchids. Although the family's many epiphytes, or tree dwellers, were once thought to be parasitic, they take no nourishment from the trees (and rocks) upon which they grow. The nutrients that their clinging roots gather with great efficiency from surface moisture are often stored in fleshy pseudobulbs—the swellings at the base of the stem. Most epidendrums are epiphytes.

Butterfly Orchid

Epidendrum tampense

SIZE:
3-30 in. tall; flower 1-1½ in. wide.

WHAT TO LOOK FOR:
flowers dull green, with scoop-shaped white lip marked with purple, fragrant, in large spray at tip of leafless stalk; leaves straplike, arising from cluster of gray-green pseudobulbs.

HABITAT:
tree trunks, branches, rocky outcrops in southern Florida.

IN BLOOM:
all year.

Phantom Orchids *Eburophyton*

Except for a yellow spot on the lip of each flower, this group's one species is ghostly white—the only North American orchid that is completely devoid of chlorophyll. Its food is drawn from the rotting humus of the forest floor, with the help of symbiotic fungi that "infect" the plant's fibrous roots, sharing nutrients with it.

Phantom Orchid

Eburophyton austinae

SIZE: 4-26 in. tall; flower ¾-1¼ in. wide.

WHAT TO LOOK FOR: flowers white with yellow spot on lip, in wandlike cluster at top of white stem; leaves scalelike, white.

HABITAT: rich mountain woods.

IN BLOOM: June-Sept.

Phantom Orchid

Cockscomb Orchids *Hexalectris*

The cockscomb orchids (named for the fleshy crests along the rear of the lip) are close cousins of the coralroots. They, too, have no roots and precious little chlorophyll, deriving nourishment from symbiotic fungi. The flowers of both groups are mostly pollinated by bees. As a bee withdraws from the nectary behind the lip, four bags of pollen (pollinia) become glued to its back.

◀ Crested Coralroot

Hexalectris spicata

SIZE: 1-2 ft. tall; flower ¾-1 in. wide.

WHAT TO LOOK FOR: flowers with dark purple stripes on yellowish tepals and scoop-shaped lavender lip, with white column in center, in wandlike cluster at top of purple to yellowish leafless stalk.

HABITAT: rich woods.

IN BLOOM: Apr.-Aug.

Vanilla Orchids *Vanilla*

Vanilla orchids are pollinated infrequently in nature—and by only a few insects and hummingbirds of the American semitropics. Commercial growers raise the vines for the popular flavoring extracted from the seedpods; and because an unpollinated flower produces no pod, they must pollinate the flowers by hand, lifting the tiny flap that separates the pollinia at the tip of the column from the stigma farther back and squeezing the two parts together.

Vanilla Orchid

Vanilla planifolia

SIZE:
2-20 ft. high; flower 3-4½ in. wide.

WHAT TO LOOK FOR:
flowers creamy green, with fringed tubular greenish-yellow lip, in clusters along climbing stem; leaves oblong, fleshy; seedpods long, green to brown.

HABITAT: forests.

IN BLOOM: all year.

Polyrrhizas *Polyrrhiza*

Only one member of this small group of leafless West Indian orchids is also found in Florida, where it clings to the trunks of Live Oaks, Royalpalms, and other trees. The green roots contain chlorophyll and manufacture food—a function that is usually performed by foliage. The flowers are pollinated by an exceptionally long-tongued hawk moth, which sips nectar from the monkey-tail spur.

Palm Polly
Polyrrhiza lindenii

SIZE:
6-13 in. long; flower 2½-3 in. wide.

WHAT TO LOOK FOR:
flowers greenish white, with white lip divided into 2 twisted lobes and long slender spur, at tip of leafless arching stalk; roots green, spreading on tree trunks.

HABITAT:
swamps, hammocks, forests in southern Florida.

IN BLOOM:
Apr.-Aug.

Helleborines *Epipactis*

The Stream Orchid is pollinated by flower flies, which land on the front half of the lip to sip nectar from the rear half. As they leave, they brush first against the stigma on the underside of the column, then against a gummy flap, and finally against the crumbly pollinia—picking up grains of pollen to carry to the stigma of the next flower.

Stream Orchid

Epipactis gigantea

SIZE:
1-4 ft. tall; flower 1½-2½ in. wide.

WHAT TO LOOK FOR:
flowers greenish to rose, with maroon veins on 2-part lip (shaped like an open mouth with outthrust tongue), borne among leaflike bracts near top of stem; leaves lance-shaped, clasping stem.

HABITAT:
streambanks, springs, shores, meadows.

IN BLOOM:
Mar.-Aug.

Index

Credits and acknowledgments for the original edition of
NORTH AMERICAN WILDLIFE

Staff
Editor: Susan J. Wernert
Art Editor: Richard J. Berenson
Associate Editors: James Dwyer, Sally French
Designers: Ken Chaya, Larissa Lawrynenko
Contributing Editor: Katharine R. O'Hare
Contributing Copy Editor: Patricia M. Godfrey

Consulting Editor
Durward L. Allen
Professor of Wildlife Ecology
Department of Forestry and Natural Resources
Purdue University

Consultants
Howard E. Bigelow
Professor of Botany
University of Massachusetts

Howard Crum
Professor of Botany and
Curator of Bryophytes and Lichens
Herbarium
The University of Michigan

William A. Daily
Herbarium Staff
Butler University

Thomas H. Everett
Senior Horticulture Specialist
The New York Botanical Garden

John M. Kingsbury
Professor of Botany
Cornell University

Alton A. Lindsey
Emeritus Professor of Ecology
Purdue University

Richard Mitchell
State Botanist of New York
New York State Museum

Charles J. Sheviak
Curator of Botany
New York State Museum

Warren Herb Wagner, Jr.
Professor of Botany and Natural Resources
The University of Michigan

Contributing Artists
Mary Kellner
Gwen Leighton
Elizabeth McClelland
Allianora Rosse
Ray Skibinski